Advance Praise for *I*

Kelly Pigott is a master modern storyteller. He is also a really good historian who doesn't know how to bore people. All of this and more is evident in this excellent book, which helps you pay attention to the signposts of Christian pilgrimage. Kelly does not provide the formulaic pop-answers we are too comfortable with. Rather, he helps you understand yourself, God, and the ancient community of faith from which we all receive life. He wants you to think more deeply, far beyond the simple answers our culture and churches provide us that have the habit of disillusioning us when life slams into our bad theology.

—John H. Armstrong
Author, *Costly Love*
Founder, The Initiative: A Community
for the Unity of All Jesus Followers

Kelly told me about this book several years ago. As a fan of history, I was excited. Seeing it now in print, I am overjoyed. Kelly brilliantly (and I use that word intentionally) weaves his humanity into the biblical narrative while adding ancient commentaries from church fathers and mothers. This book is at once comprehensive, thorough, tender, honest, coherent, piercing, human, and humorous. It is an epic work hiding out in the open under the cover of humility. I am so proud of Kelly and deeply appreciative for the creative way he has presented biblical history. This is spiritual formation at its best.

—Jim Henderson
Author of *Jim and Casper Go to Church*

With wit and wisdom, Pigott entices the reader to take seriously the Christian path of transformation. Herein lies a trustworthy guide for those seeking to live an abundant life.

—Phileena Heuertz
Founding partner, Gravity, a Center for Contemplative Activism
Author of *Pilgrimage of a Soul: Contemplative
Spirituality for the Active Life* and
Mindful Silence: The Heart of Christian Contemplation

As its subtitle implies, *From Eden to Heaven* is an adventure. That's true because *life* is an adventure, and this book is about our spiritual journey through life. Readers will be blessed by an excellent guide. Kelly Pigott employs his skills as a pastor, church historian, theologian, teacher, and friend to make sure we see all the sights that make the journey fascinating and notice the landmarks that help us find our way. Travel with wonder and awe!

—Marv Knox
Field Coordinator, Fellowship Southwest

While ideally every reader would have the privilege of calling Kelly Pigott friend, this book bridges the distance. His kindness and compassion are evident on every page, and his stories are heartwarming and eye-opening. In these pages, Pigott is a faithful, pastoral, and trustworthy guide as the reader embarks on a journey of self-discovery and spiritual transformation. May this book provoke big questions and even bigger changes as readers encounter God's transforming Spirit.

—Danielle Shroyer
Author of *Original Blessing: Putting Sin in Its
Rightful Place* and *Where Jesus Prayed:
Illuminating the Lord's Prayer in the Holy Land*

FROM EDEN TO HEAVEN

Smyth & Helwys Publishing, Inc.
6316 Peake Road
Macon, Georgia 31210-3960
1-800-747-3016
©2018 by Kelly Pigott
All rights reserved.

Library of Congress Cataloging-in-Publication Data

Names: Pigott, Kelly, author.
Title: Eden to heaven : spiritual formation for the adventurous / by Kelly
Pigott.
Description: Macon : Smyth & Helwys, 2018.
Identifiers: LCCN 2018026534 | ISBN 9781641730631 (pbk. : alk. paper)
Subjects: LCSH: Christian pilgrims and pilgrimages. | Spiritual formation. |
Christian biography.
Classification: LCC BV5067 .P54 2018 | DDC 263/.041--dc23
LC record available at https://lccn.loc.gov/2018026534

From Eden to Heaven

SPIRITUAL FORMATION FOR THE ADVENTUROUS

KELLY PIGOTT

To Susan, Nathaniel, and Eliana.
You are my resurrection place.

Acknowledgments

This work was an effort that spanned many years, so it was as much a product of a community as it was of a single author. There are several I wish to thank for their encouragement and support. First are my students, who heard much of this material as I was developing it. Your feedback and encouragement were the big reasons I wanted to get this material on paper. Some of you read my drafts and provided helpful critique. Thank you!

My friends and colleagues at Hardin-Simmons University also contributed in direct and indirect ways. I'm especially grateful for the nurturing and collegial environment on campus, particularly in Logsdon. You challenge me to love God with all of my mind. My congregations in Haskell and Stamford where I serve as pastor (yes, I'm a circuit rider) have also been a constant source of inspiration.

There are individuals who played a crucial role as well, including Steve and Ann Lacey, John Hunt, Travis Frampton, Dan Stiver, John Armstrong, Jim Henderson, Danielle Shroyer, Chris and Phileena Heuertz, and the late Phyllis Tickle. Your interest in my project and your encouraging words have meant more to me than you realize. I'd also like to thank those who endorsed the book, including Marv Knox.

I also want to thank Smyth & Helwys for publishing this work. In particular, I'd like to thank Marion Moore and Leslie Andres. Leslie, thank you for making the book so much better.

For those who are fans of Joseph Campbell, you probably have noticed that the chapters are loosely organized around his outline for the hero's journey. I have Grace Clunie at the Center for Celtic Spirituality in Armagh to thank for this insight.

Finally, I'm indebted to my wife, Susan, who has been editor and fan of my writing from the very beginning. Along with our two children, Nathaniel and Eliana, you have taught me more great theology than twelve years of undergraduate and graduate work. You challenge me to love more deeply, to enjoy life more fully, and to relish every moment. I am who I am today largely because of you.

Contents

Prologue

An Introduction to the Inward Peregrinatio

> There is meaning in every journey that is unknown to the traveler.
>
> —Dietrich Bonhoeffer

I do not remember how many times I have read J. R. R. Tolkien's *Lord of the Rings* trilogy. I know I have read the books out loud, twice, to my children. Yes, twice. And I have watched the Peter Jackson movies, extended edition, several times as well. Suffice it to say that I love the story. Little people called "hobbits" embark on a journey and find themselves in a grand conflict between good and evil. Though they are small and consider themselves insignificant, they make a major difference in the outcome of the narrative.

At the end of the story (in *The Return of the King*), the main character, a hobbit named Frodo Baggins, walks down the lane with his good friend Sam to board a ship that will take him across the sea (Tolkien's metaphor for death). It's a melancholy moment, not depressing but hopeful. And along the way, quite absentmindedly, Frodo softly begins to sing a walking song that goes like this:

> Still round the corner there may wait
> A new road or a secret gate;
> And though I oft have passed them by,
> A day will come at last when I
> Shall take the hidden paths that run
> West of the Moon, East of the Sun.

The song beautifully expresses one of the emotional threads found in the epic: wanderlust, or the unsettling desire one gets to break out of the ordinary by leaving the comfortable routine to go exploring. In other words, the desire to trod a path or enter a gate that hasn't been tried before, having no idea where it might lead. For Tolkien, this was an integral part of life. And, as I hope to demonstrate, it is also a necessary part of faith.

* * *

Early in the Christian church, men and women of faith embarked on what was known as a pilgrimage, a spiritual journey that whisked them off to a sacred place in the hopes of encountering a fresh vision of God. Sometimes the pilgrim sought God's help or guidance for a major crisis. Sometimes the pilgrim desired healing. Sometimes the pilgrim sought forgiveness, and the trip was an act of penance. These journeys grew wildly popular in the Middle Ages, becoming the impetus for many stories, including Geoffrey Chaucer's *Canterbury Tales*, the bawdy book you might have read in high school.

The notion of going on a pilgrimage, however, greatly predates Christianity. For example, evidence suggests that Egyptian temples hosted festivals that attracted the faithful from far away. Buddhist cultures practiced it as well. The roots of Christian pilgrimages can be found in the Old Testament, where the men of Israel were required to travel to Jerusalem and appear at the temple three times a year for the Feasts of Unleavened Bread, Weeks, and Tabernacles (Deut 16:16). The New Testament describes Jesus and the disciples participating in these pilgrimages, often at significant risk. The early Christians, though, felt no need to participate in them, so prescribed pilgrimages fell out of favor. However, voluntary pilgrimages gradually became more and more popular. At first, this occurred among the ascetics, especially the monks who went off into the desert as a way of exiling themselves from the world to live a holy and devoted life. Asceticism goes back to the earliest days of the Jesus movement. This group essentially renounced pleasure as a way of devoting themselves more fully to God. John the Baptist, for example, was an ascetic, and some would argue that Jesus was an ascetic as well. Following the ascetics' example, countless Christians fled to the desert as a way of exiling themselves from the world to live a more holy and devoted life. Some became famous, and Christians from all around the empire traveled to seek out their wisdom and perhaps to experience a miracle or two. After they died, their burial sites often became even more popular among the pilgrims.

In the fourth century, when Emperor Constantine ended the persecution of Christians, early believers enjoyed freedom to travel and to express their faith and piety without fear of retribution (for the most part). As a result, one of the first places they desired to visit was the very land where Jesus walked—to see the places where he was born, baptized, preached, performed miracles, and ultimately was crucified. One of the first to take such a trip was none other than Constantine's mother, Helena, who took her entourage to Jerusalem in 326 CE.

It was a grand affair, highly publicized throughout the empire. With great flourish, she gave lavishly to the poor, took Communion at each location thought to be connected to the Bible, contributed large sums of money to the churches, and graciously pardoned prisoners. What's most significant about her trip, however, is that in order to get ready for her arrival, local Christians had to figure out where Jesus was born, where he was baptized, where he preached and performed miracles, and where he was ultimately crucified. You see, the whole area we call the "Holy Land" was not a pleasant place to live for the first three centuries after Christ. It was rife with conflict and inhospitable for Christians, many of whom were forced to leave. Some oral traditions lingered regarding locations of major events in Jesus' life, but that was about it. Shrines or historical markers were rare. In fact, a temple to the goddess Venus stood on the spot where many thought Jesus had been crucified.[1]

Christian leaders scrambled to figure all this out, many times just giving it their best guess. Once they came to some semblance of an agreement, Constantine reached into his deep pockets and built new shrines (or refurbished old ones) where it was believed Jesus was born and died and taught and performed miracles. Before long, like a Hollywood map to the stars, pilgrims could follow a route that traced the life of Jesus. And on special feast days such as Christmas (first celebrated by Constantine in 326 CE), one could actually worship at the very cave (or at least at a close facsimile thereof) where Mary gave birth to the Christ child. Soon, pilgrimages became big business.

The popularity of pilgrimages inevitably led to excesses and abuses, whereby relics purporting to be, for example, the true cross of Christ or the Virgin Mary's breast milk popped up all over the place. Unscrupulous monarchs and businessmen took advantage of the piety of the pilgrims and sought to steal as much money as possible. From the beginning, pilgrimages had critics. Gregory of Nyssa, a fourth-century bishop, was discouraged by the debauchery associated with many pilgrimages and warned against them. He wrote that since God is everywhere, there's no need to travel to special places to find him.[2] In the sixteenth century, Erasmus wrote a scathing satire titled "Religious Pilgrimage." Here is a sample of his wit, a sarcastic letter written by the Virgin Mary herself about her travails when it comes to her adoring pilgrims:

> Everything was asked of me, as if my Son was always a Child, because He is painted so, and at my Breast, and therefore they take it for granted I have Him still at my Beck, and that He dares not deny me any Thing I ask of Him, for Fear I should deny Him the Bubby when He is thirsty. Nay, and they ask such Things from a Virgin, that a modest young Man would scarce dare to ask of a Bawd, and which I am ashamed to commit to Writing. A Merchant that is going on a Voyage to Spain to get Pelf, recommends to me the Chastity of his kept Mistress; and a professed Nun, having thrown away her Veil, in order to make her Escape, recommends to me the Care of her Reputation, which she at the same Time intends to prostitute. The wicked Soldier, who butchers Men for Money, bawls out to me with these Words, O Blessed Virgin, send me rich Plunder . . . . AND there is another Sort of People whose Prayers are not properly so wicked, as they are foolish: The Maid prays, Mary, give me a handsome, rich Husband; the Wife cries, Give me fine Children; and the Woman with Child, Give me a good Delivery, the old Woman prays to live without a Cough and Thirst; and the doting old Man, Send that I may grow young again . . . . If I refuse them any Thing, then presently I am hard-hearted. If I Refer them to my Son, they cry, If you'll but say the Word, I'm sure He'll do it. How is it possible for me a lone Body, a Woman, and a Virgin, to assist Sailors, Soldiers, Merchants, Gamesters, Brides and Bridegrooms, Women in Travail, Princes, Kings, and Peasants? And what I have mentioned is the least Part of what I suffer.[3]

Erasmus certainly had a point and a forceful if not provocative way of making it. As was the case with many reformers, however, he had a habit of "throwing the baby out with the bathwater," so to speak. Abuses certainly existed, but a real pilgrimage isn't about pleading for favors from relics. Nor is it about going to a place because God is *there* and God is not *here*, as Gregory of Nyssa criticized. To get at the essence of the pilgrimage, we must delve into the root of the meaning of the word itself. The Greek *paroikos* (or the Latin *pererimus*, from which the word "pilgrim" is derived) literally means "resident alien."[4] It carries the connotation, expressed often by Jesus, that we are sent into the world to be "in it" but not "of it" and that, from time to time, we must step away from it to remind ourselves of our true citizenship. The Celtic Christians referred to this as experiencing a "thin place" between heaven and earth.

A prime example often associated with the practice relates to God commanding Abraham, "Go from your country, your people and your father's household to the land I will show you" (Gen 12:1).[5] In the narrative, Abraham is a resident alien in this new land, but he holds on to the hope that one day this will become the promised land. In much the same way, Jesus sent his disciples into the world and gave them a mission to prepare for his kingdom. In his prayer for his followers, he said, "As you sent me into the world, I have sent them into the world" (John 17:18). As Paul explained, "But our citizenship is in heaven. And we eagerly await a Savior from there, the Lord Jesus Christ, who, by the power that enables him to bring everything under his control, will transform our lowly bodies so that they will be like his glorious body" (Phil 3:20-21).

Our mission as citizens of heaven, therefore, is to prepare this world for the return of its rightful King. But it's not only about transforming this world or expanding the kingdom of God here on earth as it is in heaven, as we pray in the Lord's Prayer. It is also about being transformed in the process, so that our "lowly bodies," as Paul put it, become "like his glorious body." That doesn't mean that at some point we are going to glow as if we've spent too much time near a nuclear reactor. It means rather that we are spiritually formed by "putting on Christ." But what exactly does that mean? I like the way Irenaeus, a second-century bishop of Lyon, put it: We put on Christ by ". . . following the only true and [steadfast] Teacher, the Word of God, our Lord Jesus Christ, who did, through His transcendent love, become what we are, that He might bring us to be even what He is Himself."[6] In other words, Jesus came to this world and became human to show us what real humanity looks like.

Other examples of pilgrimages abound both before and after Christ, but they all have a common theme of breaking the pilgrim of his or her preconceived notions about the smallness of God to reveal just how infinitely large God really is. Moses left his home in Egypt, traveled to the land of Midian, and found God in the burning bush where he discovered that he could not escape his destiny. Elijah fled to a mountain, where he found God not in the typical epic spectacles like fire and earthquakes but in a whisper. John the Baptist lived off locusts and honey in the wilderness near the Jordan River and preached hellfire-and-brimstone sermons about the wrath of God, and then Jesus showed up and, of all things, a dove appeared above his head. I wish I could have seen the look on John's face. He had been telling his audience for the longest time that God was mad at them, and when God showed up, he took the form of a dove, a symbol of peace and love!

And speaking of Jesus, all the disciples were required to leave home to follow him, but along the way they discovered that the Messiah wouldn't be the warrior king they had expected. This pattern continued in the Apostolic Church, when Paul traveled to Arabia and then later returned to Jerusalem (Gal 1:17). During this journey, Jesus revealed to him the message that the Jews weren't as special as Paul thought. This is another instance when I would love to have seen Paul's face when Jesus said, "I'm calling you to be an Apostle to the Gentiles. Yeah, you heard me right: the Gentiles!"

As the church expanded, the notion of going on a journey to find God became ever more popular. Ascetics like Anthony traveled to the desert, where they found God after battling with demons. Dante wrote about being led by the poet Virgil on a pilgrimage into the bowels of the Inferno, where he found God at the end of a journey after witnessing the worst of humanity. Teresa of Ávila described her pilgrimage as a room-by-room exploration of an "interior castle," where she found Jesus in the center. John of the Cross traveled through a "dark night" to unite with his Beloved after much suffering. And in *Pilgrim's Progress*, John Bunyan went on a trek past the "wicket gate," through "Vanity Fair," the "slough of despond," and the "delectable mountains," facing all kinds of trials and temptations before arriving at the "Celestial City."

In other words, a pilgrimage is an attempt to leave the comfort and safety of our routines to discover God for ourselves, uncensored and bigger than anything we had imagined. It is an attempt to disconnect from all that distracts us: cell phones, the Internet, maintenance projects, relationships, work responsibilities, and even Bible classes, worship services, family, and ministries. It is a journey to make our faith our own and not just something passed on to us from our parents or pastor. It can also be an excursion to deepen, mature, or rekindle our faith.

In many ways, too, a pilgrimage is a microcosm of what salvation is all about. This idea may not make sense to those who believe salvation is a status; you are either among the elect or one of the damned. Period. This view misses some important elements of salvation, one of them being that salvation is a work in progress. Take for example the verb tenses Paul uses when speaking of salvation. In his letters to the Corinthians, he often speaks of salvation as ongoing: "For the message about the cross is foolishness to those who are perishing, but to us who are *being saved* it is the power of God" (1 Cor 1:18, NRSV, italics mine). In several places in his letter to the Romans, he refers to it as something happening in the future, "now that we have been justified by his blood, *we will be saved* through him from the wrath of God" (Rom 5:9, NRSV, italics mine). In other words, God is not finished saving you yet. Because, honestly, look at you (okay, maybe I'm speaking more about myself).

The serious point I'm trying to make is that salvation is a process. It's like the Karate Kid doing "wax on" and "wax off." Or, as Paul put it in Philippians, it's a race we are still running: "Not that I have already obtained this or have already reached the goal; but I press on to make it my own, because Christ Jesus has made me his own" (Phil 3:12, NRSV). The main image that I present in this book is that it is an epic journey. I'm certainly not the first to do so. In fact, the Celtic Church has a special word for this: *peregrinatio.* The term stems from a story that has several versions, but essentially it involves three Celtic saints who jumped into a coracle (a small boat) and cast out into the Irish Sea because, as they explained to King Alfred in Cornwall, "we wanted for the love of God to be on pilgrimage, we cared not where."[7] The idea is that the saints wanted to be so vulnerably led by the Spirit that, after they got beyond the shore, they brought their oars in and allowed the wind and the waves to push the boat wherever God wanted them to go. Upon landing, they then continued to allow the Spirit of God to lead them to their "resurrection place"—that is, the place where God had called them to settle and to serve and to be transformed into the image of Christ.

For the Celtic Church, *peregrinatio* is the metaphor for faith, for its meaning goes way beyond just the simple pilgrimage. The *peregrinatio* is the path that all the followers of Jesus are on. As Esther de Waal explains,

> *Peregrinatio* is not undertaken at the suggestion of some monastic abbot or superior but because of an inner prompting in those who set out, a passionate conviction that they must undertake what was essentially an inner journey. Ready to go wherever the Spirit might take them, seeing themselves as *hospites mundi,* "guests of the world," what they are seeking is the place of their resurrection, the resurrected self, the true self in Christ, which is for us our true home.[8]

You have to wonder how desperate the first Cajun was who spotted a craw-fish a long time ago in some mysterious, muddy swamp in South Louisiana and came to the conclusion that it might taste good. Amazingly, he (or she) happened to be right. But then, you also have to wonder how many other critters in the swamp he (or she) tried before getting it right. Fortunately, this person was courageous and stupid enough to keep trying because his or her experiment, along with other bizarre discoveries, became the basis for the kind of cooking I grew up with.

I did not begin my life in Lafayette, Louisiana; my parents were from Wisconsin and South Dakota. At the time I came into the world, the F. W. Woolworth Company believed that the 1960s weren't chaotic enough for young families, so every few years they moved their employees from one town to the next, creating emotional and relational fruit-basket turnovers. So we made our way south, eventually settling in Lafayette about the time I started fifth grade. It was at this tender age that I went to my first crawfish boil.

Imagine walking into a backyard with tables set up in a row, lined with old copies of the *Daily Advertiser*. In the yard is a type of Bunsen burner on steroids connected to a white, banged-up propane tank. The blue flame sounds like a mini jet plane engine. On top of the burner is something that looks like a metal trash can, and the water in it is rolling wildly and bellowing steam. Bags of spices, onions, lemon halves, corn-on-the-cob, and red potatoes bob on the surface. Black eyeballs attached to red beaks peek between the vegetables every now and then, staring at you with a distant gaze before sinking beneath the gray brine. Now imagine your favorite pair of tennis shoes that you refuse to throw away because they are so comfortable, even though they are falling apart. Imagine also that you have been standing ankle deep in muddy fish heads with those shoes for years, and now you've decided to stuff them with cayenne pepper and boil them. That's what a crawfish boil smells like.

If this hasn't ruined your appetite yet, now picture a large potato bag, a little smaller than yourself, filled with hundreds of gray crawfish still alive, pinching their claws, moving in slow motion, gasping for water and secreting God knows what. Fifteen minutes later, those same creatures are bright red and steaming in a pile in the middle of the table. You are then handed a bib and a bowl of melted butter and told to dig in. I must confess that my virgin experience with crawfish was not pleasant. I may have had the guts to nibble on a potato or an ear of corn, but that was it. The image of beady eyes giving me menacing looks before dipping to their deaths ruined what little appetite I had.

In much the same way as I'm sure it was with Proto-Cajun, in South Louisiana you either learn to like crawfish or you starve. Or, at least, you go hungry until your parents take you home, which could be past midnight. Gradually, after a hundred or so crawfish boils, I got the nerve to tear off the tail, peel it, and pop it in my mouth.

Mmmm. Sweet, buttery, with a little bite from the cayenne to make your lips tingle. Aaaaiieeeee. *Laissez les bons temps rouler!* I am now a Cajun. And I even understand what they mean when they point to a cooked crawfish in a steaming pile and say with all seriousness, "Don't eat that one; it's dead."

The crawfish boil is only the beginning, though. After everyone is finished eating, you are required to sit at the table and talk, get a little tipsy on cheap wine, and peel the rest of the crawfish. You then stagger home with a bowl of leftovers that in the coming days will become crawfish étouffée or perhaps seafood gumbo. Since the latter has to fill a pot, you must add to it anything left in your refrigerator that used to be alive, swimming or crawling in the water. In addition, you toss in the holy trinity—bell pepper, onion, and celery—along with roux, a wonderful, smoky soup base made from browning flour in butter. Top it off with a generous supply of garlic, various spices, and white wine, and you have gumbo.

Right now, you could go down to the local store and buy a can of "gumbo" made by a major company. I've actually tasted it, and though I've never been to culinary school, I can authoritatively say to you that it's not gumbo. You can even go to one of the many Cajun restaurants popping up everywhere and order gumbo, and though it's better than the canned version, it's still not gumbo. You can't package gumbo, nor can you mass-produce it. If you really want to experience good gumbo, you must make it yourself. To do so, you begin with your grandmother's recipe (or one out of a cookbook if your parents weren't Cajun), and then you make it your own by adding flavors and ingredients that suit your tastes. It takes a lot of trial and error, but eventually, if you don't give up, everything comes together, and you take a sip of something that makes your feet scoot across the floor in a Cajun two-step.

Faith is like gumbo; for it to be authentic, at some point you have to make it your own.

This will be the hardest thing you've ever done in your life, which is why Jesus described the path as the "narrow way." For many, this term has been misused to connote the idea that it's narrow because "true Christians" should go around pushing off people who don't conform to *our* image. The truth is that it's narrow because it's hard and frustrating work conforming to the *image of Christ*, and very few are willing to make the effort or pay the price. Because ultimately, authentic faith requires that you go on your own peregrinatio. The scary problem with this is that no one is given detailed instructions. Just look at how befuddled the disciples were—*and they were with Jesus.* Their peregrinatio typically began with Jesus walking up to them and saying, "Follow me," and then he was off. The path he led them on was dangerous, filled with joy and hope but also with despair and doubt. Sometimes Jesus taught plainly; sometimes he spoke in riddles. Sometimes he appeared attractive and safe, sometimes scary and wild. If his followers complained, which they often did, Jesus would say something like, "Deny yourself, take up your cross, and follow me."

Well, that helps.

What many people think Jesus meant when he said "deny yourself" is that you have to go to church even when you don't want to. If you really want to deny yourself, go to Sunday school or catechism, where you will be forced to listen to someone read from a teacher's guide—and therein lies part of the problem. Spiritual formation conducted in church often comes from material written by a pastor or scholar who was given strict guidelines about how to present the content so that consistency in the product is maintained. Other pressures shape the content. The writer must assume that the reader doesn't know much about the Bible. The material must sell. It can't be too controversial, so the writer must say fairly safe things so no one is offended and the publisher won't lose customers. The material is assigned, which means that the author must contend with a specific text or topic that he or she may not even find interesting. There isn't anything necessarily wrong with this methodology, but it limits the process because it is formulated, for the most part, for novices.

The hard truth is that at some point, many church members reach a place of dissatisfaction in their faith because they begin to hear the same things over and over again and wonder, "Is this all there is?" The simple answer is, "Heavens, no." But maturing in your faith means you must venture off on your own. You must read, meditate, journal, act, serve, dialogue, and create on your own initiative. It is a good idea to find a mentor or a spiritual director who can provide guidance while refraining from telling you where to go. This will force you to take responsibility for your own peregrination, which will lead you to some uncomfortable places, even dead ends. Understand that it's only in the discomfort, struggle, and suffering that growth beyond spiritual childhood can take place. But beware. On this peregrinatio, the black and white environment you started in (and necessarily so) will give way to questions, skepticism, and doubts. It's not all painful. Ancient pilgrims enjoyed ecstatic, eureka moments. Much of your peregrinatio will thrill and exhilarate you—but these moments won't come without much struggle and effort and pain because ultimately, as J. Phillip Newell explains, "[T]he gospel of Christ leads us not into what we already know but into what we do not yet know."[9] George MacLeod continues the thought by adding, "Even if it takes you outside your preconceived ideas of God or life. Even if it takes you outside your own country into most insignificant alien places . . . ."[10]

This book is designed to help you begin such a journey and stay on it. Like the Evangelist in Bunyan's *Pilgrim's Progress* or Virgil in Dante's *Inferno*, I will attempt to lead you to signposts along the way where we will pause and reflect. We will tap into the ancient wisdom collected from others who have made this journey, both in the Bible and in Christian history. I'll toss in some of my own words of wisdom, for what that will be worth. My goal is not to give you formulas or answers or to make you feel spiritually warm and fuzzy. This journey is more about understanding yourself, God, and the ancient community of faith called the church from which we all receive our faith. It is a journey to understanding the questions of faith better and thinking beyond the simple answers that have a habit of disillusioning us when life slams into our theology.

So, to start us off, here is another song from *The Lord of the Rings*. This one is from Bilbo Baggins in *Fellowship of the Ring*:

> The Road goes ever on and on
> > Down from the door where it began.
> Now far ahead the Road has gone,
> > And I must follow, if I can,
> Pursuing it with eager feet,
> > Until it joins some larger way
> Where many paths and errands meet.
> > And whither then? I cannot say.

An Introduction to the Inward Peregrinatio

These chapters are not merely an opportunity for you to go "hmm." They are an invitation for you to roll up your sleeves and do the difficult work of going on your own peregrinatio. To help, I've created journaling exercises.

These are not Bible studies or objective questions to test your knowledge. There are no right or wrong answers (for the most part). These are simply designed to provoke an experience.

Make sure to allow the material from each chapter to sink in before going on to the next one. If you do not keep a journal, purchase one and begin practicing this important spiritual discipline. Thomas Merton was a master at journaling, and most of his books are products from his journals. If you are new to journaling, read *The Intimate Merton* published by HarperCollins and study how he wrote.

Ideally, your insights should be shared. The ancients did this in community, with a confessor or mentor or spiritual director who had years of wisdom behind him or her in order to act as a guide to the novitiates. Henri Nouwen's book *Spiritual Direction* has a great appendix offering advice for choosing a spiritual director. However, you may want to share with a group of friends or with your small group in church. By sharing your experiences, you can gain new insights you never thought of before.

The important thing to remember is that each person's journey is unique. People in the group may feel compelled to provide answers. RESIST! Remember, a major part of a peregrinatio is struggling to find the answer for yourself.

Think of this process like the metamorphosis of a caterpillar. If you try to intervene, even with the best intentions, you will kill the butterfly. The struggle that the butterfly goes through in emerging from the cocoon is a necessary workout that strengthens the wings, gives them sufficient time to dry, and prepares them for the long journey. The best you can do is to provide a safe environment for this to take place.

To that end, leaders or other members of the group must view their role as one of encouragement, listening, and only sparingly providing a little guidance through feedback. And the best way to do that is to ask questions, not to give a lecture. The group has to be a safe place for everyone to struggle. Let the tension exist. Allow for the sessions to end without closure.

And enjoy!

For each chapter, I identify a major question that the material provokes. This will be the parameter for journaling and for discussion. In addition to a question, I will identify a fear. As you jot down insights, reflect on how your fears are shaping your thoughts on the content of the chapter. As will be discussed more thoroughly in the book, if we allow our fears to be the main motivator, it will take us down paths that lead to dead ends, self-destruction, or worse! As St. Anthony taught, fears must be faced and battled. Only then will we figure out who we really are and what God has called us to do. As you identify where your fears are pushing you, push back and look to see what's on the other side. More than likely, that is where you need to go in your journaling. Look to the stories of others as your guide and inspiration.

To provide additional help, on my website, www.spilledcoffeeon ancientscrolls.com, I have a collection of exercises in a section titled "From Eden to Heaven Prompts." Here you will find readings, film clips, and thought-provoking questions to help you with your journal. These are organized by chapter titles. So after you finish a chapter, go to the corresponding page online and work through the material. Expect some of it to be helpful and some of it to flop; there is no cookie-cutter approach. Learn to trust your instincts. If an exercise disturbs you, frightens you, or moves you, there is probably something there you need to pursue. Spend some time with it, and even do some further research on your own. But don't be legalistic about it. Your inward journey may take you in a completely different direction from what I offer. Go! Just make sure to record it in your journal. Remember, you are responsible for finding your own path.

Go Deeper

"From Eden to Heaven Prompts"
at www.spilledcoffeeonancientscrolls.com

John Bunyan, *Pilgrim's Progress*

Thomas Merton, *The Seven Storey Mountain*

Notes

1. See Joseph H. Lynch, *Early Christianity* (Oxford: Oxford University Press, 2010) 187–89.

2. Bruria Bitton-Ashkelony, *Encountering the Sacred: The Debate on Christian Pilgrimage in Late Antiquity* (Berkeley: University of California Press, 2005) 53–55. It's important to note that Gregory's words were directed at fellow ascetics.

3. Desiderius Erasmus, *The Colloquies of Desiderius Erasmus: Concerning Men, Manners, and Things*, trans. N. Bailey (London: Gibbings & Company, Limited, 1900) 2:212–13.

4. "Pilgrimages," *The Oxford Dictionary of the Christian Church*, 3rd ed., rev. (Oxford: Oxford University Press, 2005) 1297.

5. Unless otherwise noted, all Scripture quotations are from the New International Version of the Bible (NIV).

6. Irenaeus, *Against Heresies* 5, preface.

7. Esther De Waal, *The Celtic Way of Prayer* (New York: Image Books, 1997) 2.

8. Ibid.

9. J. Philip Newell, *The Book of Creation* (New York: Paulist Press, 1999) 29.

10. Ibid.

Departure

The Garden of Eden

Everyone is as God has made him, and
oftentimes a great deal worse.
　　　　　　　　　　　—Miguel de Cervantes

What did God mean when he stated in Genesis 1 that he made us in his image and likeness and then plopped us in the middle of the garden of Eden? If you'll allow me to dabble in the murky world of authorial intent, I think the writer more than likely had in mind that we simply look like God, as depicted in Michelangelo's creation of Adam: God in a long white T-shirt, looking buff, extending his arm in a regal way so that it points to Adam. Adam casually points back, with a teenage "whatever" expression on his face. And thus, humanity pops into existence in the image of the Creator—though a much younger version because, judging by God's very white hair, he waited a long time before he started having kids.

But this is much too simple. Everyone who has ever read Genesis 1 has an opinion about what "image and likeness" means. Suggestions range from classical ideas found in Philo, where God created us in his image by giving us an intellect,[1] to Gregory of Nyssa, who believed God gave us virtue. Others believe that image and likeness are two different ideas. For example, Thomas Aquinas viewed the "image" as intellect/free will and likeness as grace, which was lost in the fall but can be found again in Christ. Then there are Martin Luther and John Calvin, who essentially said this debate doesn't really matter because sin has deformed us so badly that we look like a butt boil. But the Reformers also said that by the grace of God we are being recreated into pre-fallen beings for whom life with God is made possible again. I could go on and on with other ideas proffered through the centuries about what it means that we are made in God's image and likeness, like the fact that we have creative ability, reason, and authority.

Admittedly, the question has a certain allure to it. It's like finding out you were adopted and then being overwhelmed with a desire to find your birth parents because, in doing so, you can learn a lot about yourself: does baldness run in my family; do I have siblings; what genetic diseases should

I be looking for; why did my mom give me up for adoption? In the same way, answering the question, "How am I made in the image and likeness of God?" reveals vital information about us. This question, in fact, is not too far from the opinion of Augustine, who believed that in order to understand the image of God, we must first delve deep into our own souls.[2]

* * *

At this very moment I'm sitting at a Starbucks on South 14th Street in Abilene, Texas. I'm gazing out a window that overlooks a busy street, like any busy street in any town, with a grocery store, a Taco Bell next to a Wienerschnitzel, and cars zooming past. But on this day there is a child's sticky handprint on the glass window, ghostlike because of the way the sun makes it glow. It appears 3-D, as if hovering in the air. I can discern the fine lines in the fingertips, and I ponder the moment when the child slapped his hand against the window before being tugged away by a parent. My imagination conjures the scene: A mother sips coffee with a friend. The two are engrossed in a conversation while their children scramble around the table. First sitting and shoving a cinnamon roll in his mouth, then clamoring to the floor in a giggle, the toddler expresses complete boredom with the conversation of the grown-ups and complete fascination with the strange world of Starbucks. He glances outside, sees a dazzling and noisy world, smiles broadly. He then waddles to the window and scales a chair. With glee he slaps his hand against the glass. Startled, the mother rises while continuing to talk to her friend. She wraps her arms around her son and pulls him back. "No!" she commands, while still conversing fluently. He frowns, doesn't understand why this forbidden fruit is denied. He struggles to return to the window. The two wrestle for a while until the mother gets frustrated. "I said, no!" His frown turns to a tantrum. She's now embarrassed as she feels the stares of the mellow coffee drinkers. Time to go.

And now here I sit, enamored with this unique thing of beauty created by the toddler. There's not another handprint in the world exactly like it. The image represents so much potential. It displays innocence, a strong will, creativity, intelligence—in short, the image of God—yet it was produced by a human and is therefore very fragile, for it will soon disappear with a spray and a wipe.

* * *

The image of God seems to be a popular topic lately. I think it has to do with an increased interest in the plight of the marginalized. Recently, I attended a conference where social justice played a prominent role in the discussion. A stream of innovative business and ministry entrepreneurs paraded on stage to inspire us with their creative approaches to reducing suffering in the world. Almost every one of them said at some point, "I believe people are created in the image of God." While they didn't elaborate on what it means to be created in the image of God, it seems they meant that the image of God grants dignity to all people, making everyone valuable and worthy of our efforts to help. At the end of the conference, one of the final speakers said, "I too, believe in the image of God, but we do have a fallen nature. Both are true." Given the context of his message, what he meant was that though there is great potential for good in humanity, there is also great potential for evil. Sometimes we are drawn toward the dark side of our nature. In other words, this speaker was reminding the audience that, while humanity is endowed with the beautiful image of God, humans also have a rogue attitude that tends to mess things up.

In fact, "messing up" tends to be the dominant depiction of ourselves in the church. We put it in our creeds: "We acknowledge man by nature to be blind, darkened in understanding, and full of corruption and perversity of heart . . . ."[3] And we preach it in our sermons, like the famous one titled "Sinners in the Hands of an Angry God" by Jonathan Edwards, which contains this inspiring passage:

> Your wickedness makes you as it were heavy as lead, and to tend downwards with great weight and pressure towards hell; and if God should let you go, you would immediately sink and swiftly descend and plunge into the bottomless gulf, and your healthy constitution, and your own care and prudence, and best contrivance, and all your righteousness, would have no more influence to uphold you and keep you out of hell, than a spider's web would have to stop a falling rock.[4]

If both points are true—that we are mess-ups and also inhabited by the image of God—where does this leave us? Perhaps where the poet Edward Young, a favorite of hymn writer Charles Wesley, has put us: in a confused tension.

How poor? How rich? How abject? How august?
How complicate? How wonderful is Man?—

An Heir of Glory! A frail Child of Dust!
Helpless Immortal! Insect Infinite!
A Worm! A God![5]

The pendulum between viewing humanity as "a worm" or as "a god" has swung back and forth throughout the history of the church. As illustrated above, people living during the Reformation tended to have a low opinion of the nature of humanity. In fact, one of the few areas of doctrine that Catholics and Lutherans, Calvinists and Arminians could all agree on was that humankind was inherently wormish. To prove it, they launched a brutal thirty-year war of torturing and slaughtering each other, plummeting Europe into a chaos where religious fanatics knew no bounds in the treatment of the enemy, their wives, and their children. Eventually, Europeans concluded that if this is Christianity, then they wanted no part of it, giving rise to the Enlightenment and the secularization of government. At that point, many intellectuals began questioning everything about the church that had behaved so badly, calling into question the most sacred of doctrines, including the existence of God. And, as humanity advanced in science and technology, a new confidence arose that suggested that perhaps humanity wasn't so bad after all. Maybe, free from the shackles of religion, humanity could aspire to greatness. Even godhood.

Enter Friedrich Schleiermacher, the son of a Reformed chaplain born in the latter part of the eighteenth century. His father experienced a deep conversion to a pietistic faith practiced by the Moravian Brethren, and, desiring that his son experience the same, he enrolled him in a Moravian school to learn theology. Though I'm sure the faculty at this school did their best to create little saints out of the student body, Schleiermacher rebelled. He helped gather a small group of kindred spirits, and together they formed a secret club, much like the one in the movie *Dead Poets Society*, only they read the writings of philosophers instead of poets. Also, Robin Williams wasn't born yet, so it wasn't nearly as funny. Plus, there's no indication that they were obsessed with girls. They were, however, obsessed with doubt.[6] In their clandestine meetings, they spoke about it openly to one another, giving one naïve member, Samuel Oakley, the courage to challenge the "false beliefs" of the school. The faculty promptly sent him home, and in summer 1787, he drowned in a tragic accident.

This news disturbed young Schleiermacher, prompting him to reject the teachings of the school and, consequently, the heritage his father desperately wanted him to embrace. As the years went by, Schleiermacher dropped hints to his parents about his skepticism, but they went unnoticed. Finally, in 1794, Schleiermacher confronted his father, and the two got into a heated fight, causing irreparable damage to the relationship. It ended with his father declaring Friedrich a "denier of God." The young man walked away from his father's pietism and never turned back though he always considered himself to be a Moravian of a higher order.[7]

Schleiermacher went on to study theology and philosophy, becoming enamored with German Romanticism and Immanuel Kant. He desired to redefine the great doctrines of Christianity in a way that stayed true to Reformation ideas while at the same time addressing the new challenges posed by the skepticism of the Enlightenment. The result earned him the titles "Father of Modern Theology" and "Father of Liberalism." He became well known for his denial of the supernatural, what he called "magic" in an intentionally provocative way that was most likely designed to jab at the Moravian heritage he found so oppressive. But on a more serious level, Schleiermacher desired to rescue Christianity both from the traditionalists of his day, who seemed clueless that religion was becoming less and less credible to Europeans, and also from the skeptics of the day, who envisioned a world without religion. In this respect, Schleiermacher hoped to offer a third way.

And he did. His revision of Christianity captured the attention of the Western world. With respect to the image of God and the nature of humanity, Schleiermacher developed an anthropocentric theology/philosophy, emphasizing the role of the individual over any initiative by God. In effect, you must take it upon yourself to move from a state of sin, what he described as "God-forgetfulness," to a place of grace, what he called "God-consciousness." As motivation for the journey, the individual experiences a type of pain. It is not the "ow-I-banged-my-elbow-on-the-doorframe-of-my-office-for-the-third-time-today" type of pain but more like that of Neo in *The Matrix*: a "there's-something-just-not-right-with-the-world" type of pain. To escape this pain, one must achieve a higher consciousness, what he called a "feeling of absolute dependence" on God.[8]

Schleiermacher's liberalism became quite popular in the nineteenth century, and at the beginning of the twentieth century, it dominated the theological discussion of Western Christianity. With the Industrial Revolution, the invention of the horseless carriage, electricity harnessed, and flight made possible, it seemed that the inherent goodness of man was indeed creating a heaven on earth. Who really needed God?

Then the political leaders in Europe thought it would be fun to start a war. And not just any war, but one so violent and massive that they called it a World War, even though most of the world didn't actually participate. The new technology people believed would usher in a utopia was now used to inflict death and destruction on a scale never seen before in human history. Learning to fly meant that we dropped bombs from the sky. Automobiles were turned into tanks, which could shoot shells that riveted soft bodies with shrapnel. Rifles were turned into machine guns capable of mowing down a multitude. And then new technologies developed that escalated our ability to kill. Chlorine gas was carefully coaxed toward the enemy where it formed hydrochloric acid in the lungs and caused men to drown in their own fluids. Mustard gas soon followed, a more lethal chemical killer that formed huge, painful blisters on the victim, often bringing about an agonizing death. Flame throwers were also improved. Now a soldier could strap a fuel tank on his back, aim his weapon at a trench filled with men, and open up the gates of hell on his victims.

Now, who really needed Satan?

The evil of World War I was a stunning blow to Enlightenment and Liberal thinkers. Not only did they fail to adequately respond to the horrific ways human beings treated other human beings, but many of the direct descendants of Schleiermacher actually endorsed the war. This bothered Karl Barth, a thoughtful son of a Reformed pastor living in Germany. And when ninety-three German intellectuals publicly supported Kaiser Wilhelm II's war policies that plunged the country into suffering, Barth couldn't stand it anymore. He wrote,

> And to my dismay, among the signatories I discovered the names of almost all my German teachers . . . . An entire world of theological exegesis, ethics, dogmatics, and preaching, which up to that point I had accepted as basically credible, was thereby shaken to the foundations, and with it everything which flowed at that time from the pens of the German theologians.[9]

In reaction, Barth sought to remove the subjectivism that he felt was the main weakness of Liberalism. But he had to replace it with something that could be more objective. Let's see—what could the son of a Reformed pastor possibly come up with that would provide a Christian with objective truth?

How about the Bible?

But far from just resurrecting the "*sola biblia*," the old doctrine that placed the "Bible alone" as the highest authority for a Christian, Barth offered a new way of understanding and interpreting the Bible. The system he developed came to be identified by different names, but it was predominately known as "Neoorthodoxy" for the way it resurrected stalwart Reformation ideas. Far from just microwaving the theological leftovers of Martin Luther and John Calvin, Barth concocted a new recipe. For starters, he exposed what he deemed to be the main weakness of the Reformers, which was their sheer arrogance. For example, for Luther the Word of God was Jesus, and where the Bible revealed Jesus, it was the Word. This sounds great on paper, but in practice, what do you do when one person says, "I think Jesus is revealed in *this* way," and another person says, "No, you're wrong. I think Jesus is revealed *this* way"? For Luther, the obvious answer was that the correct revelation of Jesus in the Bible was *Luther's* way. So if you wanted to know the biblical answer for any question, just ask Luther!

Barth attempted to bring a little humility to the issue. For him, the Word of God provided both answers and questions. God is "wholly other" and even "unknowable." In the presence of this awesome reality, humanity is puny and clueless. God actually has to point out to us that we are sinners, and he does this by taking the initiative and intervening in our lives with grace. But this is not the kind of grace that gives us the warm fuzzies, as if God has allowed us to crawl into his lap while he rocks us to sleep. On the contrary, this grace makes us *very* uncomfortable. It convicts us and reveals to us our precarious predicament whereby on the one side is the terrible idea of God, and on the other side is the self-criticism of humanity. The individual is stuck in the middle in a great deal of tension, squirming and left with only one thing to do: move forward.[10]

One day, my seven-year-old son and I were playing basketball in front of our house. My five-year-old daughter was nearby, exploring the grass for bugs, especially roly-polies. She loves to let them crawl up her arm because they tickle, and then she collects them in the palm of her hand and rolls them around after they've curled up in a ball. But on this particular occasion, she was obviously distracted and frequently stopped to look up at the sky. Eventually she crossed the driveway and looked up again. Next, she got behind the basketball goal, grabbed the pole with one hand, and spun around, all the while gazing upward. Finally, she stopped and looked at me. "Daddy," she said with a very serious and inquisitive tone, "does the moon follow me around because I am the most beautiful girl in the world?"

What a positively wonderful question, filled with all kinds of theological insight! In that moment, I was so proud of her. I told her as emphatically as I could, hoping she would never forget, "Yes, Eliana! God placed the moon in the sky to follow you around because you are the most beautiful girl in the world!" If there were any way for me to make sure she always believes this about herself, I would do it. Because this is how I want her to think about herself.

I mention this because becoming a father completely changed the context of the questions surrounding the image and likeness of God in us. It's easy for me to see the dignity and beauty of humanity because I see it in my children. And it's hard for me to conclude that God views my children as any less than that.

However, seeing the dignity and beauty of my children also magnifies the wickedness in the world. I observe the saints my children are becoming, and my heart swells with optimism. But when I read a story in the paper about an atrocity committed by some broken person, I become pessimistic, seeing quite clearly the depravity that could very well be a threat to my children.

It seems that if history has anything to teach us about being made in the image of God, it's that an emphasis on either extreme tends to foul things up. If we emphasize goodness to an extreme, it leads us to confuse the Holy Spirit with the human spirit, as Barth explained. We begin to aspire to a utopia of supermen and superwomen with superchildren. And in the process, we create something more akin to Tolkien's Land of Mordor, where deformed creatures bent on destroying everything good and beautiful run the world. Our overconfidence in our own goodness and potential cultivates pride and idolatry, ultimately leading to world wars.

On the other hand, if we overemphasize depravity, we become vulnerable to fatalism. Like the Puritans of old, we do nothing when a house is struck with lightning, believing that God, in his good pleasure, has willed it destroyed. Why bother with a fire brigade? Who are we to question God's sovereignty? Or worse, we become self-righteous, filled with false humility and emboldened by a theological system that leads us to believe that we are the elite chosen ones, and those outside our clique are depraved and worthy of wrath. Such thinking ultimately leads to wars of religion.

Part of the problem is that in many discussions surrounding the human condition, people feel that they have to decide between two polarized ideas—that deep down, humans are bad, bad, bad or inherently good, good, good—or, as Barth put it, people live in a confused tension between the two, slinking forward. But it's important to realize that other discussions exist about the nature of humanity.

* * *

I find it fascinating that the same words for "image" and "likeness" used to describe the creation of humanity in Genesis 1 are also the words used to describe the birth of Seth in Genesis 5:3: "When Adam had lived for one hundred thirty years, he became the father of a son in his likeness, according to his image, and named him Seth" (NRSV).[11] This suggests that familial connections are a big part of the meaning. In other words, God is our Father, as Jesus taught us to pray. When we are not connected to God, the image of God within us makes us feel estranged. God has hardwired us to need him, and this is the part of our nature that then draws us back to him. But more than being drawn back, we become so enamored out of our love and respect for the Father that we want to be just like him—not in a prideful way but rather in a way that makes us one with him, as Jesus prayed (John 17:23).

Irenaeus wrote that Jesus became "what we are, that He might bring us to be even what He is Himself."[12] It is a sentiment echoed by other early church fathers, including Athanasius. Yes, we struggle with sin. To deny that is to deny an important reality that can get us into trouble, like ignoring an ugly sound coming from our car engine. But to stop there in order to beat ourselves up or to feel guilty or to fuel a dialogue on theodicy or soteriology or atonement is missing the point. The anonymous author of *The Cloud of Unknowing* called this approach "imperfect humility."[13] The better way is to become aware of our brokenness in order to be made whole—to be transformed into the image of Christ. As the psalmist beautifully explains, "Yet you have made them a little lower than God, and crowned them with glory and honor" (Ps 8:5, NRSV).

In this respect, perhaps God has purposely placed the conviction of the superlative beauty and value of a child in the heart of every parent because he wants us to learn how he feels about all of us, adults and children alike. We begin with the babies because it's easy for us to be mesmerized by their dignity. As each child is born, I hear the Father declaring, "My beloved, look! I've placed the moon in the sky to follow you around because you are the most beautiful child in the world." And the parent smiles, because he or she knows beyond a shadow of a doubt that it's true.

Then we grow up, and the moon becomes just a big rock. It gets increasingly difficult for us to believe that God still likes us, much less thinks we're beautiful. We are reminded of our brokenness, our sin. But here is where being a parent has taught me something. When my children misbehave, I never think to myself, "They are unworthy to be in my presence. I will punish them for the rest of their lives!" Rather, I think, "Okay, how do I respond to this to help them mature?" In other words, God doesn't want us flagellating ourselves every time we mess up, nor does he want us to pretend the mess-up never happened. Our inherent identity is not found in our badness or goodness but in our son-ness and daughter-ness. Like any good parent, the Father wants us to learn from our mistakes, seek reconciliation and healing, and grow up to become loving adults who make him proud.

But let's face it. We have a long journey before we get to that point.

Dietrich Bonhoeffer, a student and admirer of Karl Barth, lived in Germany when the Nazis came to power. In the early 1930s, Hitler's party began to assimilate all aspects of German culture, including the church, managing to convince many prominent theologians and pastors to support its bid for power. In their arrogance, they linked the kingdom of God with the German Reich, believing that the Nazi quest for the superior race was the divinely ordained method to bring heaven to earth. A handful of leaders, including Barth, refused to give their endorsement and even became outspoken critics of the government. In 1934, they issued the "Barmen Declaration," which urged Germans to test government propaganda against the Word of God and, where it differed, to reject it. In typical fashion, the Nazis responded with swift brutality. Pastors who signed the document were drafted into the army and sent to the front. Professors were required to sign statements of loyalty to the Third Reich, and if they refused, they were thrown in jail. Barth concluded that this would be a good time to leave, so he moved back to Switzerland, his native homeland.

However, Bonhoeffer, who lived outside Germany at the time, felt just the opposite. He was uncomfortable enjoying his safe environment while his fellow clergymen were being persecuted, so, when a group from the Confessing Church invited him back to Germany to teach at a covert seminary, Bonhoeffer accepted, despite the vocal protests of his friends in England. The young pastor found himself going from a life of ease and comfort to one of oppression and suffering. The Gestapo increasingly made things difficult for him, disbanding his seminary, exiling him from Berlin, and intimidating him to keep him silent. But Bonhoeffer continued to work against the Reich. Prior to his move to Germany, he had been an ardent pacifist. After being immersed in a culture of conflict, though, he concluded that he could not sit idly by and let others make the hard choices for him.

While men like Schleiermacher and later Barth sat at their desks contemplating the image of God in humanity, swinging the pendulum back and forth between dignity and depravity, Bonhoeffer experienced it. He came face to face with raw evil expressed in the Nazi regime. He also saw the noble courage of his fellow pastors who stood up to the SS bullies with shaky but resolute legs. In the midst of this tension, the nature of humanity was no longer an academic issue that could be intellectually explained; now it was real. Now the idealistic side of Bonhoeffer that desired a nonviolent response because this is what the Word of God taught him wrestled with the practical side that one must do something to stop evil. What is a man born in the image and likeness of God to do?

After a great deal of agonizing, Bonhoeffer chose to do what he could to disrupt the Nazis, including joining a group of conspirators who were working on a plan to assassinate Hitler (to what degree Bonhoeffer participated is debated).[14] If Jesus had been alive in Germany at this time, what would he have done? But we're not Jesus. We're not even close. And sometimes we don't have the luxury of knowing the best choice one way or the other. Jesus left us in this beautiful and broken world, filled with good and evil, and commanded us to deny ourselves, take up our cross, and follow him. As Bonhoeffer explained in *The Cost of Discipleship*, following Jesus means we must give up the comforts of shallow Christianity and its offer of "cheap grace." Bonhoeffer further explained, "When Christ calls a man, he bids him come and die."[15]

You can argue with Bonhoeffer about his theology all you want, but you have to respect a man who was willing to wrestle with his convictions in an honest way and follow through on his conclusion even though his actions were fraught with emotional conflict and tension. Bonhoeffer lived his theology, and it cost him everything when the Gestapo arrested him and threw him into prison.

Though a reluctant conspirator, Bonhoeffer was a passionate pastor. While in prison he befriended fellow prisoners and even guards and administrators, continuing to give of himself as he offered comfort and counsel to friend and enemy alike. In return, they helped him smuggle letters and other writings out of the prison, allowing him to continue to be a powerful voice in the conflict. Eventually, as the war continued and it became clear that Germany was about to lose, the government decided to exterminate prisoners it deemed most dangerous. A few days before his prison was liberated by the Americans, Bonhoeffer was hanged.

What's remarkable about Bonhoeffer's story is that it is a beautiful illustration of the struggle to understand the image of God in humanity. We like to couch it in simple terms. We want it to be clear. Humanity is depraved. Humanity is dignified. But that kind of theology doesn't harmonize well with the real world. We can debate about the great truths inherent in this subject, but in the end, like Bonhoeffer, we are all left to do the best we can, realizing that loving our neighbor isn't as simple as clothing the naked and feeding the hungry. It isn't as easy as always turning the other cheek. And that's okay. Because, as Bonhoeffer wrote, "When all is said and done, the life of faith is nothing if not an unending struggle of the spirit with every available weapon against the flesh."[16]

One spring I attended a funeral for a friend who died too young and who had left behind two daughters and a son. At the graveside, so many people were gathered that I stood a good distance from the casket and could barely hear the pastor. A woman named Connie approached me while we waited for the service to conclude. Her head barely reached my shoulder, and she had a round face with straight, brunette hair that looked a little disheveled; ironically, she owned a local beauty shop. We chatted for a while and got caught up on things. Connie had been battling cancer for years and had lived far longer than the doctors expected. She didn't like to talk about her own cancer much, except to boast about how God was confounding her oncologist.

Connie refused to be depressed or sad about her condition. Instead, she dealt with her anxiety by doing everything she could to stare down Death in a contest to make him blink first. She had a contagious, independent spirit. She refused to miss work even when she was feeling wretched. She reached out to other cancer patients in the area. Numerous times I saw her driving someone to the doctor's office for chemotherapy or visiting acquaintances at the hospital—even people she barely knew. She volunteered at the funeral home, styling the hair of the deceased before they were presented at a funeral service. Until I had met Connie, I never even thought about the need for this kind service. Somehow, this melancholic ministry gave Connie humor and strength to make it one more day. She is one of those rare individuals I have met whom I would nominate for sainthood.

Eventually we ran out of things to say and strained to listen to the pastor. He was bringing his remarks to a close, and, as he did, Connie reached out and grabbed my hand. I have to admit I was a little embarrassed at first. Here I was without my wife, and Connie was without her husband, and we were both surrounded by a mob of people, some of whom were my former church members, and we were holding hands. What would people think? I felt awkward. But after the initial shock wore off, I was able to think a little more clearly about what was going on. I turned and looked at Connie, who was crying just a little, her eyes fixated on the casket. And I don't think it was just because of sadness. She was scared—because the next funeral to take place might be her own.

How dumb could I be? Here I was, afraid of what others might think when all the while Connie was giving me a precious gift. I had been her pastor. However uncomfortable this closeness made me, I was God's representative to her. In that moment, the child in her needed the Father to hold her hand, and God had placed me there to do just that. I stepped a little closer and she rested her head on my upper arm as we watched the casket being lowered into the grave.

As I glanced up, I saw a full moon in the broad daylight—ghostlike, hovering in the air. And then I looked down at Connie.

She was beautiful. Created in the image of God. Filled with dignity. Fragile, living in a broken world and doing the best she could. A treasure in a jar of clay.

Neither worm nor god, but frightened child.

I watched as the moon followed her around for the rest of the day.

Inward Peregrinatio to the Garden of Eden

Question: Who am I?
Fear: I am nothing.

Social psychologists have a concept known as the "looking-glass self." It refers to the idea that our self-image is directly connected to the way we feel that others perceive us, especially those whom we deem to be the most important. For many of us, God plays a very important role in our lives, so what he thinks about us greatly shapes our self-identity.

In Christian circles, the discussion about God's view of humanity often boils down to two extremes: that we are depraved or dignified. I hope that, after reading the chapter, you realize that the question is much more complicated. Ultimately, this is a question about how you view yourself. Do you feel worthless? Do you feel valuable?

Who are you?

Part of the answer is found in becoming self-aware. Our culture would like us to find value in money or success or beauty or youth or ability. We value people who look good on a magazine cover or who can throw a ball 100 miles an hour.

Though most of us would agree that this is shallow on an intellectual level, moving on to a more mature way of thinking is incredibly difficult.

Our faith teaches us that value is found through relationships and character development, among other things. In the garden of Eden, Adam and Eve were secure in their self worth because their character and relationships were untainted. Contemplatives like Thomas Keating refer to this as the "true self."

Deep inside all of us is our true self—and it is the image that we all began life with, one filled with innocence and wonder. But then we grow up and leave Eden and, in so doing, develop a "false self," which is the damaged and broken image that must be covered up with fig leaves and masks.

A big part of what Eden teaches us in spiritual formation is that all of us had our beginning here. An now, we must find our way back—back to the place where we once again see the moon as a loving act of God, who placed the orb in the sky to follow us around because we are his beautiful children.

For this to happen, we must strip away pretense, remove the false self, and allow our true self to return. There is no formula for how to do this, but the ways of silence, solitude, and stillness have proven valuable practices in this endeavor. Ultimately, we must all wrestle with the the riddle, "How has God created *you* in God's image and likeness?" As you unravel this mystery, you will find yourself on a journey back to Eden, the place where you can be as God intended, naked and unashamed.

Go Deeper

"Garden of Eden" in "From Eden to Heaven Prompts" at
www.spilledcoffeeonancientscrolls.com

Dietrich Bonhoeffer, *The Cost of Discipleship*

Athanasius, *On the Incarnation of the Word*

Notes

1. Literally "*logikos*," meaning intellect, and "*nous*," meaning mind.

2. See Augustine's *Confessions*, in which he wrote,

The conversation led us towards the conclusion that the pleasure of the bodily senses, however delightful in the radiant light of this physical world, is seen by comparison with the life of eternity to be not even worth considering. Our minds were lifted up by an ardent affection towards eternal being itself. Step by step we climbed beyond all corporeal objects and the heaven itself, where sun, moon, and stars shed light on the earth. We ascended even further by internal reflection and dialogue and wonder at your works and we entered into our own minds. We moved up beyond them so as to attain to the region of inexhaustible abundance where you feed Israel eternally with truth for food. There life is the wisdom by which all creatures come into being, both things which were and which will be. But wisdom itself is not brought into being but is as it was and always will be. Furthermore, in this wisdom there is no past and future, but only being, since it is eternal. For to exist in the past or in the future is no property of the eternal. And while we talked and panted after it, we touched it in some small degree by a moment of total concentration of the heart. And we sighed and left behind us "the firstfruits of the Spirit" (Rom. 8:23). (Augustine, *Confessions* [Oxford: Oxford University Press, 1998] 171)

3. Mark Noll, *Confessions and Catechisms of the Reformation* (Grand Rapids MI: Baker Book House, 1991) 127. This comes from the Genevan Confession of 1536, but it's illustrative of many, if not most, confessions.

4. Jonathan Edwards, "Sinners in the Hands of an Angry God," digitalcommons. unl.edu/cgi/viewcontent.cgi?article=1053&context=etas (as well as many other online locations).

5. John Richard Watson, *The English Hymn* (Oxford: Oxford University Press, 1999) 251.

6. Schleiermacher and his friends weren't the first to pursue this obsession. For an in-depth look at the history of the pursuit of doubt, see Richard H. Popkin, *The History of Skepticism* (Oxford: Oxford University Press, 2003).

7. See Terrence Tice, *Schleiermacher* (Nashville: Abingdon Press, 2006) 3ff.

8. I'm indebted to Walter E. Wyman Jr.'s article "Sin and Redemption" for this material on Schleiermacher. It can be found in Jacqueline Mariña, ed., *The Cambridge Companion to Friedrich Schleiermacher* (Cambridge: Cambridge University Press, 2005) 129–47.

9. Karl Barth, *The Theology of Schleiermacher*, trans. Geoffrey W. Bromily (Grand Rapids MI: Eerdmans, 1982) 263–64.

10. See Justo L. González, *The Reformation to the Present Day*, vol. 2 of *The Story of Christianity* (New York: HarperOne, 1999) 361–64; John R. Franke, *Barth for Armchair Theologians* (Louisville: Westminster John Knox Press, 2005) 68–70.

11. My brilliant Hebrew scholar wife, Susan, pointed this out to me.

12. Irenaeus, *Against Heresies* 5, preface.

13. *The Cloud of Unknowing* (14th century; trans. Carmen Acevedo Butcher, Boston: Shambhala Publications, 2009) 37.

14. See Mark Thiessen Nation, Anthony G. Siegrist, and Daniel P. Umbel, *Bonhoeffer the Assassin? Challenging the Myth, Recovering His Call to Peacemaker* (Grand Rapids MI: Baker Academic, 2013). See also Matthew D. Kirkpatrick, ed., *Engaging Bonhoeffer: The Impact and Influence of Bonhoeffer's Life and Thought* (Minneapolis: Fortress Press, 2016).

15. Dietrich Bonhoeffer, *The Cost of Discipleship* (New York: Touchstone, 1959) 11.

16. Ibid., 171. In context, this quote is found in the middle of a point that Bonhoeffer is making about the need for struggle and discipline in order for spiritual growth to take place. His use of the word "flesh" refers to self-indulgence and laziness.

The Tree of Knowledge

One fatal Tree there stands of Knowledge called
Forbidden them to taste. Knowledge forbidden?
Suspicious reasonless. Why should their Lord
Envy them that? Can it be sin to know?
Can it be death? And do they only stand
By ignorance? Is that their happy state,
The proof of their obedience and their faith?
　　　　　　　—John Milton, *Paradise Lost*, Book 4

I saw a group of five-year-olds walk by my office window one day. Their guides looked pleasantly stern, leading the little ones by the hand. The children, stocky-legged and fair-haired, were clothed in bright colors—pink, purple, orange—that glowed in the harsh sun. They obediently traipsed along in a snake line, dragging a little because of curiosity, for the courtyard offered a number of tantalizing sights and sounds apparently invisible to the adults. For example, a bowling alley is housed in the basement of a building bordering one side of the courtyard. Vents act like speakers, amplifying crashes and whirs and creaks. I wondered if the children imagined dragons crunching and gnawing on bones.

In addition, the ground presented different textures—grass, pebbles, and bricks set in geometric patterns. Several of the children looked intently downward, spotting bugs and folded leaves. Others gazed wide-eyed at the strange students passing by, shouldering backpacks, displaying tattoos and piercings, bantering or flirting with one another.

What a bizarre and alluring Eden they passed through in that moment. I could tell they wanted to touch and smell and taste their surroundings, but they couldn't because the hand in front of them, attached to another hand, and then another, eventually reached an adult who seemed to be in a hurry. She tugged them onward.

One brave little boy, however, broke the chain and waddled toward a rock on the ground—a forbidden fruit, if you will. For a brief moment he exiled himself from the rest of the group as the two snake halves of children reattached and continued onward. The boy had only a second to make up his mind to stay and to explore by himself, or to join the group. I could tell it wasn't a difficult decision; he obviously felt he wasn't quite old enough yet to be by himself, no matter how curious he was about the rock, for as the last child exited the courtyard, the boy dropped the rock and caught up to the tail, gleefully grabbing the hand of the last child who stretched backward.

And then they were gone.

* * *

In the garden of Eden, Eve reaches out her slender hand toward a tree, plucks, and eats of the forbidden fruit, and then proceeds to pass the fruit to her husband, who had been watching the whole time, mouth gaping. He partakes as well. Immediately their eyes are opened and they perceive they are naked. They feel shame. But why? Did Eve see cellulite? Did Adam notice a beer belly? Regardless, what was once a thing of beauty crafted by the hand of God now needed covering, so in a tragically comic way, the two made fragile garments out of fig leaves. This prompted one of the earliest traditions about the identity of the forbidden fruit—that it was a fig. Over the years, others were proffered, from grapes to apples, the latter popularized by Milton and apparently derived from the pun in Latin where *malum* can mean both evil and apple.

Renowned theologian St. Augustine called this "the fall." The phrase stems from his understanding of the first real sin that took place in the garden of Eden, which was not partaking of the forbidden fruit but feeling a sense of pride. The desire to be like God led Adam and Eve to exalt themselves above God, which motivated them to break God's commandment and eat of the forbidden fruit, whereby they fell from their "true being" and from grace. Augustine's view has stuck ever since, to the degree that this episode is referred to as "The Fall," even though the word "fall" is never mentioned in the text. One has to remember that Augustine lived in a time when order was maintained with a rigid social and political hierarchy. Superiors demanded loyalty from their subjects, blessing those who proved faithful and punishing those who disobeyed. From this worldview, the Western church drew its theology and polity.

For Augustine, God was the great emperor who provided for all the needs of Adam and Eve. They lived in paradise. But how did they repay God? By joining a coup with God's enemy, Satan. The rebellion had to be punished to maintain justice. Since Adam and Eve chose evil (treason) over good (loyalty), they deserved death. And their descendants are now doomed to a hell (exile) by virtue (or rather, vice) of original sin. As Isaac Watts put it, "Would He devote that sacred head for such a worm as I?" In this interpretation, the emphasis is on how depraved (disloyal) humanity is. And also how good (benevolent) God is for allowing Adam and Eve to live though they and their descendants don't deserve it. Nonetheless, a few fortunate people get plucked from the bowels of hell and God elects (pardons) them for salvation.

Though this view has dominated the theology of Western Christianity, there have been alternatives. Believe it or not, prior to Augustine, some theologians didn't see Adam's partaking of the forbidden fruit as all that bad. The real villain of the first family was Cain. The word "sin" is used for the first time in the Bible to describe the murder of Abel, not the partaking of the forbidden fruit. And early Jewish and Christian scholars focused far more on Cain's act in plummeting the world into rebellion than on Adam's.[1] This is not to say that what Adam and Eve did in the garden was okay. The fact that God made childbirth hurt and the ground hard to till certainly expresses his displeasure. However, for rabbinical Judaism, this narrative is indicative of humanity's frailty, not depravity. If God had wanted to make us worms, he would have removed our limbs and placed opposing sex organs at either end.

So Adam and Eve were the first to disobey and the first to begin a cycle of paradise, disobedience, and restoration narratives that are repeated over and over throughout the Old Testament. A simpler way to describe this is with a theme of exile and return, or paradise lost and paradise regained.

In Genesis 4–6, Cain's sin breeds a wickedness that multiplies in his descendants and reaches a peak with the Nephilim and the way "all flesh had corrupted its ways upon the earth" (Gen 6:12, NRSV). God can't stand it anymore, so he sends a flood and starts over again with Noah. The action begins a second attempt to work with humanity, and Noah becomes Adam version 2.0. When Noah disembarks and offers a sacrifice to God, the next cycle begins. All is forgiven. To prove it, God puts a rainbow in the sky. But this doesn't work out too well either. In fact, Noah's son Ham performs the next act of disobedience for which Noah's grandson, Canaan, is cursed. Eventually, this series of events leads to God finally finding a human to work through—Abraham.

In classic rabbinic theology, it's not that sin has been passed on to each generation from Adam; it's that each generation sins. Moreover, the

cycle is not viewed as deterministic though humanity is certainly viewed as
having a propensity toward sin. Nonetheless, there is hope. The cycle *can*
be broken. Adam didn't have the right tool, which is why he lost paradise.
Later in the narrative, Israel will be given the Torah, and this gift will enable
them to live righteously as the promised land is settled.[2]

Much later in Jewish history, just prior to the first century, Jewish theologians debated whether to blame Adam for allowing sin into the world.
A minority of scholars promoted this idea, but the majority continued to
view the individual as responsible for his or her own sins. In fact, a legend
sprung up whereby each soul, upon dying, is required to visit Adam in
the cave of Machpelah, which was considered the entryway back to Eden.
Upon arrival, Adam essentially asks, "Why are you here?"

The soul then attempts, as Adam and Eve did in the garden, to pass the
blame. "I'm here because of you! This is all your fault!"

Adam coolly responds, "Ah, yes, I took a bite of the forbidden fruit.
But what sins have *you* committed?" Adam's words then force the soul into
a bit of introspection whereby it must stop blaming others for its predicament and take responsibility for its own actions.[3] If it doesn't, it is not
allowed past Adam into Eden.

This legend illustrates Jewish thought that sought to minimize the
role of Adam for humanity's woes. In fact, Adam isn't mentioned outside
the book of Genesis in the Old Testament. He represents the first human
being, period. The narrative in Genesis quickly moves on to the patriarchs
and the creation of Israel.

In the New Testament, Adam becomes a little more of a celebrity, but
he is noted more for his bad-boy status than anything else. In the Vulgate,
a fourth-century Latin Bible, Jerome translated Romans 5:12 as "all men
sin in Adam." Augustine picked this up and ran with it, coming up with
the doctrine of original sin, which says that everyone is born in Adam's
sin, therefore deserving death. But try convincing a young mother that the
newborn nursing at her breast deserves to go to hell. My guess is that you
would face a bit of postpartum rage.

Jerome didn't quite get his translation right. Modern Bibles read more
accurately, "death spreads to all because all have sinned" (NRSV). This
supports the understanding of the responsibility for sin relating directly to
the sinner, not to Adam. While the first part of Romans 5:12 does point
to Adam as the instrument by which sin entered the world, a compelling
argument can be made that even with this, Paul was using Adam not as a
scapegoat but as a common representative of all humanity. Adam serves

as a universal figure through which all nationalities trace their roots. In other words, beginning with Adam, all have sinned. Consequently, all need Christ.[4]

* * *

To sum up, we have the popular Augustinian view that sees the partaking of the forbidden fruit as a fall from grace whereby humanity became depraved, and this depravity is passed on to each generation through sex, condemning unbaptized infants to hell. There is the Pauline view, which considers Adam as the first sinner and the universal example of all sinners who need Christ. Finally, there is a classic rabbinic view that looks at the Adam and Eve narrative as the first of a series of exile and return cycles.

One thing I find interesting in the eating of the forbidden fruit narrative is how each group or theologian brings his or her own baggage to the text. The Babylonian exile dominated Jewish thought, so exile and return were what they saw taking place in Eden. Paul, who saw himself as the Apostle to the Gentiles and who preached a gospel that Jesus died for everyone (not just the Jews), viewed Adam as the universal sinner and contrasted him with Christ, the universal savior. Augustine, the theologian of the Imperial Church, pictured the Emperor God condemning the two rebels, along with the rest of their extended family, for treason.

And then there was Irenaeus. Few non-nerdy people have heard of Irenaeus of Lyon. According to tradition, he was a disciple of Polycarp, who was a disciple of the Apostle John. Polycarp was a famous Christian martyr in the second century who was burned at the stake for his courageous confrontation of an unruly mob. After the death of his mentor, Irenaeus migrated to what is now the south of France, where he flourished as a bishop. His love for the job was such that he completely immersed himself in his role as a shepherd, and this image became a dominant theme in his theology. God, the good shepherd, leads his people through the valley of the shadow of death with a rod and a staff to the place of green pasture.

A major shadow in this metaphor was the looming threat of the gnostic heresy. Gnosticism embraced elements of oriental dualism, Greek philosophy, and Christian imagery. This syncretistic approach lent itself to a myriad of variations, but inherent in the many sects was the idea that matter is evil and spirit is good. This led gnostic teachers to conclude that Jesus couldn't have been human, for in order for him to be good he had to have been composed of pure spirit. They even imagined him slightly hovering above the earth so that his being wouldn't be corrupted by the evil nature of the ground. When the Bible describes Jesus as walking, then, he wasn't really walking. It looked like he was walking, but it was all illusion for the benefit of the crowd.

Irenaeus saw a grave danger in Gnosticism and its anti-materialism, so he tended to interpret texts as a means of combating this threat. He guarded against any interpretation that might suggest that Adam and Eve were inherently evil. After all, God declared all of his creation as "very good." Rather than seeing the first couple as so wicked that they infected all of humanity, Irenaeus likened them to *children*, innocent and immature, endowed with goodness and free will. God, far from being an insecure tyrant royally ticked off over a show of disrespect to his authority, was viewed as a responsible father embracing the task of helping his children to grow up. And, in order for this to happen, at some point Adam and Eve had to learn about good and evil. So partaking of the forbidden fruit was a part of God's plan. The problem in the Genesis account is that Adam and Eve partake of the fruit too soon. They are not ready yet. It's like a preteen sneaking into an R-rated movie. He or she isn't mature enough to handle the content. Much like in real life when children grow up too fast, the young couple in the garden found themselves broken, ashamed, and unable to handle the overwhelming feelings of guilt.[5]

For Irenaeus, the "apostasy" of Adam, as he called it, had to happen.[6] God wants humanity to love him not because they have been commanded to but because they want to. Love requires free will, so God must let go. I see this happening in the narrative not on the day that Adam and Eve were sent out of the garden but rather the last time Adam and Eve met with God prior to the conversation with the serpent. In that moment, God knew that it was his last time to spend with his son and daughter without a barrier between them. He knew of the conversation that was going to take place later in the day—the arguments presented by the serpent, the decision his son and daughter would make to reject him. God knew it would break his heart and result in a great deal of emotional pain as he led them back. He could have abandoned them. He could have destroyed them and started over. He could have pouted and turned his back on them. He could have banished the serpent and kept the couple in secluded protection, but he chose to let them go, knowing what they would do, knowing it would cost him, and knowing the suffering everyone would be forced to endure.

Why did God do this? Why does any parent allow a son or daughter to attempt something that might cause pain? Because the benefit must somehow outweigh the risk. For in letting them go, God allowed Adam and Eve to grow up. He gave them independence and free will. And then he wooed them back so that they returned to him motivated out of love, not fear or obligation. This very hard lesson on love makes the risk worth it.

Here is where the story resonates with the baggage I bring to the text. As one who strives to be a loving father, it's hard for me to fathom a good parent as one who is quick to condemn his children and call them depraved. Like Irenaeus, I see in this narrative a compassionate God who desires to help his children mature. For me it is a "coming of age" story told more from the perspective of the parent, and this means it is an agonizing process of letting go, letting children make mistakes, letting them get hurt, yet always being there for them when they want to return.

I first experienced this gut-wrenching reality the day when my oldest, Nathaniel, started school. Here's my journal entry:

It's August 20th, 2003, today. You started kindergarten two days ago. Until you have your own child, you will not understand the anguish your mom and I went through dropping you off on your first day of school. For over five years now, we have been the person you have been with most of your days. Now, your teacher, Ms. Johnson, will see you seven hours, five days a week. Your mom and I both got teary-eyed on the way home. You, however, have been excited about school. At least you were excited about the first day. You were all smiles, sitting in your chair at the "red" table, though I could tell you were a little frightened. I counted the minutes until we could see you again at lunch. I brought Eliana with me, because she wanted to see you, too. You waved at us when you saw us. I said, " hello." And you said, "Go away." It was clear we were cramping your style. So I left Mom there with you and your sister and I took off to get lunch at McDonald's. When we picked you up you were all smiles. The first words out of your mouth were, "I had fun, fun, fun, fun, fun!" Your day was filled with learning the names of your classmates and baking a gingerbread man, which then mysteriously disappeared and you had to find him.

Your second day, however, was a little more traumatic. I think it dawned on you that you were going to have to do this five days a week. You were a little reluctant to get in the car in the morning. I promised you I'd see you for lunch. When I arrived and saw you in line you cried, just a little. We held hands in line while we waited to get your food. When we sat down and talked, it was clear you were homesick. After your meal you asked if you could sit in my lap. I grabbed you and snuggled you until it was time to go back to class. As the rest of your class lined up, you started to cry a little. I told you how proud I was of you and how brave you were being at school. You gave me a hug, kissed me on the cheek, then stood resolute in line, wiping back the tears. You don't know how much I wanted to scoop you up and take you home with me. It took an incredible amount of willpower to leave. But I did, holding back the tears myself.

Letting my son go that day was one of the hardest things I've ever done. By walking away, I left Nathaniel to fend for himself for the first time in his life. He was vulnerable, and I had to let him be vulnerable. If I didn't, he wouldn't grow up. My main job as a parent is to shape him into an independent, mature adult. I know I can't do that effectively unless I let him go, and it's not a matter of just letting him go this one time. I know that my relationship with him is going to be a series of letting go moments, knowing full well that in doing so he stands a good chance of getting hurt. But I do it anyway because I know the risk is worth the reward. When I put him on his bicycle for the first time and let him go, there's a good chance he's going to skin his knee. But I will let him go. The first night he spends at a friend's house, there's a good chance he'll get homesick. But I will let him go. The first time he takes a girl out on a date, there's a good chance he'll get his heart broken. But I will let him go.

In the garden of Eden, God knew that when Eve and Adam spoke to the serpent, they were going to make the wrong decision, but he let them go. Rather than seeing this moment as the "The Fall," perhaps another way of looking at it is "The Great Letting Go."

In the New Testament, Jesus addresses this same theme in his parable of the Prodigal Son (Luke 15:11-32). The narrative follows the paradise-disobedience-restoration formula found throughout the Old Testament with one striking difference—the introduction of a new character that shows up at the end of the story. In the beginning, the plot starts off as usual, with the main character in paradise living with a wealthy dad. He's bored. He rebels against his father by saying, "I wish you were dead so that I could inherit your money." I cannot overstate how horrific this would have sounded to first-century ears. Respect for elders was more than just a polite nicety. It was demanded with ruthlessness. Here's an excerpt from a popular piece of Jewish wisdom literature in Jesus' day:

> He who loves his son will whip him often, so that he may rejoice at the way he turns out . . . . Whoever spoils his son will bind up his wounds, and will suffer heartache at every cry. An unbroken horse turns out stubborn, and an unchecked son turns out headstrong. Pamper a child, and he will terrorize you; play with him, and he will grieve you. Do not laugh with him, or you will have sorrow with him, and in the end you will gnash your teeth. Give him no freedom in his youth, and do not ignore his errors. Bow down his neck in his youth, and beat his sides while he is young, or else he will become stubborn and disobey you, and you will have sorrow of soul from him. Discipline your son and make his yoke heavy, so that you may not be offended by his shamelessness.[7]

When Jesus declared that the prodigal asked for his inheritance, the Jewish listeners would have expected the son to suffer for his insolence. Perhaps the father would turn him over to some ruffians for a beating. Perhaps he would be cast out of town, penniless and naked. Perhaps the father would have him thrown in jail. Regardless, some punitive blood and guts would have been expected as part of the disobedience phase. But that's not what happens in Jesus' story. Instead, the father says, "Okay," which would have brought gasps from the audience. First-century Jews would have considered this a sign of weakness. As the passage quoted above reflects, leaders regularly condemned this kind of disrespect and chastised fathers who allowed it to pass unchecked. But Jesus continues the story with a graphic description of hedonistic living that plummets the prodigal son to the absolute lowest point of degradation for a Jew, eking out a living feeding pigs. I imagine that at this point, the religious leaders in the audience were a little satisfied though not for the reason you might expect. We read into the text that the son deserved what he got. The Jews, though, would have put the blame on the father for not being harsh enough. For them, the shame of the son's behavior was a reflection on the father's weak-willed generosity.

When Jesus described the son's decision to return, the religious leaders were probably thinking, "Well, at least the father will get a second chance to beat his son to a pulp!" But again, they were likely shocked when Jesus described the father acting in an incredibly undignified, immoral, and audacious way by running, hugging, clothing, and restoring the son. This was *not* the way the story was supposed to end. There were no bruises or lacerations or broken legs!

We have to remember that the God Jesus describes in the story of the prodigal is the same God in the garden of Eden. When God's two children ate the forbidden fruit, he could have cried, "Oh my goodness! What have I done?" and wiped out humanity with a spoken word. He could have started over with more loyal creatures, perfect even. But he didn't. He chose the painful path even though it meant having his heart broken over and over again. I never quite understood why God was willing to do this until I became a dad. Now, I read both of these stories from the standpoint of one who has had to make the hard choice of letting a child go, knowing that there's a good chance he's going to get hurt and knowing that I'm going to be hurt in the process, too. I let go anyway because the benefit outweighs the risk; I know it's the only way for him to grow up.

And it's the only way for me to grow up as well.

Henri Nouwen, a twentieth-century Catholic priest, describes an epiphany he had one year while meditating on the story of the prodigal. As part of this journey, he traveled to St. Petersburg to study Rembrandt's painting of the story. You may have seen this famous work that depicts the moment the father embraces the son immediately after his return.[8] Using dark brown tones accented by red, Rembrandt shows the son, dressed in rags, kneeling before the elderly father. The patriarch hunches over, pulling the son into his belly with a look of gentleness. Three people are in the background watching. It's hard to tell what they are focusing on. They seem a bit uncomfortable, as if they are intruding on an intimate moment. Nouwen got special permission from the St. Petersburg hermitage to spend an entire day sitting next to the painting so that he could study it in the different lighting cast by the sun. In the process, he hoped to mine spiritual insight from both the painting and the narrative, and perhaps even from himself as he tried to discern why this story resonated with him so deeply

At first light, Nouwen identified with the prodigal, empathizing with the lost, broken, and ostracized nature of this character, along with his desire to be accepted, restored, and affirmed. Certain that this was the source of his emotional connection, he shared his insight with others, only to be confronted. "Really?" his friends asked. "You, a rebel?" Henri was forced to acknowledge that he had never really indulged in debauchery and drunkenness, but he struggled with feelings of self-righteousness and resentment. Perhaps he was the older son. Then another friend pointed out that, as a priest, Henri was called to the more mature role of the father, opening his arms to the prodigals and the self-righteous in the world, embracing them and restoring them to fellowship with God's family. This insight struck him hardest of all. He wrote,

> As the Father, I have to believe that all that the human heart desires can be found at home. As the Father, I have to be free from the need to wander around curiously and to catch up with what I might otherwise perceive as missed childhood opportunities . . . . As the Father, I have to dare to carry the responsibility of a spiritually adult person and dare to trust that the real joy and real fulfillment can only come from welcoming home those who have been hurt and wounded on their life's journey, and loving them with a love that neither asks nor expects anything in return.
>
> There is a dreadful emptiness in the spiritual fatherhood. No power, no success, no popularity, no easy satisfaction. But that same dreadful emptiness is also the place of true freedom. It is the place where there is "nothing left to lose," where love has no strings attached, and where real spiritual strength is found.[9]

In the past, I read the narrative of the garden of Eden in a light that emphasized "the problem." Humanity had everything they wanted in Eden, yet they rebelled against God and were punished. And though there are certainly elements of truth in these interpretations, I am now drawn to Irenaeus who first saw this narrative in a more positive light as the path to spiritual maturity—a theme Jesus eloquently retold, and Nouwen profoundly discovered, in the story of the prodigal.

Fusing these two stories, then, when God's son and daughter take from the tree of knowledge, they are saying to him, "We wish you were dead so that we could have our inheritance." When they eat the fruit, the Father says, "Okay." When the couple realizes they are naked and become ashamed, sewing fig leaves, it's like eking out a living feeding pigs. When the Father cries, "Adam, where are you?" he is glancing out the window, hoping for the return of his prodigals. When the Father finds Adam and Eve, he puts robes on their backs and sandals on their feet in the form of garments he makes from animal skins. What a tender expression of grace. Granted, at this point in the Genesis narrative, God chastises the couple and they are exiled from Eden. But even this can be seen as an act of grace as they are protected from eating from the tree of life. Perhaps there would have been far worse consequences had this temptation been allowed to linger.

It's at this point that Jesus injects a change in the story formula as a new character is introduced. Here, Israel enters the narrative as the older son. He has been given the Torah, and he has obeyed it rigidly. In fact, he feels quite pleased and self-righteous about how good he is in comparison with everyone else in the world, especially sinners. Furthermore, the older brother can't wait for the day of reckoning when the wicked will be punished. But Jesus upsets everything when he says that the father spends a lavish amount of money throwing an audacious party for the son who has returned home. He doesn't even try to restore the boy quietly. He blatantly celebrates his return! The older brother is livid, and the narrative ends with a cliffhanger as we wonder if the older son will ever swallow his pride and join the party.

Now we, the readers, must come to the text and find our place in this recurring drama. Are we the prodigal, the older son, or the father? As Nouwen reflects, at some point in our pilgrimage we will be all three. Our journey must not only find its way to the father, but we must become the father as we take on the role of the one who lets go . . . and who welcomes home.

* * *
―――――

My children love to play at Fort Imagination, a local playground. The usual schedule involves a long time of dad pushing, spinning, and shaking a tire swing so that it becomes a tornado. Afterward we play tickle-chase, which my children never grow tired of. Fortunately, on one particular day everyone got hungry enough so that we were all ready to go eat dinner at a reasonable time. Since it was early spring, the sun was already setting, turning the clouds salmon. When we got to the parking lot, I instinctively held out my hand to Nathaniel, who grabbed it. We looked both ways and started walking to the far side where the van sat.

"Daddy," Nathaniel began in a way that let me know we were about to talk about something serious. "I'm nine years old now." This was a milestone we had recently celebrated. "Don't you think I'm old enough to walk in a parking lot by myself?"

I smiled but didn't answer right away because it was one of those moments when my brain and my heart were having an argument. Intellectually, I knew that Nathaniel was right. He was cautious and responsible and quite capable of walking in the parking lot without my assistance. He was getting older and more self-conscious about parental affection in public. I had to let him grow up. This is where my heart chimed in. *I don't want to let him grow up.* So how did I respond?

"You're right, Nathaniel," I acquiesced. "You're old enough now to walk by yourself, if you want."

He grinned. He loves to be right.

"But," I continued, "the truth is, I like holding your hand."

He paused and thought about this for a while. Then said, "Me too."

So on this day, we continued to hold hands as we walked to the van. But I cherished every second of it because I had been warned. Time was running out.

At some point, I will have to let my son go.

Inward Peregrinatio to the Tree of Knowledge

Question: Where am I going?
Fear: I am stuck or trapped.

We tend to think of the "Fall" in a negative way—that it is the cause of humanity's problems. I'm not trying to change your mind about that, but for a moment, consider Irenaeus's view that leaving Eden was (and is) a necessary part of life designed to help us mature and grow up. It's a spiritual coming-of-age story. Whether or not you agree with Irenaeus in the big theological picture, on a smaller scale there are many people who have to depart a safe existence and walk into the unknown in order to grow up. There has to be a free fall or a pit or a rock bottom before they are able to let go of the things that hold them back from becoming what they are meant to be. There are some lessons people cannot learn at home. Whether we like it or not, we have to leave and experience being let go. We have to stand at the threshold and take the first step, and then the next, and then the next, until we are far from home.

Go Deeper

"Tree of Knowledge" in "From Eden to Heaven Prompts" at
www.spilledcoffeeonancientscrolls.com

Henri Nouwen, *The Return of the Prodigal Son*

Philokalia: The Eastern Christian Spiritual Texts,
translated by Palmer, Sherrard, and Ware

Notes

1. Peter C. Bouteneff, *Beginnings: Ancient Christian Readings of the Biblical Creation Narratives* (Grand Rapids MI: Baker Academic, 2008) 7.

2. Bruce D. Chilton and Jacob Neusner, *Classical Christianity and Rabbinic Judaism* (Grand Rapids MI: Baker Academic, 2004) 43–48.

3. My account is paraphrased based on the article by Joseph Jacobs and Judah David Eisenstein, "Sin," *The Jewish Encyclopedia*, jewishencyclopedia.com/view.jsp?artid=812&letter=S&search=sin (accessed 18 October 2018).

4. For an excellent discussion of this, see Bouteneff, *Beginnings*, 38–44. See also Dan R. Stiver, *Life Together in the Way of Jesus Christ* (Waco: Baylor University Press, 2009) 229–32.

5. Bouteneff, *Beginnings*, 79–85.

6. Irenaeus, *Against Heresies* 4.37.7. ". . . for God has displayed long-suffering in the case of man's apostasy; while man has been instructed by means of it . . . . God thus determining all things beforehand for the bringing of man to perfection, for his edification, and for the revelation of His dispensations, that goodness may both be made apparent, and righteousness perfected . . . ."

7. Sirach 30:1-13 (NRSV).

8. If not, you can view it on the Internet by searching *Return of the Prodigal Son* by Rembrandt.

9. Henri Nouwen, *The Return of the Prodigal Son* (New York: Doubleday Image Books, 1994) 132.

Initiation

The Gates of Hell

"I'm a fake," she said.

"What do you mean?" I asked.

"I mean that I get up and I teach my Sunday school class when I don't even know if I believe what I'm teaching anymore. I shouldn't be teaching. I'm not even sure I should be going to church. I'm a fake!"

This snippet of a recent conversation reflects a fear I believe many Christians have about the skepticism they feel from time to time.

But when you go through such a crisis, does that mean you're a fake?

Hardly. In fact, if anything, you're in good company. Many of the greatest stalwarts of faith have gone through similar experiences. For example, after defeating the prophets of Baal at Mt. Carmel by praying for fire to fall from the sky, Elijah retreated to a cave convinced that God had abandoned him. In other words, after being a part of one of the most spectacular demonstrations of God's power, Elijah felt as if God wasn't there for him. It wasn't until he heard the whisper of a still small voice that he was comforted.

Some of us are still straining to hear the whisper.

By definition, a fake is a person who pretends to be someone they're not. Jesus ran across these kinds of people a lot in the New Testament, and he called them "hypocrites" and "whitewashed tombs" and even "snakes" (Matt 23:27, 33). But these were not people who struggled with their faith; these were people who purported to have a direct line to God, who professed super piety, or who looked down on others who were not as spiritual as they were. Perhaps they chose to deal with their doubts and fears by pretending. Whatever the case may be, Jesus reserved his strongest condemnation for them.

One of the biggest misconceptions about faith is that it requires unwavering conviction. But, as author Anne Lamott explains, this is a fallacy. The opposite of faith is *not* doubt; it's certainty.[1] Doubt is the path to faith, which is something the ancients figured out a long time ago. The one thing that Abraham, Jacob, Moses, Elijah, Hannah, Jeremiah, Mary, Paul, Peter, Augustine, Jerome, Francis, Luther, Teresa of Ávila, Wesley, and Mother Teresa of Calcutta all had in common was that they went through dark periods of doubt, skepticism, anguish, suffering, rejection, fear, confusion, oppression, and pain. This led many of the early writers on spiritual formation to conclude that if one truly wanted to get serious about heaven, one must first go through a bit of hell.

No one described this more vividly than an Italian poet from the Middle Ages named Dante.

Imagine a man who finds himself lost on a journey through a valley. Above him is a mountain that offers hope and security if he can scale it. Night encroaches, and the sun casts long shadows. The medieval Celts called this moment the magic hour, for it was supposedly when the spirits and faeries came out to play. If you looked hard enough at twilight, at precisely the moment when the line separating night and day passed, you could see them, their wings catching the last vestiges of amber glow from the sun.

But for the lost man, there are no faeries on this night; instead, there are terse growls from the woods. The man navigates away from the mysterious beast and quickens his pace, but a howl tells him he's being followed, and the animal is closer. Still faster he walks until snarls ahead cause him to skid to a stop. He turns and runs this time, but another beast blocks his way. The pale light reveals three different animals chasing him—a lion, a leopard, and a she-wolf. The man bolts in yet another direction. The animals give way, and the man scrambles down the mountain in a desperate attempt to escape.

Finally, a friendly face appears, the poet Virgil. He offers to help. Realizing that they cannot go up, the two continue down, down, and further down. Dante recounts what happened next:

> The sighs, groans and laments at first were so loud,
> Resounding through starless air, I began to weep:
> Strange languages, horrible screams, words imbued
>
> With rage or despair, cries as of troubled sleep
> Or of a tortured shrillness—they rose in a coil
> Of tumult, along with noises like the slap

Of beating hands, all fused in a ceaseless flail
That churns and frenzies that dark and timeless air
Like sand in a whirlwind.

Dante glances above him and notices words carved over a portal.

Through me you enter into the city of woes,
Through me you enter into eternal pain,
Through me you enter the population of loss . . .

Abandon all hope, you who enter here.[2]

What follows is a macabre journey where Dante travels through the bowels of hell. Among many other subjects, Dante's epic poem is a study of how monstrous humanity can be. Readers discern quickly that the people whom Dante meets are from his past. So in a way, it is an autobiography of the injustices Dante faced and even participated in. Though the journey is filled with political commentary applicable to the thirteenth century, the premise is relevant to any generation. Christian contemplatives have especially taken note of Dante's spiritual hypothesis: that, in order to be made whole, one must figure out how one is broken. It is a pilgrimage whereby the illusion of this world is removed and we become self-aware. To use evangelical terminology, we recognize we're sinners. But this is vague and generic. The contemplatives understood that this initial conviction is only the beginning. A complex and deep bit of soul searching must take place that wakes us up to the kinds of sinners we are. We must identify our broken parts before we can journey any further. Unfortunately, because this is a difficult and painful ordeal, not many are willing to pursue it, so they never really arrive at the mountain of God. This idea is counterintuitive for American Christians who have been led to believe that faith makes life easier and that if you please God he will bless you with wonderful things.

One day, my kids got in their jammies, hopped in the van, and started munching on a big bowl of popcorn while I drove them around town to look at holiday lights. We began in our own neighborhood but eventually steered toward the more fantastically decorated houses, what we call the "wahoo" houses. These are the ones who put up a gazillion lights along with all the latest technology in festive decorations: Ferris wheels, life-sized snow globes, lights that dance with schmaltzy Christmas music, bright diodes.

Eventually we made it to our first wahoo house, and as we parked on the side of the road and went "ooh" and "aahh," I noticed something that disturbed me a little. I want you to know that when I describe this to you, it's going to seem innocuous, but that's exactly my point. In the center of the yard was a plastic nativity set. Very simple. Just Mary, Joseph, a faux wooden frame, and the head and hand of baby Jesus peeking out the top of a manger crowned with straw. But then, right next to the manger, as if he was a part of the narrative, gazing down at the baby, was Frosty the Snowman. On the other side of him were Santa and the elves, waving next to the sleigh. Reindeer frolicked around the nativity, frozen in play. Some creepy clowns were in the backdrop, twirling around on a trapeze, along with a dozen other fantasy creatures that have been added to the Christmas drama of late.

At that moment I realized that, like the Israelites of old who combined stories of Baal and stories of Yahweh to create a syncretistic religion of their own, the American church has, for the most part, created her own deity.

I call him "Santa Jesus."

Despite the fact that Jesus warned us in the Sermon on the Mount that one cannot serve both God and mammon, the American church has decided that perhaps Jesus was exaggerating a bit here. He didn't *really* mean we can't serve both God and money. After all, we have to have money to buy food, clothes, shoes, a house, a college education, cars, iPhones, kitchen gadgets, high-def TVs, Internet and cable service, lawn mowers, bikes, subscriptions, movie tickets, cruise vacations, more shoes, braces, prescriptions, more clothes, and, well, you get the idea.

Why?

Because we have turned the accumulation of stuff into a virtue. Ironically, this is the opposite of the message of the incarnation. Jesus gave up heaven to come to earth. He humbled his deity and became a man. He willingly gave up status to be God with us. But here's the important part: In doing so, he showed us the way. To be a citizen of his kingdom, we must embrace poverty.

Poverty has become a sin in our culture. It's something that we feel needs to be fixed. When I say "poverty," I'm not talking about becoming homeless and dependent on welfare. I understand that there is a degree of hyperbole in Jesus' teaching, but Jesus often used hyperbole to warn us about some very real dangers, and at the heart of this one is our attitude toward money and material goods.

As we start off in life, we begin with a valid desire for the basics in our culture: an education, a job, a home. But if we are not careful, this can quickly turn into an obsession and even an addiction for more and more stuff. Before long, our credit cards are maxed out. In fact, we've changed the definition of a "Scrooge" from one who is heartless toward his employees and the poor to someone who hasn't reached his credit limit buying presents.

Jesus taught his disciples to "store up . . . treasures in heaven" by recognizing that money and status are an illusion (Matt 6:19-21). True wealth comes from embracing poverty, that is, by simply being content. By stopping and saying, "You know, I have enough. I don't want anything more." And then taking the next step, which is saying, "I need to start giving up some of this stuff."

This is becoming increasingly hard in a church culture that encourages belief in a Santa Jesus who tells us to want more so that he can bless us more. Every now and then, I hear a practical sermon explaining to us how to avoid the "naughty" list and ensure that we have won God's favor by being placed on the "nice" list. Consequently, our prayers have become long Christmas lists of things we want or think we need. We ask Santa Jesus for good grades, a handsome spouse, a well-paying job, healing of Grandma's shingles, and on and on. We've been taught that Santa Jesus wants us to be blessed in life, which we interpret to mean that he wants us to have everything. After all, we serve an infinite God who has very deep pockets.

We take out of context phrases like "You have not because you ask not" (Jas 4:2, KJV), and we run with it while ignoring passages like the one where Jesus tells the rich young ruler that if he truly wants salvation, he must give away all of his possessions to the poor (Matt 19:21). We conclude that this is "works theology"—a view that we must earn God's saving grace by doing certain things. We insist that we are saved by faith, which means we don't have to do anything. Besides, we think, Jesus wants us to be rich. Jesus was just coming down hard on this guy because he was greedy. He didn't mean for everyone to follow this command. That's impractical. Anyway, I'm not greedy.

Santa Jesus even inspires church leaders with the notion that in order to "be the church," we must have large buildings with padded pews, air-conditioning and heating, a top-quality sound system, lighting, tasteful decorations, a coffee bar, a bowling alley, tennis courts, a driving range, and a beach volleyball court. Since that's what it takes in our culture to reach the lost—or so we think—we figure Santa Jesus must want us to have all of it.

Santa Jesus has even changed our motivation for giving. No longer do we give to become poorer, simpler, more focused on the things that matter. Now we give so that Santa Jesus can bless us two-, three-, even four-fold. The idea is that if we give someone in need ten dollars, then we can expect Santa Jesus to send us a fifty-dollar present, like a cosmic pyramid scheme.

As a former church planter, I'm fully aware of the need to be culturally relevant. Church leaders are in a catch-22 of sorts. If we don't provide air-conditioning and a place to sit, people aren't going to show up. But as a church historian, I've often wondered what would happen if we could magically transport one hundred American Christians back to the first century. How many of them would still be attending church in a year? How many of them could endure a faith community that demanded real risk and sacrifice in the face of a truly hostile society? Today, sacrifice might mean putting up with a pastor who preaches boring sermons or giving to the building fund the money we set aside for a dream vacation. This is a far cry from the kind of commitment pastors like Polycarp and Ignatius expected from their flocks.

Recently, I watched a news program where Bob Simon interviewed Bartholomew, the head of the Orthodox Church. He resides in Istanbul, Turkey, a place that is 99 percent Muslim. Over the decades, he has watched the church in his country dwindle from a couple million to about four thousand, mainly due to the expulsion of his members by the Turkish government but also because of the cultural oppression his people face just by showing up at church. In fact, during the interview, Bartholomew had to cut a visit short because of a death threat.

Here's an excerpt from the transcript:

Simon: Do you sometimes fear that the community will be wiped out?

Bartholomew: Not really. We survived. We do believe in miracles. . . . This is the continuation of Jerusalem. And for us, it is equally a holy and sacred land. We prefer to stay here, even crucified sometimes. Because in the gospel, it is written that it is given to us not only to believe in Christ, but also to suffer for Christ.[3]

Hmmm. Really? That's not what Santa Jesus says.

I'm not suggesting that believers must purposely seek out hardship. This actually became a problem in the history of the church, as I'll discuss later; well-meaning, devout believers tortured themselves because they thought it somehow made them more pious. On the other hand, hardship is very much a necessary ingredient for spiritual formation. I'm not sure exactly why this is so. Perhaps our nature needs it, like a slap on a newborn's butt to get her to breathe. Or perhaps in order to truly understand a Messiah who allowed himself to be crucified, we must share in his passion. Regardless, it is a familiar pattern, and the ancients called this the "dark night of the soul." Thomas à Kempis put it this way:

> And if it lies in your choice, you should choose rather to suffer hardships for Christ's sake, than to be refreshed by many consolations; for thus you will more closely resemble Christ and all His saints. For our merit and spiritual progress does not consist in enjoying such sweetness and consolation, but rather in the bearing of great burdens and troubles.[4]

Teresa of Ávila grew up in sixteenth-century Spain during a time of tremendous turmoil in the church.[5] Martin Luther led much of Germany to break from Catholicism. Other reformers were doing the same, and alliances were forming politically and religiously, with Spain being a stronghold for the pope. His secret weapon in this war was the Inquisition. Led by the Dominicans and enforced by the state, the Inquisition sought to scare people into submission through torture and executions, mainly by burning at the stake. And in Spain, they were especially ruthless.

Teresa was brilliant, beautiful, wealthy, and passionate. Add to this mix a father who was a converted Jew, and one has the ingredients for the kind of recipe the Inquisition found most delectable: an intimidating woman with a shady bloodline. One could argue that her greatest miracle (and there were many attributed to her) was that Teresa escaped the torture chamber of the Inquisition.

The Inquisition wasn't the only stress haunting her life. As a child, Teresa watched her mother suffer through one pregnancy after another until she finally died in her early thirties. Teresa was only thirteen. Soon after, she had a love affair with a cousin whom she had wrestled from a rival (though it's unclear how far the *love* part of the affair went). As she wrote about this period later, she referred to it as a dark three months that nearly ruined her family.[6] At a time when honor among Castilians was at a premium, her assessment was quite literally true. Presumably because of this threat, her father sent her to a local convent. Eventually, Teresa became convinced that she wanted to be a nun, so she joined the Carmelite Convent of the Incarnation outside of Ávila. We have to get out of our minds the notion of a building filled with pious women praying and helping the poor. This particular place was more like a sorority where young debutantes went to gossip and flirt with boys. The nuns actually sported expensive jewelry and owned lap dogs, and the sisters were encouraged to nurture *devotos*— men who came to meet with them in the parlor for "spiritual" guidance. Granted, most of the relationships remained platonic, but private "prayer sessions" in darkened corners occurred as well.[7]

Despite the fleshly atmosphere of the convent, Teresa's spiritual journey began here. Though she didn't have a mentor to guide her, she became interested in reading books on prayer and the contemplative lifestyle. To her dismay, she found the books banned by the Inquisition to be the ones she liked the best. At first this was the cause of great anguish, but then Jesus appeared to her in a vision and reassured her by saying, "Fear not, for I shall be to you like an open book."[8]

Her spiritual journey progressed slowly, with constant setbacks that more often than not were caused by agonizing health issues. We don't really know what ailed her, but she had painful fits, sometimes lasting for long periods. The other challenges Teresa faced in life fill several books. Suffice it to say that she endured severe loneliness, persecution, slander, malice, and, most challenging, increasingly dramatic visions that many believed were from the devil, despite her intuition that they were from God. Most of her confessors counseled her to do everything she could to dissuade the visions, with one even commanding her to exorcise them with a rude gesture, similar to what we in Texas call "the finger."[9] Teresa wisely sought another confessor.

The visions of Teresa became both banes and blessings to her. They frightened her, sometimes caused pain, and at other times brought ecstasy. And sometimes they transported her to places that seemed quite real. The following is her description of one such vision where she was whisked to hell.

> The entrance seemed to me like a very long, narrow passage, or a very low, dark, and constricted furnace. The ground appeared to be covered with a filthy wet mud, which smelt abominably and contained many wicked reptiles. At the end was a cavity scooped out of the wall, like a cupboard, and I found myself closely confined in it . . . .

> I felt a fire inside my soul, the nature of which is beyond my powers of description, and my physical tortures were intolerable. I have endured the severest bodily pains in the course of my life, the worst, so the doctors say, that it is possible to suffer and live, among them the contraction of my nerves during my paralysis, and many other agonies of various kinds, including some, as I have said, caused by the devil. But none of them was in any way comparable to the pains I felt at that time, especially when I realized that they would be endless unceasing.[10]

After exhibiting a little bit of sorrow for the poor Lutherans who would have to suffer this pain forever,[11] Teresa did some soul searching to determine why she had been shown this vision, and eventually she deemed it as a calling that would make evangelist Billy Graham proud:

> Indeed, I believe that if I could free a single one from these dreadful tortures, I would most willingly suffer many deaths. For if we see someone on earth whom we especially love suffering great trials or pains, our very nature seems to awaken our compassion, and the more dire his sufferings the greater our distress Who, then, could bear to see a soul endlessly tormented in this most terrible trial of all.[12]

At first, Teresa attempted to fulfill this calling in her own convent, but the lax atmosphere soon led to frustration. She founded a new convent nearby that would be more rigorous in its pursuits. After facing fierce opposition from the establishment, she finally was granted permission to start the Discalced ("barefoot," though actually they wore sandals) Carmelites. Though the move brought limited spiritual renewal in Teresa's day, her writings have significantly shaped countless others ever since—so much so that today she is recognized as one of only three female Doctors of the Catholic Church.

By the time of her death, Teresa was much revered. As a token of their affection, admiring Catholics chopped up her body into little pieces and shipped them all over Europe as relics. Gracian, one of her favorite confessors and a fellow reformer, carried her little pinky with him wherever he went. (This makes me wonder if the confessor who commanded the rude gesture got the middle finger.)

Over time, Teresa was able to see her suffering as a part of God's love for her. It's hard for us to fathom this in our culture, where pain is typically associated with evil. Even Teresa struggled to comprehend it fully. During an especially painful vision, God tried to console her by saying, "Do you not know, Teresa, that this is how I treat My friends?" She retorted, "Well, if that's so, then it's not surprising that You don't have many of them."[13] Nevertheless, Teresa came to understand that her journey through hell gave her a spiritual clarity that would have been impossible otherwise.

In her classic work, *The Interior Castle*, Teresa imagines the soul as a diamond castle with many rooms. As a person journeys from one room to the next, he or she goes deeper to the center, where the King awaits his beloved. It is a metaphor for the spiritual journey that reflects her own experience. In the first chapter, echoing Dante, Teresa explains that one must enter a room called "self-knowledge." Here, we take a good hard look at ourselves to identify our brokenness so that we might become humble. This is *the* most important step, as Teresa explains, for

> . . . without humility all will be lost. Still, we should remember that the bee is constantly flying about from flower to flower, and in the same way, believe me, the soul must sometimes emerge from self-knowledge and soar aloft in the meditation upon the greatness and the majesty of its God. Doing this will help it to realize its own baseness better than thinking of its own nature, and it will be freer from the reptiles [demons] that enter the first rooms—that is the rooms of self-knowledge.[14]

In other words, Teresa understood the painful experiences of life to be like the fire that burns the dross from the soul to purify it and so free it to move ever closer to the center room, where God is.

The one who popularized this idea perhaps better than anyone else was Teresa's friend and fellow reformer, John of the Cross. John's trip to hell began in a closet when his fellow Carmelites, who did not share his vision for reform, imprisoned him. They beat and tortured John in an attempt to get him to renounce his efforts, but the young friar remained strong. He nearly froze in his cell during the winter, and in the summer his only change of clothes began to rot from the sweat of his body. The few times the brothers allowed John to leave his cell was when they took him to the dining hall during a meal, where he was strapped to a chair and flogged while the other friars looked on, eating the food John's starving body desperately needed. The only thing that allowed him to keep his sanity was working on a poem in his head, where he painstakingly memorized it line by line. Even this exercise wasn't enough, and he finally resolved to escape, figuring that if he was caught and killed then at least he wouldn't suffer anymore.

At last the moment came, and John tied linens together to form a crude rope, which he used to scale down the wall and flee to safety.

Eventually he arrived at a nunnery several miles away. Emaciated, weak, sick, near death, he staggered through an archway. He could hear the sisters recite the morning Angelus, "Hail Mary, full of grace, the Lord is with thee . . . ." John leaned against the wall, closed his eyes, and wept uncontrollably.

The nuns took him and nursed him back to health. After he regained his strength, John wrote down the poem he had worked on from memory in his cell. It's titled "The Dark Night of the Soul," and today its influence continues to be widely significant. John joined the reform efforts of Teresa of Ávila, and he was instrumental in renewing the male Carmelites—though Teresa had some reservation in teaming up with him at first. You see, John was quite short in stature. At their introduction, Teresa reportedly said, "Lord, I asked you for a monk and you sent me half of one."[15]

Getting back to Dante's journey into the inferno, the deeper the poet goes, the more of his enemies he finds, and you would think this would bring him some sense of satisfaction, knowing that they are all suffering. But instead he is sympathetic toward most of them because of the gross predicaments in which they find themselves. In fact, some scholars argue that *The Inferno* is the first of the horror genre, laying the foundation for such movie classics as George Romero's *Night of the Living Dead*, where flesh-eating zombies terrorize a household of young people in a small Pennsylvania town. The "living dead" are mutilated by decay, with body parts gone or unnaturally twisted. And they are after you! Watch out, because if they touch you, you become like them. So in some sense, the fear that the horror story elicits is the fear of becoming like the monsters that are after us.

In the inferno, the monsters are the dead people whose sufferings are not random but are directly related to their crimes. This notion is known in Italian as *contrapasso*: murderers are boiled in blood; gluttons find themselves as perpetual food for Cerberus, the three-headed dog; diviners of the future, who used illicit means to look far ahead, now must walk around with their heads stuck on backwards. All of them beg Dante for the same thing: "Please, please warn my loved ones that this is their fate if they don't turn from their ways." Dante's message warns about how our sins literally mutilate us and others. And if that weren't bad enough, our greatest fear is realized as it turns us into the very monsters we fear.

As a child attending a Catholic church, I was reminded of this effect of sin as I gazed at a crucifix of Jesus during Mass. He was emaciated, his body positioned unnaturally on the cross. Blood oozed from his wounds. His hair was matted against his face. His head was lowered, his eyes sunken and sad . . . deeply sad. Often in Mass I was reminded that I put Jesus on that cross. I was the monster who mutilated his body. At the time this was difficult for me to comprehend. I didn't do that! I wasn't even alive when Jesus walked the earth a long, long time ago. How could I have done that to him?

* * *

When I was in first grade, I met a boy who was quite different from me. If I think about it hard enough, his face pops into my mind as a clearly as a photograph. He had short, curly brown hair, hazel eyes, a long face, and a wiry body. What made him different was that he had a speech impediment and likely a developmental delay. I remember he had a nasal whine, and his words were heavily slurred. He was goofy too. He acted more like a toddler than a first grader, so the other boys and I made fun of him on the playground during recess. We mimicked the way he talked and the way he acted until he ran away crying, at which time we'd all laugh raucously. One day our victim ignored us. The others got bored and ran off to find something else to do. But not me. I stayed because I wanted to see him cry. So I ran after him and tackled him. I grabbed either side of his head, and, with a kind of evil rage one wouldn't think a six-year-old could exhibit, I banged his head several times on the hard, mud-packed dirt.

He cried.

I got up and ran away. The boy found one of the teachers, but because he was so traumatized, he had a hard time verbalizing what had happened. I saw him point to me, and the teacher came over and asked what had happened. I plastered the most innocent expression on my face and shrugged my shoulders. Since the teacher couldn't understand what he was saying, she decided to let it go and walked away.

I smiled, knowing that I had gotten away with it. Or so I thought. I realize now that in that moment I mutilated an innocent boy. This is not to say that there was permanent physical damage. I wanted to scare him, not wound him. What I didn't know as a first-grader is that there are many ways to wound someone, and some of the worst ways don't involve physical contact. I also didn't know that whenever wounding takes place, it goes both ways. I have damaged myself as well.

Fifty years later, I struggle with guilt and remorse over this memory. I realize I have no excuse, no justification for what I did. What's worse is that now I fear that my children will be mutilated by some monster like me on the playground.

As my first-grade victim walks through his inferno, I wonder how he pictures me: perhaps as one caught in a perpetual chase scene, like in Hitchcock's *The Birds* but with huge, leathery creatures with hammers as beaks, pounding my head. My skull is swollen, disfigured with bumps and purple bruises. However I look in his nightmares, I certainly deserve it.

Psalm 139 ends in verses many are familiar with—"Search me, O God, and know my heart; test me and know my thoughts. See if there is any wicked way in me, and lead me in the way everlasting" (vv. 23-24, NRSV). It sounds nice, doesn't it? But look at the verses that precede it:

> O that you would kill the wicked, O God,
> and that the bloodthirsty would depart from me—
> those who speak of you maliciously,
> and lift themselves up against you for evil!
> Do I not hate those who hate you, O LORD?
> And do I not loathe those who rise up against you?
> I hate them with perfect hatred . . . . (vv. 18-22a, NRSV)

That doesn't sound very Jesus-like, and there is no transition between this passage and "Search me, O God." What's going on here? I've often wondered if, as the psalmist railed against the monsters he hated, he suddenly realized that maybe he wasn't any better. In other words, I picture him shaking his fist in the air and crying out, "O that you would kill the wicked," and a swell of self-righteousness fills him. "Do I not hate those who hate you, O LORD? And do I not loathe those who rise up against you? I hate them with perfect hatred; I count them," he says. Then the first grader he bullied pops up in his mind. "I count them," he says, losing steam, "my . . . enemy." Then he reflects for a moment on how much he is like the enemy. "Search me, O God, and know my heart," he says, lowering his head. "Test me and know my thoughts," he continues as he closes his eyes, and the self-righteousness is replaced with grief and guilt as he pictures the boy he bullied running away and crying. "See if there is any wicked way in me," he says with a tear.

It's what Jesus referred to when he said, "First take the log out of your own eye, and then you will see clearly to take the speck out of your neighbor's eye" (Matt 7:5, NRSV). In the very process of removing our "logs," as Jesus put them, we realize that in some ways we are the enemy. We are the monsters. We are the mutilators. In discovering this, we become self-aware, humble, and we enter the first room of the interior castle.

But it doesn't end there. For, as Dante put it, now we return to ground zero and must continue with our prayer. "Lead me in the way of the everlasting." What I believe the psalmist meant by this is to be led far, far away from the hurtful way (Hebrew, *oatsev*). For Dante, this meant scaling the seven-storied mountain where God lived. For Teresa, it meant wandering from room to room, seeking the inner sanctuary where her Spouse awaited. For John of the Cross, it meant penning a poem that still brings comfort to those agonized by dark nights. As author Jennifer Michael Hecht explains, doubt is the hallmark of great awakenings. Rather than viewing ourselves as people of faith who have doubts, sometimes it's better to recognize ourselves as people of doubt who have faith.[16]

I think it's safe to say that none of the saints would have accomplished what they did with the same measure of success had they not first traveled through their bit of hell. I think it's also safe to say that if we want to grow into adulthood in our faith, the way of suffering is a necessary path. But I must warn you that there are great risks. There are some who have wandered on it all their lives and found little comfort in their faith. Mother Teresa was one such person. In a moment of brutal honesty, she wrote,

> Lord, my God, who am I that You should forsake me? The Child of your Love—and now become as the most hated one—the one—You have thrown away as unwanted—unloved. I call, I cling, I want—and there is no One to answer—no One on Whom I can cling—no, No One.—Alone . . . Where is my Faith—even deep down right in there is nothing, but emptiness & darkness—My God—how painful is this unknown pain—I have no Faith—I dare not utter the words & thoughts that crowd in my heart—& make me suffer untold agony.[17]

Inward Peregrinatio to the Gates of Hell

Question: What's wrong with the world?
Fear: It's me, and I'm broken beyond repair.

In many epic journeys, there is a point at which the protagonist realizes that there is something wrong. In the movie *The Wizard of Oz*, Dorothy's world is black and white, and she is unhappy though she doesn't know why. She sings of a world beyond the rainbow. In *The Lord of the Rings*, Frodo and Gandalf have a chilling conversation at the beginning about the One Ring and Mordor. It's at this point that we discover that Middle Earth is under attack and will be ravaged unless someone can stop an evil, disembodied eye.

Our "something wrong" probably isn't so epic (though there have been times in history when the fate of the world really was on the line). In most cases it can be something quite simple, yet it is shaping our lives and our future. It's a pebble in our shoe that's annoying us and distracting us and slowing us down. It may very well be making us miss the moment when we meet the love of our life, or the contact that opens an opportunity for a dream job, or the friend who helps us face our cancer. More significantly, it may keep us from the moment that turns the tide in a battle that decides the fate of humanity with respect to poverty, disease, warfare, or the environment—so it must be dealt with.

This is where the "gates of hell" play a role. We have to figure out what's wrong. We have to take the annoying feeling seriously. It is human nature to assume that there is something wrong with the system, and sometimes there is. But many times what is wrong is *us*. That's the fear we have to conquer. We have a feeling of insecurity, a wound, a traumatic memory, a weakness, a dark side, and it's getting the best of us. Left unattended, it will shape us into the monsters that inhabit hell, so we take the journey to sober up a bit. We have to envision our worst nightmare and ask, "What is it about me that could easily lead to this?"

Dorothy has to learn that color doesn't really bring happiness. Colorful people can be wicked. Frodo learned that there is a thin line separating himself and the decaying world of Mordor, so he must do what all the other ring-bearers found impossible—resist the lust for power and destroy the object he desires most.

Realize, though, that you may not be ready to begin this journey. Or this journey may take a long time, as in years or decades. Or you may have "been there, done that" so you need to move on. Whatever the case, you are responsible for your own journey. Don't expect to be taken by the hand and shown the way. You have to find it for yourself.

Go Deeper

"Gates of Hell" in "From Eden to Heaven Prompts" at
www.spilledcoffeeonancientscrolls.com

Teresa of Ávila, *The Interior Castle*

John of the Cross, *The Dark Night of the Soul*

John Milton, *Paradise Lost*

Notes

1. Anne Lamott, *Plan B: Further Thoughts on Faith* (New York: Riverhead Trade, 2006) 256–57.

2. Dante, *The Inferno of Dante*, trans. Robert Pinsky (New York: Farrar, Straus and Giroux, 1994) 19.

3. Patriarch Bartholomew, "Peter Bartholomew Feels Crucified," *CBS News*, interview by Bob Simon, 17 December 2009, cbsnews.com/news/patriarch-bartholomew-feels-crucified-17-12-2009/ (accessed 11 May 2018).

4. *The Imitation of Christ*, trans. Leo Sherley-Price (New York: Pengin Books, 1952) 2:12.

5. Much of the biographical content in this section is taken from Deirdre Green, *Gold in the Crucible* (Longmead, England: Element Books, 1989) 1–35.

6. Teresa of Ávila, *The Book of My Life*, trans. Mirabai Starr (c. 1562; Boston: New Seeds, 2007) 8–12.

7. Green, *Gold in the Crucible*, 6.

8. Justo L. González, *The Reformation to the Present Day*, vol. 2 of *The Story of Christianity* (San Francisco: Harper & Row, 1985) 115.

9. Ibid.

10. Teresa of Ávila, *The Life of Saint Teresa of Ávila by Herself*, trans. J. M. Cohen (16th century; London: Penguin Books, 1987) 233.

11. Teresa was astute and mindful of the ever-watchful eye of the Inquisition. This may have been said to divert their attention from the fact that she had admitted to visiting hell, a risky confession given the fact that Inquisitors loved to link women to the devil and burn them as witches.

12. Teresa, *The Life of Saint Teresa of Ávila by Herself*, 237.

13. In Green, *Gold in the Crucible*, 31. The story is probably apocryphal, but, as Green points out, it is congruent enough with Teresa's character that a conversation similar to this must have taken place.

14. Teresa of Ávila, *The Interior Castle*, trans. E. Allison Peers (16th century; Dover Publications, 2007).

15. González, *Reformation to the Present Day*, 115.

16. Jennifer Michael Hecht, *Doubt: A History* (San Francisco: HarperSanFrancisco, 2003) 473, along with comments she made in her talk, "Doubt Is the New Faith," Christianity 21 conference, Minneapolis MN, 10 October 2009.

17. Quoted in David Van Biema, "Mother Teresa's Crisis of Faith," *Time*, 23 August 2007.

The Cross

See how in the Cross all things consist, and in dying on it all things depend. There is no other way to life and to true inner peace, than the way of the Cross....

—Thomas à Kempis

At the end of the crucifixion event described in the books of Mark and Matthew, Jesus utters one of the most profound and baffling questions ever to face those of us who believe in a loving God.[1] On the last day of his life, Jesus was beaten several times. He was whipped with a cat o' nine tails, an especially gruesome torture device consisting of leather straps and sharp fragments of bone and pottery used to inflict the maximum amount of pain on the victim. He then had to carry a heavy cross to Golgotha, all the while jeered and spat upon by the crowd, and probably pelted with objects. He endured all of this before being nailed to two pieces of wood and facing one of the most horrific ways to die: crucifixion. I won't go into detail about all the agony inflicted on a person's body as a result of this form of torture.

At that moment, the Son of Man looked to heaven and asked, "My God, my God, why have you forsaken me?" If this doesn't move you, consider also the fact that after he yelled his brutally raw interrogative/accusation, he was answered with silence.

My seven-year-old daughter entered the bedroom in the middle of the night in tears. "Daddy, my tummy hurts."

I sat up, rubbing my eyes. "Do you feel like you're going to throw up?" This is always my first question when it comes to tummy troubles.

She nodded her head.

"Ugh," I thought. There are few things worse than this. I know this is going to sound selfish, but as I searched for the throw-up bowl and a towel, I reflected over the day to review how much contact I'd had with her in order to calculate the odds of catching the stomach virus myself. I eventually wound up in her bedroom, sitting next to her as she moaned and cried. I knew she was miserable, and I felt helpless because there was nothing I could do. This was going to be a long, sleepless night.

"Daddy?" She sounded pitiful.

"Yeah, baby."

"Can you pray and ask God to take my sickness away?"

My heart sank because now, on top of feeling helpless, I felt like a hypocrite. Understand that I believe in the power of prayer. I believe that God sometimes heals people. But after a couple of decades of pastoral ministry, I also know that sometimes people get sick and they don't get better, despite our most fervent petitions. My anxiety increased because I feared that my daughter was about to learn this lesson the hard way. I prepared to lead her in a prayer that I didn't expect God to answer, and I figured this would break her heart.

We prayed. I mustered all the sincerity I could. But her tummy just got worse and worse. She cried harder and moaned deeper. I tried patting her, wiping her brow with a wet cloth, letting her chew mint gum. Nothing worked. Finally, in a heart-wrenching voice, she stared at me with narrow, red eyes and asked in dismay, "Why did God make sickness!?"

Then she threw up.

Her question fits under a general category called *theodicy*, whereby theologians and seven-year-old girls ponder why a good and loving God allows evil and suffering to exist. Put plainly, why does God allow people like Hitler to slaughter the innocent; why doesn't God just take Grandma when she's in such pain; why does God send or allow tornadoes to wipe out entire towns? The dirty little secret of theology is that no one has been able to come up with a satisfying answer. A lot of smart people have tried, and many have come up with something that satisfies them. Ultimately we are left with one of two untenable positions: either God is not all loving, or he is not all powerful. In a simplistic way, this is the problem of theodicy.

To illustrate the problem, imagine God standing on the front lawn of a house that is burning. In the bay window overlooking the street, a child pounds on the glass, looking straight at God, crying. The flames are getting closer. She's coughing, begging God to do something, but he just stands there, immobile. Why? On one side of the equation, God desperately wants to do something because he is all-loving. The fact that he simply stands there must mean that something is holding him back. Perhaps there's nothing he can do; in that case, God is not all-powerful. On the other side of the equation, God can do something about it easily. He can break the glass and grab the child and even make all the pain go away in an instant. But he doesn't. No matter the justification, what kind of a God is that? Obviously he is not a very loving one.

The Bible gives us little hints and clues to help us understand the dilemma, but it doesn't provide an answer. Instead, what we get is like a connect-the-dot drawing without numbers to guide us. Essentially, we gaze at a page full of dots with labels like "sin," "broken," "love," "sovereign," "Satan," "free will," "grace," "guilt," and "evil," just to name a few. God gives each person a crayon with which to connect the dots. Some draw a King who commands everything to happen. He sends the earthquakes, tsunamis, dictators, and diseases, and if people get in the way and die, they deserve it for being a bunch of dirty rotten sinners. It's a disturbing picture but one that attempts to satisfy the problem of theodicy by emphasizing God's power and justice. In the process, though, God comes across as mean and cranky. Did God really send the pedophile into the five-year-old's room because she deserved it?

Others connect the dots and create a picture of a loving Father who grieves when tragedy strikes. They blame our broken world on humanity's propensity to choose sin. In other words, evil exists because of the evil choices people make. Some believe that even God suffers because of people behaving badly. Sometimes he intervenes to relieve the pain. His overall presence keeps things from getting really bad. But sometimes he doesn't do anything and allows evil to reign. This last part is problematic. A truly loving God would want to save everyone from extreme pain and suffering, not just a few. The fact that God *doesn't* must mean that he *can't*.

There are other ways to connect the dots, but there's always a part of the picture that doesn't make sense. It's out of proportion with the rest of the figure, or unfinished sections remain. Therefore, we must approach the subject with a great deal of humility, realizing that our picture may help us but not necessarily someone else. When people suffer, they tend to become emotionally invested in their picture, or else they become traumatized over the fact that their picture isn't working, so they must redraw it. The problem of theodicy is one of the reasons why faith is faith. It's an area where understanding the question may be far more important than coming up with an answer.

Put another way, perhaps understanding the question better *is* the answer. For the great picture of theodicy is Jesus hanging on the cross after hours and hours of excruciating pain, rejection, and injustice, at which point he gazes to heaven with a tear-and-blood-streaked face and asks, "Why?"

Real damage occurs when well-meaning friends feel compelled to provide the answers that they've come up with, convinced that their wisdom will resolve the tension and make the victim feel better. They say things like, "God always has a reason." "Something good will come of this." "God won't test you beyond your ability." "If you just have faith, things will get better." "Maybe there's unconfessed sin in your life." There may be some truth in a few of these statements, but most of the time the words come across as callous and trite. When people suffer, the last thing they want you to do is to connect the dots for them.

* * *

On the radio, a young college student described how a tornado ripped into her dorm room while she and her friends huddled in the bathroom. "God is sovereign," she bravely proclaimed several times throughout the interview. "And if he wanted to take us, he could take us." Her voice was filled with emotion—fear, relief (none of them got hurt), shock. My heart melted for her. I pictured in my mind a group of girls clinging to one another, shaking, praying, eventually screaming in the dark while the building creaked and crashed around them from the tornado that God had sent.

At the end of the conversation, though, the interviewer asked an interesting question. He said, "As you look at the pile of rubble that was once your dorm, what are you looking for?"

She had an immediate answer. "I don't care about my car or my computer; that can all be replaced." She paused, choking back tears. "But I really want to find my Winnie-the-Pooh doll that I sleep with at night." She hesitated, trying hard not to break down on national radio. Then she added, "It's the one thing I have that I can't replace."

Another image emerged in my head: a traumatized young woman, scanning brick, broken glass, and busted furniture looking for a tattered, golden stuffed animal. I wondered how her faith would be affected if she wasn't able to find her doll. In her mind, though, I'm sure getting a chance to hug her doll again was the only thing she was really thinking about. She wasn't psychoanalyzing her behavior as she searched. She wasn't trying to figure out why finding this doll was so important to her. But I was.

Her words haunted me for the rest of the day. I rooted for her to find her doll, and I found myself wondering from time to time if the joyous reunion had occurred. I also pondered how her connect-the-dot picture of God had changed after experiencing such a devastating, near-death ordeal, now that the question of theodicy was no longer academic and she felt drawn to her doll for comfort rather than to the Sovereign who, in her Calvinistic belief system, sends tornadoes.

I imagine that her connected dots looked a little more like Winnie-the-Pooh.[2]

My daughter is involved in a church soccer league, which the organizers view as a great opportunity to witness to the kids and parents. During halftime, some brave soul attempts to hold everyone's attention for ten minutes with a devotional. It's always an uncomfortable time because the kids are rambunctious and thirsty, and the parents are trying to tend to them. You can tell that people don't want to be rude, but it's obvious that few are listening. The devotionalizers then resort to various gimmicks or humor or hyperbolic statements to engage their audience. During one such halftime, the man speaking made a bold declaration—"God is your super-hero! You can always count on him to rescue you!" The man said it with such confidence, too, proclaiming, "The Bible and all of history testify that God always comes through for people." I bristled when I heard this taught so emphatically.

Ironically, I had just read an article that morning about an army chaplain who was going through a crisis of faith in Iraq. He had been taught in his Sunday school class that God always rescues us, yet his earnest prayers for the protection of the men and women he ministered to didn't seem to have any effect. At first, even though he didn't understand, he continued to pray dutifully, believing that with enough patience and diligence, God would answer.

Months went by, and there was still no change: people continued to be riddled with bullets and ripped apart by bombs. The suffering was senseless—soldiers, citizens, children. The chaplain invoked his God for protection. The terrorists invoked their God to wreak vengeance. It didn't seem to matter who prayed or what doctrine they believed; the killing and the suffering continued. Eventually, the daily trauma whittled away at the chaplain's faith to the point that he didn't know if he believed anymore. In a brutally honest confession, he said that some days he did, and other days he didn't. No matter how he felt, he did his best to pray and minister to the men and women under his charge, all the while hiding the inner turmoil caused by his experience suggesting that God didn't seem to be rescuing *anyone.*

* * *

The book of Job struggles with the problem of theodicy perhaps more than any other book in the Bible. I find it interesting that despite his reputation, Job is far from patient. He's vitriolic in the way he speaks up for himself, even to the point of accusing God of being mean and unfair. We, the readers, sympathize with him because God does seem mean and unfair. He makes Job suffer horribly, and all over a bet with Satan.

The drama is filled with characters who respond in different ways to suffering. Job throws a fit, yet God's ultimate restoration of Job teaches us that it's okay to be honest, to yell at God when our world is crumbling around us. God understands. Job's wife nags her husband to curse God and get it over with. He'll get zapped, but at least he won't be in pain anymore. She's not very sympathetic, but in the end she too reaps Job's blessing. After wreaking havoc in Job's life, destroying his children, livestock, and even his health, Satan is nowhere to be seen at the end of the book. He has lost the bet, so that's understandable.

Then we get to Job's friends. Out of all the characters, they are the only ones who get into big trouble with God. God says to Eliphaz, "My wrath is kindled against you and your two friends; for you have not spoken of me what is right, as my servant Job has" (Job 42:7b, NRSV). It's interesting that the friends get into trouble for spouting the then-orthodox answer for suffering: you must have done something wrong to make God so mad at you. In other words, they attempted to connect the dots for Job, creating a picture of a just God punishing a deserving sinner. In the end, Job is vindicated. The friends were wrong.

Job's vindication leaves us with a great deal of tension. If Job was right in that he didn't deserve all the horrible things that happened to him, then why did he suffer? Perhaps one lesson can be gleaned from Job's friends, who teach us what *not* to do. In other words, God doesn't want us speaking for him in these situations, regardless of the current orthodox theology on

suffering. There are enough preachers who claim to be speaking for God—
too many, in fact. Maybe God wants more people like his son who spoke
for humanity by defending the woman caught in adultery, the man with a
withered hand, and the sinful woman who anointed his feet with her tears.

Still, an honest assessment of Job's story recognizes a conflicting tension:
Jesus demonstrated great tenderness and grace toward humanity, but God
in the book of Job appears cruel. For one, I can't get past the torture of Job
and the execution of his family. All for what? To teach Job a lesson? To show
up Satan? To prove that God was right about Job's integrity? To demonstrate that people must love God even if everything is taken from them? Do
torture and the deaths of innocent children justify such cruelty?

In his poem "Edward's Anecdote," Donald Hall describes a scene he
read in a newspaper in which a father physically abused his one-year-old
daughter by beating her with a broomstick:

> breaking rib bone, and as
> she screamed she kept crawling
> back to her father: Where else
> should she look for comfort?[3]

One of the tough questions I ask myself is, how is this scene any different
from the way God treated Job? Granted, in the poem the father is drunk.
God doesn't get drunk, but the behavior seems eerily similar. God, through
Satan, inflicts horrible pain and suffering on Job to see if he comes crawling
back. Compare Hall's verse with Job's complaint against God:

> With violence he seizes my garment;
> he grasps me by the collar of my tunic.
> He has cast me into the mire,
> And I have become like dust and ashes.
> I cry to you and you do not answer me;
> I stand, and you merely look at me.
> You have turned cruel to me . . . . (Job 30:18-21a, NRSV)

Today we throw people in jail for such abuse of their children. Even
Job recognizes the injustice, so he demands an opportunity to argue his case
before an impartial judge; Job is confident he can win (see Job 23:3-7). I
think the majority of us would agree that God is *not* an abuser. I certainly
don't believe that God goes around siccing Satan on people, but sometimes life gets so traumatic that God can seem to act this way. The writer

of Job knew this all too well, which is what makes his book so profound. Even so, it leaves me with a difficult task: how do I reconcile the God Job experienced with the Father Jesus described in his parable of the Prodigal Son? Job was innocent, but he suffered at God's hands. The prodigal was guilty, but he was embraced by God. Both stories portray God in radically different ways. Both represent an element of the truth. Both have happy endings in that Job and the prodigal are restored. I have to admit, as much as I struggle with the way God treated Job, at the end of the book Job is satisfied with the new connect-the-dot picture of God he has received. Before the suffering, Job had just *heard* of God. After the suffering, Job could now *see* God (Job 42:5).

* * *

Evil and suffering in a world created by a loving God make no sense on many levels, and the events of the twentieth and twenty-first centuries have only made the theological conundrum worse: two world wars, droughts, political upheavals, religious violence, and terrorism are only some of the things that have caused atrocities resulting in countless deaths. Where is God in all this? It's a question many of the brightest theologians of late have attempted to answer, but without much success.[4] This leaves you and me with a difficult challenge as we all must make peace with the tension found when we come face to face with evil. Perhaps that's the point. Though we may not arrive at a satisfactory answer as to why evil and suffering exist, we can at least determine how we are going to respond to life in a broken world. To get guidance here, we turn to the most significant symbol on the matter—the cross.

When one pictures the crucifixion, it's an intensely emotional scene: an innocent man, the Son of God, suffers horribly. It's easy to get so enamored in the drama and the sacredness of the moment that we are willing to move on to the happy ending, the resurrection. But if we want to mature in our faith, we must do the uncomfortable work of staying for a while and pondering the cross. To get started, let's begin by asking the question, "Who is responsible for the crucifixion of Jesus?"

One popular view is presented by people called "Calvinists," who tend to emphasize the sovereignty or power of God and the depravity or wickedness of humanity. Calvinists are followers of John Calvin, a famous sixteenth-century reformer in Geneva who wrote one of the most eloquent summaries of Reformation theology titled *The Institutes of the Christian*

Religion. In it, Calvin concludes that God the Father was behind the cruci-fixion of Jesus the Son. It was the logical outcome of an implicit belief that God is sovereign, meaning that nothing can happen without God's causing it to happen; otherwise, God wouldn't be sovereign. God's justice demanded that Jesus face the full wrath of the Father in order to atone for the utter depravity of humanity. In fact, utter depravity is something Calvinists love to apply to everything about themselves—except, of course, to their theology.

Another popular approach (often viewed as an opposing view) is main-tained by Arminians, named after Jacobus Arminius, who, believe it or not, considered himself a Calvinist. Arminius was concerned with the possibility that Calvinism might devolve into a type of unattractive fatalism. If God causes everything to happen, then there's nothing I can do about anything, so why bother? *C'est la vie.* Or more accurately (if Google translate is to be trusted), *Tel est Dieu*—"Such is God."

To keep Calvinism from devolving into fatalism, Arminius attempted to retain the sovereignty of God while at the same time elevating free will in humanity. The crux of the problem, he correctly surmised, was in how Calvinists understood predestination. Perhaps, Arminius mused, predes-tination doesn't necessarily mean that God causes everything to happen, but that God knows ahead of time what's going to happen. In other words, predestination is really foreknowledge, so, when you fall down the stairs, it isn't because God pushed you but because God knows you're a klutz. This gave Arminius the freedom to proclaim that you and I actually have some power to make choices in life because God gives us just enough grace to decide between good and evil. When they apply this idea to the cross, Arminians tend to see not God but humans causing the suffering. Armin-ians tend to blame all that is wrong with the world on the bad choices people make—especially the choice that many make to become Calvinists.

There is a third major viewpoint. For the first thousand years of Chris-tianity, this view was the most popular among those who pondered the "passion," or suffering, surrounding the cross. It's an idea at the heart of C. S. Lewis's book, *The Lion, the Witch, and the Wardrobe,* where Aslan took on the role of Jesus, Edmund took on the role of humanity, and the White Witch took on the role of Satan.

In this scenario, when humanity sinned, we committed treason, and whether we knew it or not, we joined Satan's side. He has power and authority over us and can do whatever he wants. Naturally, he'd like to wipe us out, so he is well at work in the world doing just that. Since God still loves us even though we have betrayed him, God strikes a deal with Satan. God offers Jesus in exchange for humanity. In this way, Jesus becomes our ransom (Matt 20:28; Heb 9:15) that allows God to buy us back. We are no longer under the dominion of Satan. However, Satan can now do whatever he wants with Jesus, and the Son of God isn't allowed to fight back, which is why the crucifixion takes place. Satan believes he is removing Jesus from the universe for good as he uses his evil powers to torture and kill Jesus. Afterward, Satan believes he has won, but what he doesn't know about is the power of the resurrection. When Jesus comes back from the dead, the Father not only gets humanity back but gets Jesus back as well. Satan winds up the big loser, and he's a really sore loser, which is why he keeps pestering Christians. It's only a matter of time before he will be thrown into the Lake of Fire, and he knows it.

I don't want to make light of a serious question. The truth is, behind my overly simplistic and slightly irreverent attempt at explaining these three grand ideas is a sober desire for you to understand the problem of evil and suffering as it was displayed at the cross. You may argue that there is no greater picture of evil than the senseless torture and execution of the innocent, but the crucifixion has multiple facets. One is that Jesus paid for our sins on the cross, thus revoking our death sentence. It's an idea made popular by eleventh-century scholar Anselm of Canterbury, who viewed the crucifixion of Jesus as compensation to the Father for the way humanity has dishonored him. What many do not know is that this view was based on the medieval understanding of justice, whereby important people (kings, nobility) were considered far more valuable than unimportant people (serfs). Therefore, if you stole from a serf, you might just get jail time or have your hand cut off. But if you stole from the king, you probably would be executed. Punishment for a crime was based on the nature of the crime *and* the value of the person against whom the crime was committed.

When it comes to humanity's sin, we have a big problem because we are finite in value and God is infinite in value. Even if we are executed, it isn't sufficient to pay for our crime against a priceless Being. In other words, we're toast (or, more appropriately, roasted in hell) no matter what we do. But Jesus, as a human, can pay for the sins of humanity and, as God, has infinite value, making his sacrifice sufficient. This is called "substitutionary atonement." But there are many problems with this view. For starters, we now tend to reject the notion that the rich and powerful are more valuable than the poor and weak. Second, we also tend to reject the notion that an innocent person can pay for the crime of the guilty. Imagine how a judge would respond to a loving mother who begs to be sent to the electric chair in place of her guilty, serial-killer son. Again, in our world, that's not justice. It wasn't even justice in Anselm's world, which is why many people criticized him and offered alternative views.[5] Nonetheless, his view is so popular today that some traditions proclaim that if you don't believe in substitutionary atonement, then you are not a Christian.[6]

I wonder if part of our problem in comprehending the crucifixion stems from the fact that in our day, the vocabulary most used to describe what happened comes from the legal world. For to me, describing the cross in strictly punitive terms is a lot like letting lawyers define marriage. Are they really the best people for the job? Granted, at one level marriage is a legal contract between two parties, but whenever a judge is called into the conversation it's usually because things have broken down so badly that the law must intervene. It's sad. But you can't understand marriage by only studying what happens when you dial 911.

When we want to learn about marriage, most of us turn to our parents or a counselor or Shakespeare or *Shrek 3* or that husband and wife in our church who have been married for fifty years and who still stroll down the street at sunset holding hands.

My guess is that few of us, if any, turn to a law book.

Before Neil deGrasse Tyson showed us the universe, there was Carl Sagan. As a teenager, I watched the original *Cosmos* series on PBS, and I still remember the wonder that Sagan conjured. It motivated me to read his books, including his science-fiction novel, *Contact.* You may have seen the movie starring Jodie Foster as a radio astronomer name Ellie Arroway. The story begins with her praising the scientific method to a group of children. As the narrative progresses, Ellie defiantly defends science as the only legitimate way to understand truth, yet her credentials as a scientist are questioned by her more serious counterparts because Ellie has devoted her career to listening for aliens. The bad guys shut her down.

In true Hollywood fashion, Ellie is saved by an eccentric and insanely wealthy patron who gives her a second chance. She is soon vindicated as the aliens she has been searching for give humanity a call. They send a message that describes how to build an enigmatic machine with a capsule that will seat one person. (Spoiler alert: Ellie fights for the seat in the capsule, and in the end she gets her chance.) As the capsule drops into a monstrous contraption of spinning and rotating rings (which turns out to be a gate into a wormhole), Ellie is yanked on a journey through the cosmos. The capsule dips and turns like one's worst nightmare of a roller-coaster ride, stopping from time to time to give Ellie an awe-inspiring view. In short, she is shown what awaits the future of humanity. She narrates her experience into a video recorder, hoping that at least her journal survives even if she does not.

At the climax of her journey, Ellie sees an especially inexplicable scene. It's at this point that she's confronted with the fact that all of her training as a scientist is failing her in perhaps the most important moment of all of human history. As tears form in her eyes, and in a rare moment of humility, she whispers, "They should have sent a poet."

Maybe one of the reasons atonement has been so problematic to understand is that the language of law breaks down before the inexplicable image of the cross. Maybe the language of literature is better suited to allow for all the nuances and complexities. The cross, after all, is not found in a courtroom presided over by a judge. It's on a hill, surrounded by humanity, with God in the center, and it's the most important moment in all of human history. Like all good dramas, evil and good are on full display at the cross, and the fate of the world is at hand.

Indulge me a little as we contemplate the cross as part of a grand love story. Let's go back in this narrative to the beginning, where we trace the word "sin" to its first usage: when Cain murdered Abel—a horrific act of violence between two men who were brothers. As Cain went off to other people groups, the Bible describes how violence followed him. This teaches us that unjustified violence is at the heart of humanity's first sin, and the violence escalates throughout the story as one reads the Old Testament. It becomes our universal language. It is what we resort to when all else fails. All communication. All love. All civility. All law. All order. All humanity. Remove all of these things, and we are left with violence. Put two people in a room who speak completely different languages, and I promise you that if one of them hits the other, both will understand exactly what's going on.

As our narrative continues, violence reaches a fevered pitch when Jesus enters the Roman world. To illustrate how bad things got, Herod had toddlers put to death in Bethlehem, and no supervisor called him into the office to explain. This is not to say that Herod's actions failed to incite anger. Actually, at the point when Jesus began his ministry, tension in Jerusalem had reached a critical point. Many were looking for just the right moment, and just the right military ruler, to lead Israel into war against the Romans, putting "tactical genius" at the top of the qualifications for the long-expected messiah. They were looking for a Patton or, more precisely, another David. Jesus proved to be not even close. Instead of filling his sermons with images of the wicked getting punished, Jesus preached about peace and reconciliation. Literally, he said if some Roman slaps you on one side of the face, you should offer him the other side. And if he takes your coat, you should offer him your shirt. What kind of language is that? To make matters worse, Jesus commanded his followers to "Forgive one another." To add force to it, he said, "If you do not forgive others, your Father will not forgive your sins" (Matt 6:15). Does Jesus wish for us to be cowards? We want plagues and fire and brimstone and angels smiting the Gentile Romans!

The crowds eventually had enough of Jesus. After being threatened, abandoned, persecuted, tortured, and brought out to the crowd for an opportunity to repent, Jesus went silent. He had explained his revolutionary ideas about the kingdom in every way possible, and his audience still didn't get it. There was only one thing left to do, and Jesus agonized over this decision in the garden of Gethsemane, suggesting that even he struggled with why a loving Father would send his Son to be tortured. But by the time the crowd showed up with swords and lanterns, Jesus had submitted to the Father's plan.

In this meditation on the crucifixion, God chose the cross because humanity chose violence as its universal language, making execution and torture the only way for God to communicate an important message to us.

Therefore, the cross becomes the one place where all peoples—Greeks, Jews, Romans, Ethiopians, Egyptians, Anglos, Germans, French, Americans, Mexicans, Iranians, Palestinians, Peruvians, Koreans, Chinese, Indians, Eskimos, Russians, etc.—can understand what God has been trying to say to us all along. We all speak the language of violence displayed on the cross, and consequently we are all able to understand what's happening at a primitive level. But rather than striking with a legion of angels, as some taunted the "King of the Jews" to do, God chose this moment to do something most beautiful and profound. Right in the middle of our tirade and tantrum where we unleashed our most violent acts, Jesus said, "Father, forgive them." In doing so he taught us a new universal language: love.

In some respects, this makes the cross like a Rosetta stone. On one side, humanity spoke violence. On the other, God spoke love, making Golgotha the one place where we could finally understand one another.

Put two people in a room who cannot verbally communicate with one another, and when one offers tea and cookies with a genuine smile to the other, they both will understand what's going on. But now the world has two universal languages. At the cross are both the ultimate ugliness of evil and suffering spoken in the language of violence and the ultimate beauty of grace and hope spoken in the language of love. They represent two paths for us: the wide one that leads to death and the narrow one that leads to life.

Just like the two trees in Eden.

Peter, harkening back to Isaiah, explained it more eloquently when he preached, "By his wounds you have been healed" (1 Pet 2:24; see Isa 53:5). In order for this to happen, however, we must follow Jesus on the cross. He has set the bar very, very high. The odds are that we will never face evil and suffering at the level Jesus faced, yet he was still able to say, "Father, forgive them," and by doing so, he led the way. For if Jesus could forgive his enemies while nailed to a cross, then any excuse we might offer for why we can't do the same looks anemic, even ridiculous.

Forgiveness and grace are at the heart of Jesus' teaching. They are an integral part of the strategy with which the kingdom of God will prevail over the gates of hell and will come to earth as it is in heaven. Jesus wasn't kidding when he said, "Love your enemies." Many first-century Christians understood this. This kind of love became a litmus test for inclusion in the community of faith. Ever since Cain murdered Abel, humanity has used violence to protect itself, to further its interests, even to bring about peace. But ultimately, violence begets violence, and any peace is short-lived.

Imagine a world in which, through the power of the Holy Spirit, the church convinces the more than seven billion inhabitants to forgive, to respond to all evil and suffering inflicted on us by others with grace. We could even pick a day, like next Friday, when we would all wake up that morning and offer love and grace to our enemies—when we would literally turn the other cheek. What would our world look like?

> The wolf will live with the lamb,
> the leopard will lie down with the goat,
> the calf and the lion and the yearling together;
> and a little child will lead them. (Isa 11:6)

Perhaps the most powerful lesson of the cross is not so much about *answering questions* concerning atonement or theodicy (though these are important), but about *showing us how to respond* to the very real suffering and evil in the world—and in us. My guess is that if God were to administer a doctrinal test at the gates of heaven, not many would get a passing grade. But I think God will be looking not at our answers but at our actions, to determine whether or not we truly grasp the Son. How did we respond to the heretic? To the unfaithful spouse? To the corrupt politician? To the immoral pastor? To the office or school bully? How did we respond to them even after they deeply hurt us? Did our actions lead to redemption or condemnation? Did we advance the kingdom or expand the boundaries of hell?

* * *

After four years of college as a religion major, eight years at seminary to get a master's degree and a PhD, and twenty years in pastoral ministry, I got stumped by a nauseated seven-year-old girl who asked, "Why did God make sickness?" In that moment, I really wish I had had an answer, but if the Father refused to give Job and Jesus an answer as they faced suffering, then what could I possibly say? I just had to hug her tightly and confess, "I don't know." As I did, I wondered how my daughter connected the dots to create her picture of God. I decided a long time ago that I can't speak for God about why he created sickness. I have no idea what he would say. But I can respond to my child's trauma with the language of love. I can snuggle her and share her frustration. I can speak to God on her behalf. I can clean out the throw-up bowl, place a cold washcloth on her forehead, and sit with her through the night. I can tenderly hold her hair back as she throws up again and again, all the while hoping that as she connects the dots picturing God, she remembers that God didn't just make sickness.

He made daddies, too.

Inward Peregrinatio to the Cross

Question: Why have I experienced evil and suffering?
Fear: I have been abandoned by God and/or others because I'm unwanted.

We live in a culture that promotes conditional love. Many women believe they have to be young and pretty to be wanted. Many men believe they have to be wealthy and successful. When it comes to our relationship with God, we believe we have to be perfect.

The problem is that we can never be pretty enough. Or successful enough. Or perfect enough. So for those who have been swayed by this thinking, they feel they can never be lovable.

When we experience deep suffering in life, the temptation is to believe that we have been abandoned because we are unlovable and unwanted and imperfect. She broke up with me because I'm a failure. He wants a divorce because he doesn't find me attractive anymore. I have this ailment because God is punishing me for not living up to his expectations. Our approach to suffering, then, seeks to answer the question "Why?"

Rather than giving us answers, God gave us the cross.

The cross is where Christ suffered and where he invites us to follow him on a path of passion. In doing so, we find that suffering can be redemptive. It represents the moment where, having identified our baggage in the depths of hell, we begin to dump it: the things that make us feel insecure and guilty; the critical voices that tell us we are no good, unlovable, unwanted, imperfect; the feeling that we will never amount to anything. It's the place where we find humility and grace for all the mistakes and sins and weaknesses and wounds that make us feel like we are big failures, and we finally let them go.

Let go of all the baggage. Leave it there at the foot of the cross. Strip naked. And then, rather than curling up in the fetal position believing that you have been abandoned, take action by abandoning yourself to the Father. Push through the pain like a marathon runner hitting the proverbial wall and getting through it one step at a time.

In order for this to happen, a value change or a character change or a theological change has to take place within us. We have to take out our big pink eraser and remove the old connect-the-dot picture of God we drew as children and replace it with a new one that fits our maturing theology.

The cross represents the place for this to happen because we are most motivated to do this kind of work when we have reached rock bottom. When we are in the pit. When have have wandered into hell. Fortunately, Jesus is there to meet us. Jesus traveled here on the road to Golgotha to be there for us when we arrived. While hanging above, he looks down with great compassion and teaches us a new language—love.

This is the way out.

Contemplatives explain that this is the time to recognize the false self for all of its ugliness. We have to take responsibility for it, and then we have to let it go. Letting go is easier said than done because the false self wants to assert itself constantly. But Jesus meets us in our hell to set us free. The true self emerges as we learn the new language of love and grace and forgiveness of the cross.

Go Deeper

"The Cross" in "From Eden to Heaven Prompts" at
www.spilledcoffeeonancientscrolls.com

Jürgen Moltmann, *The Crucified God*

C. S. Lewis, *The Problem of Pain* and *A Grief Observed*

Notes

1. The material in this chapter was originally posted in a six-part series on "The Cross" on Patheos in 2014: "The Problem of Evil," patheos.com/blogs/faithforward/2014/03/the-cross-the-problem-of-evil/; "The God Who Sends Tornadoes and Fails to Save Soldiers," patheos.com/blogs/faithforward/2014/03/the-cross-part-2-the-god-who-sends-tornados-and-fails-to-protect-soldiers/; "Was Job Right in Declaring God Unfair?," patheos.com/blogs/faithforward/2014/03/the-cross-part-3-was-job-right-in-declaring-god-un-fair/; "The Views of Calvin, Arminius, and Aslan, Described Somewhat Snarkily," patheos.com/blogs/faithforward/2014/03/the-cross-part-4-the-views-of-calvin-arminius-and-aslan-described-somewhat-snarkily/; "My Answer to my Daughter's Question: Why Did God Make Sickness?," patheos.com/blogs/faithforward/2014/04/the-cross-my-answer-to-my-daughters-question-why-did-god-make-sickness/; "They Should Have Sent a Poet," patheos.com/blogs/faithforward/2014/04/the-cross-they-should-have-sent-a-poet/.

2. C. S. Lewis addressed this issue when he responded to a parent in a letter and attempted to calm the anxieties of a boy who feared he loved Aslan more than he loved Jesus. I found his response especially insightful.

> "But Laurence can't really love Aslan more than Jesus, even if he feels that's what he is doing. For the things he loves Aslan for doing or saying are simply the things Jesus really did and said. So that when Laurence thinks he is loving Aslan, he is really loving Jesus: and perhaps loving Him more than he ever did before. . . . Now if Laurence is bothered because he finds the lion-body seems nicer to him than the man-body, I don't think he need be bothered at all. God knows all about the way a little boy's imagination works (He made it, after all) and knows that at a certain age the idea of a talking and friendly animal is very attractive. So I don't think He minds if Laurence likes the lion-body. And anyway, Laurence will find as he grows older, that feeling (liking the lion-body better) will die away of itself, without his taking any trouble about it." (*Narnia, Cambridge, and Joy, 1950–1963*, vol. 3 of *The Collected Letters of C. S. Lewis* [New York: HarperOne, 2007] 603)

3. Donald Hall, *White Apples and the Taste of Stone: Selected Poems, 1946–2006* (New York: Houghton Mifflin Co., 2006) 139.

4. For an excellent resource, see Philip Kennedy, *Twentieth-Century Theologians* (New York: I. B. Taurus, 2010).

5. For an excellent summary of these views, see Dan R. Stiver, *Life Together in the Way of Jesus Christ* (Waco: Baylor University Press, 2009) 314ff.

6. A. C. Dixon and R. A. Torrey famously popularized the idea that substitutionary atonement is one of the "fundamentals" of the faith. To reject it places one outside the bounds of salvation. This idea launched the Fundamentalist movement, which still exists today in a variety of forms.

Transubstantiation

The Altar

As the grain from which the bread we break was
made were once scattered over the fields, and then
gathered together and made one, so may your
Church be gathered from all over the earth into your
kingdom.
— A Communion prayer from the *Didache*
(or *The Teachings of the Twelve*)

Unless one is referring to the Old Testament sacrificial system, or a place where wedding vows are made, it seems that the word "altar" has fallen out of favor with many Protestants.[1] The reason dates to the Reformation when a huge dispute arose over the concept known as the "Sacrifice of the Mass." Essentially, the Eucharist (or the bread of the Lord's Supper) is understood to be an additional sacrifice once the priest prays over it so that it has the power to atone for sins. In other words, every time a mass is said, Jesus is sacrificed all over again. Protestants rejected this idea, claiming that Jesus' sacrifice on the cross was a "once-for-all" sacrifice that covered all of our sins, and no additional sacrifices were needed. The idea that Jesus was sacrificed again at each mass in the Eucharist actually offended them, and Protestants became quite grumpy about it. Catholics responded to Protestant grumpiness by calling the Council of Trent. In 1562 this council published no less than nine canons affirming the Sacrifice of the Mass, declaring that it not only atoned for the sins of the living but also for the dead (at least those in Purgatory, another doctrine Protestants tended to get grumpy about). Suffice it to say that it was a long time before Protestants and Catholics were able to speak civilly about this matter to one another.

Since the priest consecrated the Eucharist while holding the host (the bread) over the altar, Protestants connected the two ideas and assumed that the reason it was called an altar was because of the doctrine of the Sacrifice of the Mass. Ever since then, they have preferred to refer to it as a "table." But long before the doctrine of the Sacrifice of the Mass originated, early Christians referred to the Communion table as an altar. One of the earliest references comes from a letter written by Ignatius, a first-century bishop of Antioch.[2] Other church fathers also regularly referred to it as such, and they even spoke of the Eucharist as a "sacrifice."[3] They don't go into much detail, for they were satisfied in understanding the Eucharist or the Sacrifice as a great mystery, designed to elicit awe and gratitude in the worshiper over the willingness of Jesus to die for them. It is clear that words such as "sacrifice" and "altar" were important in their understanding of what happened during Communion from the very beginning, despite later misconceptions.[4]

"Table" is a good word, too. In fact, both "altar" and "table" were used interchangeably. All of this is to say that there were many layers of meaning to this most ancient place where Jesus originally met with his disciples for a meal and then declared that the bread was his body and the wine was his blood, commanding his followers to consume them in remembrance of him. When the place is viewed as an altar, the elements become the body and blood of Christ, and the worshiper is vividly reminded of the ultimate sacrifice Jesus made out of his deep love for us. When the place is viewed as a table, the elements are bread and wine, offering the worshiper spiritual food to be consumed in community with his or her brothers and sisters in Christ. It is in this context that the word "Eucharist" or literally "to give thanks" makes the most sense, because it is at this table that God is providing for our deepest needs physically, spiritually, and emotionally, for which we are giving thanks.

Ironically, however, the table or altar also quickly became a place where some of the fiercest debates and fights occurred, even though today many have forgotten these family feuds as the table has become more of an enigma. As modern Christians ponder the table, they view it more like an odd antique one would find in a grandparent's house. It looks pretty, but it doesn't seem to have any practical purpose anymore. As a result, in many contemporary church buildings, one would be hard pressed to find a Communion table at all. This is a far cry from the first century when early pastors regularly approached the table and prayed, "But to us Thou has vouchsafed spiritual food and drink and eternal life through Jesus, Thy Servant,"[5] and were not talking about the sermon or the Bible or the praise music but about an altar where the bread and the cup resided as the focal point of the room and the highest point of worship. What happened to this tradition?

In *The Ten Commandments*, Cecil B. DeMille portrayed Moses receiving the Law in a dramatic way, with wind and fire and Charlton Heston's over-acting as Moses. When I picture Moses receiving the Law, I see it as a far more subdued affair, with Moses perched on a rock scribbling on papyrus. I've often wondered how much arguing actually took place between the two because, as we see in many passages, Moses clearly felt free to quarrel with God, which was fortunate for the Israelites who were on the verge of being completely destroyed on several occasions.

For example, a discussion over which foods are kosher may have gone something like this:

God: Anything that chews the cud, you may not eat.
Moses: Forgive me LORD, but I love double cheese animal-that-chews-the-cud burgers.
God: You may not eat double cheese animal-that-chews-the-cud burgers anymore. I declare it nonkosher.
Moses: But LORD, if we can't eat the animal-that-chews-the-cud, that would also eliminate pot roasts of animal-that-chews-the-cud. If women weren't allowed to put a roast in the oven before church so that the family could come home and eat, this would be a hardship and they might have to work on the Sabbath.
God: Okay, I relent. You may eat the animal-that-chews-the-cud, but do not put the cheese on it.
Moses: What's wrong with a little cheese? I foresee a day when people wear cheese on their heads at sporting events.
God: You may wear cheese on your head, but don't put it on the animal-that-chews-the-cud, because the milk of the mother is in the cheese.
Moses: Oh, all right, no cheese animal-that-chews-the-cud burgers. At least I can still have bacon animal-that-chews-the-cud burgers.
God: I think I need to rest now.

Most Christians completely ignore the list of unclean foods in Leviticus 11. We feel justified in this because in Acts 15 the Apostles decide not to burden Gentiles with this aspect of the law, with two exceptions. We are not to eat meats sacrificed to idols—not a problem. And we are not to eat meat with the blood in it. This was before the invention of the Food Network, so the Apostles did not know that if you cook a steak well-done it will dry out. Despite the fact that this command had the full support of the Apostles and Elders backing it, many Christians place it under the "stupid cultural laws I can ignore" category. Isn't it interesting, though, that out of all the commands mentioned in the Old Testament, this was one of a rare few chosen for the Gentiles to obey? Why?

To find out, we have to delve into the legal sections in the Torah that we usually skip because they're boring. Here we find descriptions of the various sacrifices with names like "whole burnt offering" and "purification offering" and "reparation offering" (see Leviticus 1–7). When an animal was slaughtered for these offerings, strict orders were given to allow the blood to be poured on the ground. Sometimes the blood was sprinkled on various items to ritually purify them, but for the most part, the blood of the animal was to return to the earth from which it came because the blood literally represented the life of the animal. This life was the sole property of Yahweh. He created it, and he demanded it back with warnings and actions that sent the clear message: "Don't mess with the blood." To ensure that no blood was consumed, YHWH (the proper name for God in the Old Testament, usually pronounced *Yah-weh*) even demanded that the animals be slaughtered a specific way and cooked well done.[6]

Skip to the New Testament. Now that the long history has been established under the Old Covenant that the blood equals life, Jesus holds up the cup of wine in front of his disciples the night before he is to be sacrificed and says to them, "This is my blood of the covenant, which is poured out for many" (Mark 14:24, NRSV). He then has them drink from the cup. Now remember, up until this moment, humanity was not allowed to drink the blood. It belonged to YHWH. When Noah exited the ark, God proclaimed it off limits; for those who dared to disobey, YHWH threatened to set his "face against that person" (Lev 17:10, NRSV). I'm not sure what that means, but I don't want to find out.

Now, though, Jesus has made it possible for us to drink blood because it is no longer blood but wine. In other words, perhaps the issue is *not* that the wine has been changed into blood but that the blood has been changed into wine, making it permissible to drink and accessible to everyone, both Jew and Gentile, you and me, saint and sinner. And in consuming it, we receive life.

* * *

When the early Christians walked into the room where worship took place, the focal point was a table—not a pulpit or a baptistery or a cross or a computer screen but a table. This is where the Lord's Supper was celebrated, which was the pinnacle of their worship experience. The practice was simple, spontaneous, joyous, and deeply meaningful. The altar/table was where one communed with Jesus by remembering his sacrifice, by recognizing his presence in the room, and by looking forward to the day when all the church will gather with her groom at the messianic banquet. A meal was served as well, and these became known as "agape [love] feasts."[7]

Over the decades and then centuries, the Lord's Supper morphed. To some degree, this is understandable and necessary. What I find tragically ironic, though, is how quickly the church strayed from the simple meanings surrounding the altar/table to emphasize practices that communicated almost the exact opposite of what appears to be the original intent.

To begin with, one of the scant texts in the New Testament describing how early Christians practiced the Lord's Supper specifically mentions that bringing the church together was a major purpose behind Communion: "Because there is one loaf, we who are many, are one body, for we all share the one loaf" (1 Cor 10:17). This became so important to the early church that, as congregations outgrew their initial meeting places and resorted to satellite congregations in town, the bishop baked one huge loaf of bread and then distributed the pieces, called the *fragmentum*, to each group as a sign that though the church met at different locations, they were still a unified body. It's clear from the picture of the first Lord's Supper Jesus celebrated with his disciples that, more than anything, Jesus meant for the meal to be a moment of grace. Just look at the group he gathered that night. It's safe to say that all of them were having doubts about Jesus, especially after a challenging week where just about everyone, except those gathered in the room, had abandoned Jesus. For some of them, the disillusionment was beginning to take its toll, yet they were all invited to this meal where Jesus stood and said, "This is my body, broken for you . . . . This is my blood, shed for you." Jesus offered himself, body and blood, bread and wine, to a group of skeptics, sinners, apostates, and one who was about to betray him. And then he commanded the church to "do this in remembrance of me" (see Luke 22).

Unfortunately, it didn't take long for the church to forget. As early as the second century, a document titled *The First Apology*, written by Justin Martyr, detailed some of the initial stipulations put on those who could participate in the Lord's Supper:

And this food is called the Eucharist, of which no one is allowed to partake but the man who believes that the things which we teach are true, and who has been washed with the washing that is for the remission of sins, and unto regeneration, and who is so living as Christ has enjoined.[8]

In other words, despite the unworthiness of the initial group at the Lord's table, now the church started to demand that people demonstrate their worthiness by being baptized (which took up to three years of instructions before it could occur), by passing a doctrinal test, and by proving that they were living a moral life (i.e., no sinners allowed). Had Jesus demanded this, he would have been eating alone.

It gets worse. In the late second century, Victor of Rome wanted to withhold Communion from those who celebrated Easter on the fourteenth of Nissan instead of on Sunday like the rest of the church. Fortunately, he was forced to back down. But in the second and third centuries, one could permanently be denied Communion for certain sins, like fornication, idolatry, or watching Harry Potter movies (well, actually, for dabbling in magic).

After Christianity became the dominant religion of the empire, Communion was used to make political statements. When an angry mob of Christians destroyed a Jewish synagogue at Callinicum, Emperor Theodosius wrote to the bishop and demanded that he punish the rioters and make them build another synagogue. The following Sunday, Theodosius's pastor, Ambrose, preached a sermon directed at the emperor with the following three points and a poem:

(1) Jews are heretics.
(2) Heretics deserve to have their places of heresy destroyed.
(3) It's immoral for Christians to use their resources to build buildings for heretics.

And anyone who disagrees with what I just said
Next Sunday, will not receive the wine and the bread.

Okay, I made up the poem. But the threat was real, and Theodosius was forced to repent. At that point the Lord's Supper was used to discipline members of the congregation who not only got out of line theologically or morally but who also made political decisions the pastor didn't like.

It gets worse. As worship became far more formalized, complicated, and difficult to understand, Communion became a privilege restricted to only orthodox, baptized believers who had properly consecrated themselves. The means of consecration grew increasingly strict, limiting the number of people "worthy" to partake. Granted, the strictness of this practice varied by location, but more and more Communion was viewed as a blessing only for the elite. As a result, it was celebrated less and less by the masses. Before long, the average congregant was celebrating Communion only on popular holy days, but even that was eventually whittled down until many were only taking Communion on Easter.

It gets worse. Fairly soon, the wine was taken away from the masses for fear that someone might accidently spill the blood of Christ on the floor, a risk considered too great to take. Only the religious professionals were allowed access to the cup, thus denying the average worshiper a chance to obey Christ's command to "take and drink." It appears they weren't "taking and eating" much, either. In the fifth century, church leaders actually discussed whether one who didn't partake of Communion at least once a year should even be allowed to be called a Christian.[9]

It gets worse. In 1054, the Patriarch of Constantinople, Michael Cerularius, picked a fight with Pope Leo IX. Cardinal Humbert was sent to Constantinople to try to work things out. He was absolutely the wrong person to send. He already had a reputation for being a bit of a hatchet man for his strict approach to reforming the church, so when Patriarch Cerularius made Humbert wait a long time before granting an audience, the cardinal lost patience. The following Sunday, Humbert marched down the aisle during mass at Saint Sophia's and slapped papers of excommunication on the altar. He then shook the dust from his sandals and stormed out. Never mind that Pope Leo IX had been dead for some time. Nonetheless, Cerularius retaliated by excommunicating Humbert and his posse. From that moment on, the Western Catholic Church and the Eastern Orthodox Church were separate institutions, and the occasion of their split was the Lord's Supper.

It gets worse. As the Reformation approached, in order to accommodate laypeople, a curious practice developed called "ocular Communion," whereby a worshiper received a blessing merely by *looking* at the host. No "taking and eating" or "taking and drinking," and therefore no need to go through the overwhelming preparations (including sexual abstinence) in order to be consecrated enough to receive the elements. With ocular Communion, you could come just as you are and venerate the host that was placed on display in a monstrance (imagine a sun with tendril rays made of gold on a stand with the wafer at the center).[10] Gazing at it might be a businessman praying for healthy profits or a pregnant woman pleading for a healthy child, and nearby would be a priest taking donations, encouraging the sinners to peer through the "elevation squint" to receive their answers to prayer.[11] The church had apparently rewritten the narrative of the Lord's Supper so that Jesus lifted the bread and the wine in front of his disciples and commanded, "Squint and look."

Fueling this idea was a subtle shift in the way the Eucharist was understood. At the Fourth Lateran Council, the term "transubstantiation" was used to describe what happens to the Eucharist when it is consecrated. Essentially, this is the notion that when the priest says, "*hoc est corpus meum*" during mass, the bread literally changes into flesh.[12] By the way, if you say the Latin really fast, as many priests in the Middle Ages did, you'll discover where the magic words "hocus pocus" came from—or so some believe.

John Wycliffe, an Oxford professor who lived during the fourteenth century, called into question the doctrine of transubstantiation by essentially saying, "I don't care what the Pope says; bread is bread, no matter what magic words are uttered by the priest!" He then came up with the doctrine of the *real presence*, which denied a literal transformation of the bread but acknowledged that the presence of Christ was still in the host.

Then in the sixteenth century, a man named Ulrich Zwingli came along and challenged even this notion. Zwingli was considered the leader of what's known as the Swiss Reformation. He became pastor of a church in Zurich after promising not to seduce a virgin, a nun, or a married woman (the implication being that the rest of womankind was fair game).

In a famous meeting with Martin Luther at Marburg, the two reformers debated heatedly. Luther grabbed a piece of chalk and scribbled on a table, "*hoc est corpus meum*" and emphatically declared that one must interpret this phrase literally. The bread *is* the body of Christ.[13]

Zwingli shot back that it all depends on what your definition of "is" is. In this case, "is" means "signifies," allowing for a symbolic understanding of the bread. He then referred to John 6:63 where Jesus states, "It is the spirit that gives life; the flesh is useless" (NRSV). Essentially, Zwingli made the case that Communion was merely a memorial meal. The focus should be to *remember* the sacrifice of Christ, nothing more. He was very proud of himself, and he boasted menacingly that his argument was so good it would break Luther's neck. Luther's response was something along the lines of, "Oh yeah, you and what army?" The two never spoke to one another again, thus ensuring that from then on there would be Protestant churches, not the Protestant church.[14]

Unfortunately, Zwingli never lost his predilection for breaking necks. When he returned to Zurich, his rhetoric incensed the Catholics enough that they raised an army and attacked the city. Lacking the patience, wisdom, and common sense to wait for help, Zwingli led a ragtag group of fanatic townsmen on a desperate attempt to rescue a group of soldiers stationed outside the city gates. They were slaughtered. Zwingli himself was knocked off his horse, run through with a sword, and decapitated; then each of his limbs was tied to four horses, which were slapped on the butt to make them bolt in four different directions. I imagine you have a fine picture in your mind right now of the outcome. However, this gruesome act wasn't sufficient for Zwingli's enemies. They burned his quartered body into ashes, mixed it with dung and pig entrails, and scattered it over the countryside.

The message to other would-be reformers: don't mess with transubstantiation. Unfortunately, as is the case with some of Zwingli's followers who become known as the Anabaptists, the message wasn't heeded. During this period of Christian history, tens of thousands of Christians were brutally tortured and killed by their fellow believers because they differed over Eucharistic theology, among other things. No group suffered more than the Anabaptists, who were hunted by Lutherans, Calvinists, and Catholics to such a degree that more Anabaptists were probably killed during the Reformation than all the early Christians combined during the first three centuries.[15] And the Anabaptists were pacifists!

But—you got it—it gets worse! John Wesley, founder of Methodism, hero of Pietism, one of the leaders of the Great Awakening, served as pastor in the Georgia Colony during his early years. While there, he fell in love with a young woman in his congregation. The two dated for a while, but the young woman eventually decided that Wesley was not the one, and she let him know by telling him to his face that he wasn't spiritual enough (ouch). The following Sunday, still fuming from the rejection, Wesley scowled as his ex-girlfriend gingerly stepped down the aisle to receive Communion. To the gasps of many in the room, Wesley skipped over her, thus refusing to offer her the wafer.

This was a serious declaration of church discipline. It was supposed to be done by a pastor when he deemed that there was some great immorality in a person's life that needed repentance. Essentially, it was a public slap in the face. The family, understandably, was outraged, and demanded that Wesley explain his actions. To them, and to the leaders of the church,

Wesley coolly declared that the woman was, and I quote, "frivolous." But we all know the real reason.

OK, so this last story wasn't as epic as the others. But an interesting shift began to take place at this point with respect to the Eucharist as it enjoyed a brief period of reinstatement. With Luther, the bread and the wine were once again offered to the average sinner in the congregation. But Luther changed other elements of worship as well that put the early emphasis of the Lord's Supper in jeopardy, for the Wittenberg scholar felt compelled (and rightly so) to completely renovate worship to make it more understandable. He translated the Bible into German and wrote hymns that everyone could sing. Significantly, he added a pulpit on the side to elevate the role of preaching. This was considered necessary to combat the perceived heretical theology of the Roman Catholic Church. Later, that pulpit would be moved by many Protestants to the center of the stage and considered the place to combat not just the Catholics but also everyone else who thought differently from "us." The "us" became defined in increasingly narrow ways, which resulted in shouting matches, church splits, and even violence.

Now, as worshipers entered the room, an ornate pulpit stood front and center. This sacred piece of furniture would eventually be wired for sound and plugged into a transmitter so that not only the people in the room but also everyone in radio and TV land could hear the sermon. In most traditional churches, the table was placed at the foot of the pulpit, a not-so-subtle shift establishing the preacher as the focal point of worship because he was now the guardian of the truth. Along with that came the pressure for pastors to wow the audience. Members often left the service judging how good worship was that day by how well the pastor preached.

Jump to today, where the pulpit has, believe it or not, been removed. In many cases, it has been replaced with a drum set, microphones, guitars, a keyboard, and, most important, a projector screen overwhelming just about everything else on stage. When the service starts, a band kicks things off, with software projecting the words high overhead. There is still preaching, but hour-long sermons like in the "old days" have now been whittled down to about twenty minutes. People are likely to judge the service by how well the praise band led them into the "presence of the Lord."

Other churches have replaced the pulpit and even the praise band with more creative devices. One church in Houston has used car crashes, cooking demonstrations, and live elephants in an attempt to wow the audience.[16]

Oh, and the table is nowhere to be found.[17]

I believe worship ought to be relevant and understandable. I love creative worship, including contemporary. But I wonder if we've placed so much emphasis on attracting audiences in our market-driven society that we've done them a great disservice. We've created a type of spiritual codependency where the preachers and the worship leaders want to be wanted, and the crowds who follow these men and women feel that they cannot grow spiritually without such leaders. But here's the scary thing. Remove all references to Jesus from the preaching and the music, and my guess is that people would still show up, Sunday after Sunday. Remove the preacher and the worship team, and suggest to the crowd that they just show up to read Scripture, pray, and celebrate the Lord's Supper, and one wonders how many people would still be around after a year?

The foundation of worship is not to be wowed but to be united with God. And for much of church history, the primary place this happened was at the altar, or the table.

St. John of the Cross lived in the sixteenth century, and he was deeply concerned about helping people find God. He wrote the following words, sensing a great danger in worship designed to lead people to experience merely a "sensory sweetness," what I call the "warm fuzzies":

> They [novices in worship] think prayer is all about finding pleasure and sensual devotion. Through great effort, they struggle to acquire that sweetness, exhausting their energy and confounding their heads. When they cannot find what they hunger for they become discouraged, convinced they have accomplished nothing. In light of this yearning, they lose true devotion and spirituality, which lie in humble and patient perseverance, in self-doubt, in the desire only to serve God.
>
> Such souls give everything over to the pursuit of spiritual gratification and consolation. Beginners like these never get tired of reading sacred literature. They dedicate themselves to one meditation and then another, in constant search of some pleasure of the things of God. Justly and with loving care, God denies them this kind of satisfaction. If indulged, their spiritual gluttony and attachment to that sweetness would lead them into countless troubles. Those who are inclined toward gratification are generally lazy and reluctant to tread the rough road to union. A soul in search

of sensory sweetness will naturally turn her face away from the bitterness of self-denial.[18]

The problem is that today it's quite easy to find another exciting church service, podcast, book, or album to feed our addiction to the "sensory sweetness" of which John of the Cross speaks. In other words, we've become addicted to spiritual junk food.

Jesus taught us to pray, "Give us this day our daily bread." In other words, we need spiritual food in order to maintain our faith. When Jesus was tempted in the wilderness to turn stone into bread, he quoted from Deuteronomy 8 by saying, "One does not live by bread alone, but by every word that comes from the mouth of God" (Matt 4:4, NRSV). His last command to Peter while strolling on the shore of Galilee just prior to his ascension was to "feed my sheep" (John 21:17). Most important, during his last meal with the disciples, he held up the bread and wine and commanded, "Take and eat," proclaiming these elements to be his flesh and blood (Matt 26:26-28).

Ironically, this command has been the source of great division, brokenness, bloodshed, and judgmentalism. Is that what Jesus intended when he ate for the last time with his disciples?

C. S. Lewis expressed a similar dismay when he wrote,

> I could wish that no definitions had ever been felt to be necessary; and, still more, that none had been allowed to make divisions between churches . . . . I do not know and can't imagine what the disciples understood Our Lord to mean when, His body still unbroken and His blood unshed, He handed them the bread and wine, saying *they* [my emphasis] were His body and blood . . .
>
> I hope I do not offend God by making my Communions in the frame of mind I have been describing. The command, after all, was Take, eat: not Take, understand. Particularly, I hope I need not be tormented by the question "What is this?"—this wafer, this sip of wine. That has a dreadful effect on me. It invites me to take "this" out of its holy context and regard it as an object among objects, indeed as part of nature. It is like taking a red coal out of the fire to examine it: it becomes a dead coal.[19]

As odd as it may sound, perhaps it's easier for us to talk about what happens to the bread and wine than it is to do the real work that Communion demands, which is to follow Jesus by becoming living sacrifices. Because for this to happen, we must focus our attention on things that makes us uncomfortable, like David declaring his guilt in Psalm 51. This is hard to do, especially of late since it goes against the grain of popular Christian culture where the priority seems to be that worship should make us happy.

Worship isn't about an attitude adjustment, nor is it about exclusion. It's about union with God. In the context of Communion, it's about processing spiritual food for ourselves by meditating on the Word and by listening to the Spirit. It's hard, very hard, because here the truths we learn about God and about ourselves must be fleshed out. For example, it is not enough to believe because you've been told to believe that Jesus died for your sins. You must experience it here in his presence as you agonize over a horrible mistake you've made that has tragic consequences. It is not enough to believe because you've been told to believe that Jesus loves you. You must find him here even though you cannot physically hug him. You believe that God is always with you, but you will not truly believe this until you cry to him at the table, "My God, why have you forsaken me?"

Many modern Christians have been led to believe that worship will satiate us, like the gorged feeling one gets after eating a supersized combo meal. The truth is, true spiritual food, like what happens when we consume the bread and the wine, burns us, like the hot coals on Isaiah's lips. It breaks us, like when Jacob wrestled with God and his hip was dislocated. It frightens us, as when Moses hid his face after he heard the voice speak from the burning bush. It reveals our neediness more than anything else, as Job discovered when he proclaimed, "By the hearing of the ear I heard Thee, And now mine eye hath seen Thee. Therefore do I loathe [it], And I have repented on dust and ashes" (Job 42:5-6, Young's Literal Translation).

When we consume the bread and the wine we become naked, vulnerable, compelled to draw near to a God who instills both dread and affection. Beware. When we acquiesce, *we* become that which is truly transubstantiated as we share in the very passion of Christ. The eternal question one must ask of Communion is not, am I worthy? Nor is it, what happens to the bread and the wine? It is, rather, what happens to me? Do I change into the flesh and blood of Jesus? If in some small way this happens, more often than not we will find ourselves walking away from the service not commenting on the preacher or the band or the drama but being silent because we have become intimate with the One who understood himself to be the "man of sorrows."

As Thomas à Kempis wrote when he imagined Jesus speaking to us from the cross,

Naked I hung on the Cross with arms outstretched, offering Myself freely to God the Father for your sins, My whole Person a sacrifice of divine propitiation: you, too, must willingly offer yourself daily to Me in the Eucharist with all your powers and affections as a pure and holy offering. I require nothing less of you than that you should strive to yield yourself wholly to Me. Whatever you offer to Me besides yourself, I account as nothing; as I seek not your gift, but yourself.[20]

It's amazing to see how far we've come from that first night when Jesus invited a group of unworthy individuals and offered them him body and blood, commanding them to "remember me." In "remembering," we should meditate on the fact that the altar/table is a place designed to unify the church, not split it apart. The bread and wine served as spiritual food to nourish us. In this, Christ sacrificed himself for us so that we might have grace. We respond by placing ourselves on the altar as a living sacrifice. And finally, the table is a place where all are welcome. Jesus turned the blood into wine so that all may partake—not just the religious elite but also the tax collectors and the fishermen, the doubters and the deniers.

And the enemy. For let us also remember that even Judas was invited to the table, where he ate and drank.

Henri Nouwen was a Catholic priest who suffered as one who craved intimacy but found it to be just out of reach. He spent the latter years of his life working with those challenged with mental disabilities at L'Arche Daybreak Community in Toronto, Canada. As he sought to relate to a God who always seemed distant, Nouwen, like many of us, believed that there must be something wrong because of his constant battle with emptiness. Then one day Nouwen realized that there wasn't anything wrong with him at all. Rather, he was misunderstanding what it meant to eat the body and blood of Christ. He wrote,

When He reaches out to us and puts the bread in our hands and brings the cup to our lips, Jesus asks us to let go of the easier friendship we have had with Him so far and to let go of the feelings, emotions, and even thoughts that belong to that friendship. When we eat of His body and drink of His blood, we accept the loneliness of not having Him any longer at our table as a consoling partner in our conversation, helping us to deal with the losses of our daily life. It is the loneliness of the spiritual life, the loneliness of knowing that He is closer to us than we ever can be to ourselves. It's the loneliness of faith.[21]

Inward Peregrinatio to the Altar

Question: What am I looking for?
Fear: I'll never find it.

While wandering the streets of the Las Vegas strip—a symbol of American vice, greed, and materialism—Bono shot a music video where he famously sang, "I still haven't found what I'm looking for." In doing so, he identified the gut feeling of his generation. Okay, my generation. But it's not a new one. The context certainly changes, but as one studies the great men and women of the past, even characters of the Bible, one sees that this nagging dissatisfaction is everywhere in history. In spiritual formation, it eventually leads to an altar, a place of sacrifice, where we are forced to go beyond the narcissism to find the answer.

This is no easy task, and sometimes what works for one person will flop with someone else. Perhaps this is why Paul said you had to "work out your own salvation with fear and trembling" (Phil 2:12).

One common pattern that emerges, though, is a moment of *transubstantiation*, suggesting that the "what" we are looking for isn't so much the dream job or the dream lover or the dream house but more of a metamorphosis. This might lead to nice things, and it might not. But through the process we will discover that what we attain or achieve is no longer what is important.

The important thing is becoming who we were meant to be.

Transubstantiation, then, is what happens to you when you push through your fear and pain, abandon the baggage that has been holding you back, and move forward in the direction you were meant to go, thus becoming what you were meant to become—your true self.

It sometimes involves a moment of clarity where you are able to see clearly before you the path you need to take. I don't want to sound as if there is only one moment. There are many course corrections along the way, but the altar becomes the place for us to experience them.

At the altar, we consume the flesh and blood of Christ that then becomes our source of nourishment for our journey. We make our offering, which is nothing less than ourselves, so that we can be intimately joined with God, who is Father, Son, and Spirit, the perfect union of love. We revisit this sacred place over and over again, not always in church or corporate worship, but most often in silence and solitude. It is there that we recall our own passion (suffering) in light of Christ's. We dump any baggage that we have picked up again. We correct our course to make sure we are heading where we are supposed to be heading, and we move forward, having received the grace and power to do so through the gift of God.

The problem is that it's easy to get distracted. We procrastinate. We get busy with families, church, and jobs, and in the process we get lost. Hungry. Discouraged. If we are not careful, we can attempt to satisfy our hunger and thirst with easier substitutes—what C. S. Lewis called "the sweet poison of the false infinite."

The altar, however, demands that we become the living sacrifice again and again.

Go Deeper

"The Altar" in "From Eden to Heaven Prompts" at
www.spilledcoffeeonancientscrolls.com

Thomas à Kempis, *The Imitation of Christ*

Henri Nouwen, *Spiritual Direction*

Notes

1. Much of the material in this chapter was published in a series titled "The Battle Over the Body and Blood of Christ," posted on Patheos in 2015: "Stale Crackers and Fruit Juice," patheos.com/blogs/faithforward/2015/03/stale-crackers-and-fruit-juice-the-battle-over-the-body-and-blood-of-christ/; "When This is my Body Became Words to Kill For," patheos.com/blogs/faithforward/2015/03/when-this-is-my-body-became-words-to-kill-for-the-battle-over-the-body-and-blood-of-christ/; "Altar or Table?," patheos.com/blogs/faithforward/2015/02/the-battle-over-the-body-and-blood-of-christ-altar-or-table/; "Blood Becomes Wine," patheos.com/blogs/faithforward/2015/03/the-battle-over-the-body-and-blood-of-christ-the-blood-becomes-wine/; "No Sinners Allowed," patheos.com/blogs/faithforward/2015/03/no-sinners-allowed-the-battle-over-the-body-and-blood-of-christ/.

2. Ignatius, *Letter to the Magnesians* 7. See also *Letter to the Ephesians* 5 and Hebrews 13:10.

3. See *Didache* 14.

4. See Edmond Bishop, *Liturgica Historica* (Oxford: Clarendon Press, 1918) 21.

5. *Didache* 10:3.

6. For an interesting discussion on this, though a bit technical, see William K. Gilders, *Blood Ritual in the Hebrew Bible* (Baltimore: Johns Hopkins University Press, 2004). The truth is that we have no idea how the ancient Jews (as in long before the first century) applied the biblical texts on dietary laws. I am told that modern Jews have no qualms about eating rare steak and consider it kosher as long as it has been butchered properly. But because of the serious way that this subject is discussed in the Old and New Testaments, I can't imagine that the ancient Jews took any chances. Still, I could be wrong.

7. J. G. Davies, *The Early Christian Church* (Grand Rapids MI: Baker, 1965) 61–62.

8. Justin Martyr, *First Apology* 66.

9. Joseph Dougherty, *From Altar-Throne to Table* (Lanham MD: American Theological Library Association, 2010) 1–3.

10. Nathan Mitchell, *Cult and Controversy: The Worship of the Eucharist Outside Mass*, Studies in the Reformed Rites of the Catholic Church (Collegeville MN: The Liturgical Press, 1990) 180–81.

11. Dougherty, *From Altar-Throne to Table*, 4–5.

12. Based on Aristotle's view on matter, the "literal" transformation was of substance, not appearance (accident), according to the Council of Trent (1545–1563). In other words, it still looks and tastes like bread (accident), but its "substance" literally changes.

13. Luther didn't believe in transubstantiation. He believed in what is sometimes referred to as "consubstantiation" though that word isn't entirely accurate. Essentially, Luther held that both bread and flesh coexisted in the host, like fire and metal both reside in a white-hot iron.

14. See discussion in William R. Estep, *Renaissance and Reformation* (Grand Rapids MI: William B. Eerdmans, 1986) 150–51, 189–90.

15. Justo L. González, *The Reformation to the Present Day*, vol. 2 of *The Story of Christianity* (San Francisco: Harper & Row, 1985) 56.

16. Alex Cohen, "Using Cooking Demos, Elephants to Fill the Pews," radio broadcast on NPR, 27 October 2006. Transcript available at npr.org/templates/transcript/transcript.php?storyId=6392770.

17. For an excellent discussion on the theology behind worship practices in American Christianity as they pertain to baptism, the Lord's Supper, and preaching, see Jeanne Halgren Kilde, "Space, Time, and Performance: Constitutive Components of American Christian Worship," in *American Christianities*, ed. Catherine A. Brekus and W. Clark Gilpin (Chapel Hill: University of North Carolina Press, 2011).

18. John of the Cross, *Dark Night of the Soul*, trans. Mirabai Starr (New York: Riverhead Books, 2002) 54.

19. C. S. Lewis, *The Joyful Christian* (New York: Macmillan Publishing Company, 1977) 82.

20. Thomas à Kempis, *The Imitation of Christ*, trans. Leo Sherley-Price (New York: Pengin Books, 1952) 4:198.

21. In Robert Jonas, ed., *Henri Nouwen: Writings Selected with an Introduction by Robert A. Jonas*, Modern Spiritual Masters Series (Maryknoll NY: Orbis Books, 1998) 91.

The Holy of Holies

You talk to God, you're religious. God talks to you,
you're psychotic.

—Doris Egan

"Are you happy to be in God's house today?" the worship leader, bathed in the spotlight, shouted into the microphone as he picked up his guitar. Three attractive girls paraded out, picked up microphones, and assumed the trance pose with bright smiles. The drummer pounded away on his set, which launched the praise team into a pop-inspired song. I looked around at the young crowd as it rose to its feet and began singing and clapping. Most of them, indeed, seemed happy to be in God's house—but not all of them, including me.

To be honest, I felt uncomfortable at the way the worship leader phrased his question, which made it seem that if you weren't happy to be in God's house, then you weren't going to be included. Because he was happy, the backup singers were happy, the drummer—well, the drummer was in his own little world but seemed happy in it. If you wanted to be part of this very spiritual group, you had to be happy, too. If you weren't, then there was obviously something wrong with you. Go home and come back when you're happy.

I can't fault the young worship leader for his approach. Contemporary worship has its roots in the revivalist tradition of the New Lights, echoes of which can be found in songs still sung today by Charles Wesley: "Christ the Lord Is Risen Today" and "Rejoice, the Lord Is King," decidedly happy songs. But the psalmist prayed, "My soul is cast down within me" (Ps 42:6a, NRSV). And Jeremiah prayed, "Why did I come forth from the womb to see toil and sorrow, and spend my days in shame?" (Jer 20:18, NRSV).

Those of us who struggle to show up with smiles on our faces at church all the time will be reassured to know that the most popular type of psalm in the Old Testament is neither a praise psalm nor a thanksgiving psalm. It's a *lament*, or a prayer expressing deep sadness over a loss. I doubt you will ever hear a worship leader stand up and cry out, "Are you lamenting in God's house today?"

Don't get me wrong. Joy is great, and finding contentment is certainly a worthy goal as we work through grief and sadness (which I will point out in a later chapter). The point I'm trying to make is that worship doesn't have to be mono-emotive. Prayer and worship are an invitation to plumb the depths of our soul, which includes all of our emotions and not just the so-called positive ones. It's important to let go of the unrealistic expectation to always be joyful, as well as the guilt associated with the times when we end our prayers feeling a little down. It's perfectly okay to be sad or frustrated or even angry. It doesn't mean we are somehow less faithful. The point of worship is not just to experience some sort of an attitude adjustment; it's to be united with God.

During the time of Jesus, many good Jews believed that if you wanted to unite with God, you had to visit Herod's temple. There, in the holy of holies, God resided, and by performing certain rituals the worshiper could meet with YHWH. In the minds of some, uniting with God was limited to location. The Samaritan woman at the well in John 4 points this out in her debate with Jesus when she says, "Our ancestors worshiped on this mountain, but you [meaning the Jews] say that the place where people must worship is in Jerusalem" (v. 20, NRSV). In response, Jesus presents us with a wonderful discourse on what must take place in order to unite with God: "God is spirit, and those who worship him must worship in spirit and truth" (John 4:24, NRSV). In other words, worship is not limited to location. It doesn't have to take place in a temple or a church. Instead, true worship is a journey inward. As a dramatic expression of this teaching, Matthew records that after the crucifixion the curtain separating the holy of holies from the rest of the temple was ripped from top to bottom (Matt 27:51). And Paul declares in 1 Corinthians 3:16, "you yourselves are God's temple." In other words, you are the holy of holies. You are where God resides. And part of the nature of worship is to journey inward to discover this reality.

Before we do, Jesus mentioned two criteria: "spirit" and "truth." Let's start with the latter. In order for us to be true, we must be real or authentic. To use a more graphic term that better fits the ancient discussion of this topic, we must be naked. Not literally naked, though a second-century group of Christians who called themselves the "Adamites" believed that God wanted them to live like Adam and Eve in the garden of Eden, which meant attending church sans clothing and even fig leaves. The metaphorical nakedness implied by the word "truth" means approaching God having removed all pretenses. We strip the masks and the bravado we hide behind in order to survive in the world, and we enter into the holy of holies vulnerable, trusting, and completely exposed.

As we do, we discover, perhaps to our surprise, that entering the holy of holies in this manner reveals that union with God is not something that happens. It's something that already exists. The masks we wear have blinded us to the fact that God has been there all the time. By becoming naked, we finally become aware of our true self, which is intertwined with God. As Paul put it, "For in him we live and move and have our being" (Acts 17:28).

A second important characteristic of worship described by Jesus is that it must be done "in spirit," because God is spirit. Granted, this phrase is quite nebulous and open to a wide variety of interpretations. What did Jesus mean? Part of the answer lies in an ancient tradition in which people turned to silence and solitude to solve this riddle. Those who were most serious about worshiping in spirit sought increasingly isolated places to simply be with God without any distractions. As they soon discovered, silence itself could be one of the most challenging distractions of all. But once it was overcome, the ancients learned that God often chooses to relate to us using a vocabulary of silence on a path known as the "*via negativa*" or the "negative way." In an overly simplistic description, this refers to the notion of approaching God by stripping our prayer and worship of all images, thoughts, and even words—because all of these things limit God. The *via negativa* attempts to let God be God by understanding him through what he is not. In more practical terms, it refers to silence and solitude.

The Desert Fathers and Mothers are viewed by many as the ones who initially popularized this approach in the church, yet their ideas and practices have roots in the Bible.[1] In 1 Kings 19:12-13, Elijah finds God in a whisper (silence). In Acts 10:9ff, Peter is on the roof when he enters into a trance and has his vision of the unclean animals (solitude). And several times, Jesus leaves the crowd and his disciples to be alone with the Father (Mark 1:35; Luke 5:16).

In following these examples, the Desert Christians became enthusiastic about forsaking everything and pursuing God. Some of them also wrote extensively about what they learned, providing a wealth of information that on one end of the spectrum describes keen psychological insights but on the other end describes sheer lunacy. Therefore, one must read the literature of these monks with a critical eye. But, with a great deal of patience, one can find that the *Sayings of the Fathers* produces some truly priceless gems.

As early as the second and third centuries, men such as Clement, Origen, and Athanasius created a powerful intellectual center for Christianity in Alexandria. Despite this ancient beginning, people today don't often associate Egypt with Christianity. Among these men, Origen was perhaps one of the most prolific. He was one of the few early church fathers who actually knew Greek and Hebrew, the original languages of the Bible. He wrote extensive commentaries and the first systematic theology of the church, yet Origen had his quirky side. For example, one tradition describes that when he was young, he desired to follow in his father's footsteps by becoming a martyr. So one day when persecutions broke out in Alexandria, he fully intended to walk outside and preach to the authorities. His worried mother foiled the plan when she hid his clothes. Apparently it is embarrassing to be martyred while improperly dressed. For a teen, embarrassment is a fate worse than death—which, in Origen's case, saved his life.

Another quirky story surrounding Origen involves how he took Jesus quite literally when he taught, "there are eunuchs who have made themselves eunuchs for the sake of the kingdom of heaven. Let anyone accept this who can" (Matt 19:12b, NRSV). Origen accepted this by castrating himself. To be fair, this particular scandalous detail was recorded by Eusebius, who didn't particularly like Egyptian Christians and who had an agenda to discredit Origin. So its truthiness is questionable. Unfortunately, over time, Origen's teachings became more and more maligned and misrepresented, until the Second Council of Constantinople condemned them in AD 553. All of this is to say that even today Origen is controversial. Still, there is much that Origen taught that became foundational for Christian theology, as his teachings greatly influenced other early church theologians, like the Cappadocians, leading some to suggest that his significance is as great, if not greater, than Augustine's.[2]

With respect to the Desert Christians, Origen taught that the life of discipleship was a journey consisting of stages of maturity. Indeed, he categorized members of the church into two camps. First were the "milk drinkers," the "simple" believers stuck at an immature level of development. They tended to interpret the Scriptures literally and to be weighed down with legalism and worldly concerns. Second were the "solid food eaters," consisting of those more serious about their faith and willing to make necessary sacrifices to grow, including living a life free from the cares of this world.[3]

Creating a map of this process became the great obsession of the Desert Christians, so men and women ventured into remote areas to forge a path to God in silence and solitude. They were called "anchorites," or solitary monks, and the origin of this term actually comes from those who fled the government to keep from having to pay taxes. To be honest, some of the early Christian anchorites may have been simply tax evaders.[4]

Ironically, the ones who were really good at this lifestyle soon found themselves quite popular, surrounded by novices seeking their wisdom. Typically, in response the monks fled to find an even more remote location, only to be discovered again. Finally, in exasperation, most would work out a compromise, taking on novices with conditions that limited the amount of access time.

Others, however, got more creative in their search for solitude. Take Simeon Stylites, for example. Realizing that putting horizontal distance between himself and the crowds seemed futile, he decided to try vertical distance. Near Telanissos, he climbed a pillar with only enough room for one at the top. This, at least, kept people from getting too close, but he soon felt it wasn't enough, so he increased the height, eventually settling on a pillar sixty feet up in the air. Ironically, Simeon became a major tourist attraction and started a fad with other monks who become known as the Stylites in his honor. Soon, hundreds of copycat monks were claiming their own pillars on which to live. The beauty of this approach was that it allowed Simeon to stand and preach to the crowds whenever he felt the urge. Then, when he was done, he could simply sit in the center of his pillar and pray in his creative version of silence and solitude.

Life on top of a pillar tended to affect one's mental state after a while. Simeon was fond of inflicting himself with wounds as an act of penance. To spread the love and grace of God to all of creation, he invited maggots to feed on his open sores, admonishing the bugs to "eat what God has given you." After thirty-six years of this, Simeon eventually descended from his pillar and died.[5]

Believe it or not, other ascetics went to even more bizarre extremes. Thalelaeus of Cilicia spent ten years in a barrel. Macarus the Alexandrian felt so guilty about killing a gnat that he spent six months in a swamp allowing the insects to feast on his body. Still others used whips and chains and uncomfortable locations like chest-sized caves to live as austere a life as possible in their pursuit of holiness.[6] What started out as a good idea soon led to laughable extremes. I mention this because the *via negativa* has at times fallen out of favor because of the exploits of fanatics like these. A movement known as Quietism became popular in the seventeenth century; it basically taught that the way to spiritual perfection was literally to sit and do nothing. Don't think. Don't speak. Don't go to church. Don't read. Just spend your days being completely passive. It was condemned by Innocent XI in 1687, and it spooked Protestants as well—so much so that for both traditions, the idea of being quiet before God for long periods was discouraged and looked upon with great scandal.

By denying the benefits of the *via negativa*, the modern church neglects an important part of her heritage, a tradition that has biblical roots and historical precedence. From a practical standpoint, the way of the negative can bring a much-needed balance. We live in a world where more and more people are living frenetic, 24/7 lives constantly connected to input from the Internet, TV, games, cell phones, and the like. Even the church has become a place so programmed that thirty-second blocks of time are mapped out in a service to ensure that there is no wasted "dead air." Consequently, we have become addicted to noise. Without a constant feed running through our minds during our waking moments, we feel at a loss. If we pause just for a moment and reflect upon this obsession, it will become apparent that perhaps we are no less crazy than the bizarre monks with their whips and pillars, albeit on the other end of the spectrum. Where they aggressively sought quiet, we compulsively seek input.

For Christian contemplatives, speaking to God in spirit entailed using a more intuitive part of the mind. For example, Augustine described a "lower" part of the mind that used reason and a "higher" portion of the mind that was capable of contemplating God. Though today speaking about the brain this way might be a bit unsophisticated, there is some truth in this idea. A Desert Father by the name of Evagrius the Solitary called this higher portion the *nous*, which can be defined as a type of "intuitive spiritual intelligence."[7] He wrote, "Undistracted prayer is the highest intellection of the intellect. Prayer is the ascent of the intellect to God. If you long for prayer renounce all to gain all."[8] Fundamental to this definition is the idea that prayer is a journey that begins within. As one ventures forth, one removes distractions, whether external or internal, and that process then leads to the edge of one's self. Evagrius explained, "Do not pray only with outward forms and gestures, but with reverence and awe try to make your intellect conscious of spiritual prayer."[9] In other words, as one sits in silence and slowly calms the mind so that the to-do list, the worries, the fears, the yearning to check email, to turn on the TV, to browse the web become more and more distant, one becomes more aware of the important presence of God. As one creates distance from even such distractions as words, one discovers that prayer is not a matter of running through a shopping list of requests or of constantly chattering about this or that but, as Evagrius described it, a state of being. One doesn't pray. One enters the state of prayer.[10]

The prayer of silence or the wordless prayer or contemplative prayer (*contemplatio*) is certainly not the only type of prayer, but, as we will discover, it was considered an essential element of worship that has largely been forgotten.[11] In this approach, the worshiper seeks to remove all thoughts and words from the mind so that he or she can become more aware of God. In this, we recognize that to relate to God more intimately, we must escape the limitations of words and gestures. Paul explains,

> In the same way, the Spirit helps us in our weakness. We do not know what we ought to pray for, but the Spirit himself intercedes for us [with groans that words cannot express]. And he who searches our hearts knows the mind of the Spirit, because the Spirit intercedes for [the saints] in accordance with [God's will]. (Rom 8:26-27)

As early anchorite monasticism continued to grow and become a bit unruly, there were those who sought to tame it a little and make it more effective in its purpose of separating oneself to live a life of devotion to God. More than anyone else, Benedict of Nursia accomplished this as he organized groups of monks into communities and established a set of guidelines, literally *The Rule*, to help monks live as Jesus and the disciples lived. An essential part of their practice was prayer. Through trial and error, Benedict came up with a beautiful approach that became known as "the office," or the "Opus Dei," the "divine work."[12]

"Pray without ceasing," Paul admonished (1 Thess 5:17, NRSV), and these three little words became a serious concern of the monastics. Taking their cue from a few biblical passages, including Psalm 119:164 where the psalmist boasts that he prays seven times a day, and references in the New Testament that indicate that the disciples prayed at certain times (Acts 3:1; 10:9), the monastics set out to create a routine of prayer. Learning from the

Desert Fathers, Benedict created a schedule whereby the monastics began their day in prayer at six in the morning (*lauds* or *matins*), and then prayed again every three hours (*terse, sext, non, vespers*), ending at midnight with the *compline*. The monastic would then be allowed six hours of uninterrupted sleep until he or she started all over again with the morning *matins*. A myriad of variations exist for this today, with different expectations for those who are cloistered with a little more time on their hands, and for those who are trying to figure out how to hack the laws of space and time by inserting more hours in the day.

In addition to the daily office, Benedict also came up with an approach to worship that became known as the *lectio divina*, or the "divine reading." The approach became a template for monastics and ultimately for the church over the centuries. It thrives today in many forms. In essence, the divine reading begins with the *lectio*, which is a devotional reading of Scripture. In this respect, the worshiper approaches the text more as a conversation than as something to study. We recognize God speaking to us, specifically to us, in the text. No longer are the ideas static or stuck in the past. They leap from the page and grab us, probing our thoughts and memories, finding something from our experiences and actions to latch onto. Suddenly, the verse or the phrase or the word has incarnated into our lives as we become a participant with the text.

The *lectio* then leads us to the *meditatio* where we spend time mulling over the verse or word or phrase that has latched onto us. Why has this jumped out at me? How should I respond? What do I do with this? Sometimes the answer is to tuck it away for later. Other times, the Word demands action. And in between there are many ways that ultimately lead to edification and transformation.

Next, the *oratio* brings us to a moment of response. This can stem directly from the reading, or it may come from our life experiences. The *oratio* can be expressed in many forms—singing, chanting, praising, intercession, petition, lament, repentance. My favorite is to journal. If you ever want to study a master at work in this endeavor, read Thomas Merton, a Trappist monk who lived in Kentucky in the twentieth century at Our Lady of Gethsemani. His journals have become classics in the contemplative tradition.

Finally, the *lectio divina* leads us to the *contemplatio*, or the silent prayer, as mentioned earlier in this chapter. Every author who writes on this discipline has a slightly different way of explaining it. I would recommend that you read several works until you find one that resonates with you. I think different personalities find different metaphors and similes meaningful. In essence, the *contemplatio* is resting in God. There are two parts to it. There is a negative aspect that removes all words and images as one enters the silence. As the author of *The Cloud of Unknowing* explained, "When we reach the end of what we know, that's where we find God."[13] The positive aspect is where the worshiper becomes vulnerable, allowing the love of God to do its work. St. Maximos the Confessor explained, "at the very onset of prayer the intellect is so ravished by the divine and infinite light that it is aware neither of itself nor of any other created thing, but only of Him who through love has activated such radiance in it."[14]

The *contemplatio* is the moment when you recognize that you are the holy of holies. It is taking time to pause, to sit still in silence and solitude, and to become aware that God is indeed with you. At times it can be dreadful or empty or frustrating. And at other moments, it is like being wrapped in a warm blanket by a fire ignited by heaven. Thomas Merton explained in detail:

> In the Christian tradition, as we have already observed, contemplation is simply the "experience" (or better, the quasi-experiential knowledge) of God in a luminous darkness which is the perfection of faith illuminating our inmost self. It is the "meeting" of the spirit with God in a communion of love and understanding which is a gift of the Holy Spirit and a penetration into the mystery of Christ. The word "contemplation" suggests lingering enjoyment, timelessness, and a kind of suave passivity. All these elements are there, but they smack rather of pagan *theoria*. The important thing in contemplation is not enjoyment, not pleasure, not happiness, not peace, but the transcendent experience of reality and truth in the act of a supreme and liberated spiritual love. The important thing in contemplation is not gratification and rest but awareness, life, creativity and freedom. In fact, contemplation is man's highest and most essential spiritual activity. It is his most creative and dynamic affirmation of his divine sonship. It is not just the sleepy, suave, restful embrace of "being" in a dark, generalized contentment: it is a flash of the lightning of divinity piercing the darkness of nothingness and sin. Not something general and abstract, but something on the contrary as concrete, particular and "existential" as it can possibly be. It is the confrontation of man with his God, of the Son with his Father. It is the awakening of Christ within us, the establishment of the Kingdom of God in our own soul, the triumph of the Truth and of Divine Freedom in the inmost "I" in which the Father becomes one with the Son in the Spirit who is given to the believer.[15]

* * *
—

Protestants have their own version of purgatory known as "theological German." It's a class that people who have doctorates make people who don't have doctorates take for purposes of hazing. If you have really poor judgment, as I apparently do, then you take a year's worth of theological German in one summer while attempting to minister to youth at a small country church. In theological German they make you memorize words like *bekenntniskirche* ("denominational church") and *ungerechtigkeit* ("injustice"), which you would never use in a normal conversation but nonetheless you must use in your seminar classes in order to demonstrate to your professor that you are a worthy candidate for a doctorate. The problem is that every now and then one of these words pops out of your mouth while you're leading a Bible study with your high school students about love, sex, and dating, at which point they look at you strangely, timidly raise their hands, and ask if this is another stupid Greek word or an STD they have never heard of.

It was during this same summer when I found myself at a youth camp at Lake Lavon. I spent my mornings learning German vocabulary and translating a single sentence that went on for pages and pages. In the evenings I learned hand motions to silly songs designed to make you feel awkward and endured flatulence jokes told by the camp pastor. Finally, I had enough. I escaped through the back door of the auditorium while the crowd was singing a song with the chorus, "Dead puppies aren't much fun," and I walked down to the shoreline of the lake, where I sat on the prickly brown grass. The sun burned a hazy orange across the water, and it reminded me of Moses' theophany at the burning bush. I suddenly became jealous. Why did he get a burning bush, and a voice, and a clear outline of what God had called him to do? Why couldn't I? What made him so special?

Eventually I found myself wondering, "Why am I here?" More than that, I felt empty, burned-out, and I questioned whether I had made a big mistake going into the ministry. My questions didn't stop there. I began to wonder if all of this—faith, the church, the Bible, even God himself— was essentially one massive Jedi mind trick. And I was just another duped, stupid Stormtrooper who couldn't hit the side of a transport ship with a blaster if it were ten feet in front of me.

At that moment, what I thought I needed was a theophany of my own—a dramatic appearance of God. He spoke to Saul on the way to

Damascus; he gave Ezekiel the wheel within a wheel; and he gave Elijah fire from heaven. I honestly didn't need something that dramatic. Maybe just an audible voice proclaiming, "I am here." Or a smiling, white-robed figure that popped in and out of thin air, or . . . I don't know. Surprise me.

So I closed my eyes, and with all the sincerity I could conjure, I asked God for a sign—something to prove in that moment that he was really there and really listening and really concerned about me. I waited. Peeked one eye open and then the other.

Nothing.

I prayed again, pleading. Begging. I was serious. I wasn't asking for much. Just something tangible. Some physical assurance that I could take with me from that lonely spot next to the water. It didn't have to be much. Something simple would suffice.

Again, nothing.

I don't think I have ever felt more disillusioned and abandoned than I did sitting on that shoreline, listening to the water gently lap up the slope, feeling the wind brush my face, and fearing that I was truly, utterly, alone.

I got up and walked back into the auditorium, but emotionally I had checked out. It was all I could do to go through the motions and finish out the week, and then the summer, and then eventually the years, trying to figure out what to make of the silence. Because at that time in my life, silence either meant that God wasn't there or that he was so deeply disappointed in me that he wasn't talking to me anymore. Either way, how was I to respond?

What I did was what every overachieving, approval-addicted person going through a crisis of faith does. I immersed myself in working for God as a way to numb my soul. I figured that as long as I kept busy doing things for God, I didn't have to think about whether he still liked me or, worse, whether I still believed in him.

As I found out the hard way, working for God takes you only so far. It takes more and more out of you, and the recovery time between moments of despair get longer and longer, deeper and deeper, until eventually you find yourself in a pit so deep that there is no way out. At the time I was clueless about where my journey was leading. I dutifully planted a church, started a family, taught Bible and church history classes at a couple of universities, and found ever more creative ways to stay busy doing things for God in the hopes that at some point he would finally approve of me and start talking.

But still there was silence.

The day finally came when my fragile truce with God broke down and I realized where I was. I had found my "inferno," my "dark night." There appeared to be no way out. I was sitting in the hall of an office building after leading a service for the church I had planted. Every Sunday the church was growing smaller and smaller, and I knew its time was limited. I was helpless to stop it. I felt very small. The only sound came from the hum of the air-conditioner. Harsh fluorescent lights lined the ceilings, and the walls had been painted a dark maroon. Before we took over the place it had been a fitness club.

As I sat on the musty, high-traffic carpet, I drew my knees to my chest, holding them with both arms. Everyone was gone, even my wife, and I was left with only my thoughts. No matter how I tried to put a positive spin on my experience, an oppressive weight, an actual physical heaviness, made me feel that this had all been one big failure. Even as I tried to redirect my thoughts to the future, the question, "what now?" only made me more depressed. The last ounce of respect I was able to muster had just been poured out as an oblation. There was nothing left, and I knew it.

At seminary they teach you how to study the Bible and preach and baptize people and bury people and even speak a little Greek and Hebrew. You can take a course on how to grow a church or plant a church. What they don't teach you is how to close a church: what to do next after you have spent the last several years watching your congregation dwindle to a few loving, precious friends, whom you know would be better off joining a more vibrant community. You make the decision to send them away with your blessing, which becomes the euphemistic way of proclaiming the death of the church.

John of the Cross beautifully explains where I was in my pilgrimage.

> The deep suffering of the soul in the night of sense comes not so much from the aridity she must endure but from this growing suspicion that she has lost her way. She thinks that all spiritual blessing is over and that God has abandoned her. She finds neither support nor delight in holy things. Growing weary, she struggles in vain to practice the tricks that used to yield results, applying her faculties to some object of meditation in hopes of finding satisfaction. She thinks that if she is making a conscious effort to do this and still feels nothing, then she must be accomplishing nothing. Nevertheless, she perseveres.[16]

Persevere I did, but only because I felt a deep obligation to my children, who were preschoolers at the time. Since my wife had a good job that paid the bills, I became a stay-at-home dad. There was a part of me that relished the opportunity. Playing with my children all day was cathartic. But I also discovered that a large part of my identity, my source of feeling good about myself, came from my career. I felt as if I were walking around with a big scarlet "F" on my shirt. Also, West Texas is a little behind the rest of the country when it comes to cultural shifts. A stay-at-home dad was a rare thing, so when I answered the inevitable question that seemed to pop up quite a bit, "What do you do?" with "I take care of the babies," I sensed a great deal of confusion and embarrassment from people about how to respond. Around those parts, a man who stayed home and watched the kids was just plain unnatural, and surely there was a Bible verse somewhere that warned against such things.

I had now become relegated to the island of misfit toys. Unfortunately, I was the only one there. I didn't even have other misfits to commiserate with. So, out of desperation, I turned to books. I started out with works by Thomas Merton. I had used a few quotes from him in my sermons that I had found from reading other authors, and I felt strangely drawn to his ideas.

One afternoon while my children were in a fittingly named "mother's day out" program, I went to a local coffee shop and started reading. Slowly, something started to heal inside me. As strange as it may sound, I felt a kinship to this monk who had died soon after I was born and who had lived most of his life in seclusion. I furiously underlined passages and later copied them down in a notebook. As I did, I noticed something a bit odd. Every time Merton said something about silence, I highlighted it. Something about his teachings on silence drew me to a place that I longed for though I had no idea why. I was drawn to passages like this one:

> One might say I had decided to marry the silence of the forest. The sweet dark warmth of the whole world will have to be my wife. Out of the heart of that dark warmth comes the secret that is heard only in silence, but it is the root of all the secrets that are whispered by all the lovers in their beds all over the world. So perhaps I have an obligation to preserve the stillness, the silence, the poverty, the virginal point of pure nothingness which is at the center of all other loves. I attempt to cultivate this plant without comment in the middle of the night and water it with psalms and prophecies in silence.[17]

I now believe that God was lovingly, gently, patiently, gracefully leading me into the holy of holies. Habakkuk declared, "The LORD is in his holy temple, let all the earth be silent before him" (Hab 2:20). My problem was that I didn't understand God because I didn't understand the language of silence and of love. Because of that, I didn't recognize that on the shore of Lake Lavon, God indeed answered my prayer. He was inviting me into the silence, into what an anonymous author described as a "cloud of unknowing," a darkness that represents the closest we can approach God.

> You won't know that this is. You'll only know that in your will you feel a simple reaching out to God. You must also know that this darkness and this cloud will always be between you and your God, whatever you do. They will always keep you from seeing Him clearly by the light of understanding in our intellect and will block you from feeling Him fully in the sweetness of love in your emotions. So, be sure you make your home in this darkness.[18]

What I didn't realize I had to do at the time was to learn the language of silence and love. Fortunately, I discovered the spiritual masters like Thomas à Kempis, the author of *The Cloud of Unknowing*, John of the Cross, Teresa of Ávila, Benedict, and Augustine, and the more I read them, the more fluent I became. It soon dawned on me that I had one thing helping me in my endeavor that these ancient writers did not.

I was a dad.

* * *

There is something about holding your infant son and daughter and experiencing the overwhelming joy over the fact that this living being is somehow bonded to you. It goes far beyond words. There are other moments in life that mirror this intimacy—a couple flush with love silently holding one another at sunset, for example. But since I was a young dad during my "dark night of the soul," it was this experience that spoke to me. My favorite moment of the day was rocking my children to sleep, knowing that as they clung to me and slowly nodded off that I was communicating with them in a way that transcended sound. Eventually my dull mind finally came to the realization that the reason Jesus taught his disciples to refer to God as Father was to give them a way of understanding the kind of intimacy God desires with his children. He wants to relish us, just like I love to relish my children.

This is what the ancients called *contemplatio*. To go there I have to strip naked, void of pretense and expectations. I have to be silent, alone. I have to leave behind the desires to please, to do, to help, to cajole.

I have to stop working for God and simply be.

And in the being become aware.

And in the awareness find the Father.

Who has never stopped relishing me.

As Thomas Merton prayed, "You, who sleep in my breast, are not met with words but in the emergence of life within a life and of wisdom within wisdom. With You there is no longer any dialogue, any contest, any opposition."[19]

Inward Peregrinatio to the Holy of Holies

Question: Where is God?
Fear: God is not speaking to me.

Transubstantiation is not something that just happens to us once. It is a constant process that can sometimes feel like two steps forward and one step back. One of the ways we make sure it's progressing in the right direction is by having a vibrant life of prayer and worship that includes silence and solitude.

The problem is that prayer and worship do not come naturally. In fact, most people must unlearn before they can relearn because the kind of popular devotion that they have practiced is closer to what C. S. Lewis called "the sweet poison of the false infinite." The journey to worship "in spirit and in truth" often leads people to places that are quite frustrating and unnerving. In the discouragement, it's easy to conclude that God is not on the other line, so to speak.

To fill up the awkwardness, we talk. We bring out our laundry list of petitions and intercessions. We sing our songs. We lecture God. We offer thanksgiving and praise. And then we leave.

Eventually, the notion creeps into the back of our mind: "Am I just talking to myself?"

The truth is, prayer is hard work. It involves listening and awareness more than it involves talking. As I said above, Evagrius the Solitary explained that prayer demands using a part of our mind that he called the *nous*, which he defined as a type of intuitive spiritual intelligence. He wrote, "Undistracted prayer is the highest intellection of the intellect. Prayer is the ascent of the intellect to God. If you long for prayer renounce all to gain all."[20] A simpler way to put it can be found in Simone Weil's words, "Absolute attention is prayer."[21]

These books listed below are designed to introduce you to various approaches to prayer and worship that were mentioned in the chapter and that trace their roots back to the most ancient traditions in Christianity. Hopefully they will whet your appetite for further study.

Go Deeper

"Holy of Holies" in "From Eden to Heaven Prompts" at
www.spilledcoffeeonancientscrolls.com

Phyllis Tickle, *The Divine Hours*

Thomas Keating, *Open Mind, Open Hearts*

Thomas Merton, *Contemplative Prayer* and *New Seeds of Contemplation*

Anonymous, *The Cloud of Unknowing*

Cynthia Bourgeault, *Centering Prayer and Inner Awakening*

Notes

1. Somewhere around the third century, a group of ascetics decided to seek God in the deserts of Egypt. They became known as the Desert Fathers (and Mothers), and their practices and wisdom greatly influenced monasticism. Even though their approach to silence, solitude, and stillness seems extreme to us, their ideas and practices have roots in the Bible.

2. See "Origen," *Encyclopedia of Early Christianity*, 2nd ed. (New York: Routledge Taylor & Francis Group, 1999) 835–36.

3. Joseph H. Lynch, *Early Christianity* (Oxford: Oxford University Press, 2010) 102.

4. William Harmless, *Desert Christians: An Introduction to the Literature of Early Monasticism* (Oxford: Oxford University Press, 2004) 10.

5. Stephen Tomkins, *A Short History of Christianity* (Grand Rapids MI: Eerdmans Publishing Co., 2005) 56.

6. Ibid., 54.

7. Martin Laird, *Into the Silent Land* (Oxford: Oxford University Press, 2006) 26.

8. *Philokalia*, trans. G. E. H. Palmer, Philip Sherrard, and Bishop Kallistos Ware (Woodstock VT: Skylight Paths Publishing, 2006) 73.

9. Ibid.

10. Harmless, *Desert Christians*, 352.

11. Many books have been written on this subject. Here are a few of my favorites: Martin Laird, *Into the Silent Land*; Thomas Merton, *Contemplative Prayer*; and Thomas Keating, *Open Mind, Open Heart*.

12. Phyllis Tickle has written extensively on this subject, and I encourage you to take advantage of her works, in particular the *Divine Hours* series and her book *The Shaping of a Life*.

13. Anonymous, *The Cloud of Unknowing*, trans. Carmen Acevedo Butcher (Boston: Shambhala Publications, 2009) 156.

14. *Philokalia*, 83.

15. Thomas Merton, *Thomas Merton: Spiritual Master, The Essential Writings*, ed. Lawrence S. Cunningham (New York: Paulist Press, 1992) 324–35.

16. John of the Cross, *Dark Night of the Soul*, trans. Mirabai Starr (New York: Riverhead Books, 2002) 67.

17. Thomas Merton, *Thomas Merton: Spiritual Master, The Essential Writings*, 219.

18. *The Cloud of Unknowing*, 12.

19. Thomas Merton, *The Intimate Merton*, ed. Patrick Hart and Jonathan Montaldo (San Francisco: HarperSanFrancisco, 1999) 101.

20. *Philokalia*, 72.

21. Quotation appears in Esther de Waal, *The Celtic Way of Prayer* (New York: Image Books, 1997) 196.

Struggle

The Wilderness

And if you are a fake, don't tell me. I don't wanna
know.

—Linus to the Great Pumpkin in
It's the Great Pumpkin, Charlie Brown

On the last day of school before the winter break in December 2007, I
picked up my son to drive him home. On the way, he announced that he
had gotten into an argument with his fourth-grade friends at lunch about
the existence of Santa Claus.

"Dad, they were all saying that the parents put out the toys, but I know
that's not true. There's no way you and Mom could do all of that without
me knowing about it. I know Santa exists!" When Nathaniel gets excited,
he gets loud. And on that day, he was really loud. He continued, "And to
prove it to them, I'm going to email Santa and ask that this Christmas he
give me a reindeer hoofprint on a piece of paper. Then I'll take it to school
and show them. I'll prove it to them!" I could see in the rear-view mirror
that he had his wild look of obscene determination that wouldn't rest until
he had tested his hypothesis.

In his nine-year-old mind, a reindeer hoofprint was definitive proof
that Santa existed. Never mind that this experiment was riddled with logical
holes. In Nathaniel's world, it was his kite in a thunderstorm dangling a
brass key. And I, as the great hypocrite driving him home, agonized about
how to keep my son from getting electrocuted. I'm sure I said something
innocuous like, "Okay," but deep down inside I felt disturbed. One part
of me wanted so badly to continue the illusion of Santa for my son as a
way of extending his childhood. I didn't want him to grow up too fast. No
longer believing in Santa was a milestone that I wasn't ready for yet. But the
other side of me didn't want my son to embarrass himself by arguing for an
illusion. The only way to spare him was to reveal the truth, and once that
happened, Christmas would never be the same.

I talked it over with my wife, and we decided that it was time—but not
quite yet. We wanted him to have one more magical Christmas. To make

it a great make-believe moment, on Christmas Eve I took a red potato and carved a reindeer hoofprint. I then grabbed one of my daughter's many stamp pads, dabbed the potato on it, and made a very convincing hoofprint on a piece of paper. I hung the artwork next to his stocking on the mantle.

The next day when Nathaniel came down the stairs, he immediately snatched the picture of the hoofprint and danced around. "I knew it! I knew it! Santa does exist! They were wrong and I was right! I can't wait to show them!" He did a victory dance around the den.

I thought to myself, "I am such a horrible dad."

My only option for the moment was to let Nathaniel enjoy his Christmas, but as the back-to-school day loomed, I knew I had to have my little talk with him. As a good nerd, I did my homework and studied "Yes, Virginia, There Is a Santa Claus" over and over again as a foundation for my argument. I even delved into a little hagiography, studying what we know about Saint Nicholas, which is about as much as we know about Santa Claus. Then, at an opportune moment, I took Nathaniel into my bedroom so that we could have some privacy, and I gave him "the talk."

"Nathaniel," I began, trying to sound gentle. "You know that picture of a reindeer hoofprint that you got for Christmas?"

"Yeah," he responded. His lower lip quivered as if he knew what I was about to say.

"Well, I want you to know that I made it."

"NO!" He sounded incredulous. "You couldn't have made it! It's a real reindeer hoofprint!"

"It's actually a stamp of a hoofprint that I made out of a red potato. I can even show it to you if you'd like."

"What do you mean a *stamp*?"

"I mean that I cut a small potato in half, carved a little notch in it to make it look like a hoofprint, dabbed ink on it, and pressed it to the paper."

His eyes darted back and forth as he worked the image through in his mind and realized that it was plausible. Now his eyes started to water. "So Santa doesn't exist?"

This was the cue for my prepared speech. "Well, actually, the character of Santa comes from a real saint in the church named Saint Nicholas. He was the Bishop of Myra in the fourth century, and he is the patron saint of children. There are lots of stories about how he put gold coins in people's shoes to help them through hard times. And on one occasion he helped a very poor young girl who didn't have a dowry, which meant she couldn't get married. She was very much in love with a young man in town, so one night, Saint Nicholas threw a bag of coins in her window. Fortunately, it was open, so no glass was broken. And the next morning she found it and was so glad because now she could go from being a slave of her father to a slave of her husband! Which may not sound like much of an improvement, but it was. And Saint Nicholas made it happen. He was known for his generosity, except for that time at the Council of Nicaea where rumor has it that he decked Arius in the face for being a heretic. But that's a whole other story . . . ."

I was blowing it, and it knew it. So I switched to the "Yes, Virginia" article.

"You see," I said when I finished reading it, "Saint Nicholas still inspires people today to be generous, so the spirit of Santa is alive and well in all of those who give presents during the holiday season, especially to those in need!"

There was an awkward silence. Nathaniel sniffed. "So does *Saint Nicholas* live at the North Pole?"

"No, Saint Nicholas died a long time ago."

He whimpered, "So does *Santa Claus* live at the North Pole?"

"No. Nobody lives at the North Pole. It's actually just a sheet of moving ice that's pretty desolate."

"Does this mean Santa doesn't exist?"

I sighed. "No, Nathaniel. Santa doesn't exist. Your mom and I put the toys out."

"But how?"

I gave him an explanation of the Christmas Eve routine. He listened attentively and became very somber. I held him as close as I could while he fought to hold back the tears. Afterward, we sat there together for a long, long time. Then he said, "Does this mean I don't get toys?" He wiped tears from his eyes.

"No! Not at all. You'll still get toys on Christmas."

His face brightened a little. "And even though I know Santa doesn't exist, can I still pretend that he does?"

"Of course! In fact, now you get to be a part of the make-believe fun so that Eliana doesn't find out."

This seemed to satisfy him. He now had something over his sister.

"Okay," he said, then slipped off the bed and scampered down the stairs.

As I crawled out of bed, I have to admit that I felt horrible. It's never easy helping your children to grow up.

* * *
—

The wilderness in the Bible was wild, dangerous, and chaotic. In the Old Testament, the Israelites were forced to wander around in it for forty years, eating only bread and quail meat. As you conjure that image in your mind, remember that much of this area was desolate. The Israelites felt punished. Often, they asked, "'Was it because there were no graves in Egypt that you have taken us away to die in the wilderness?" (Exod 14:11, NRSV).

Though the forty-year excursion of the Israelites is perhaps the most famous, many others in the Bible found themselves in the wilderness. Abraham had to cross it to get to the land of promise (Genesis 12). Elijah fled into it to escape being found by Jezebel's men (1 Kings 19). And King David took his men there to escape Saul's army (beginning in 1 Samuel 21).

The wilderness is a place of extremes, and as such, it is a difficult place to survive; those who wander into it will find themselves tested. In the Bible, this wilderness takes on different forms. The Israelites faced hostile armies and snakes among other hardship in Deuteronomy, and they griped about it most of the way. This prompted the text's alternative title in Hebrew literature as "The Book of Complaints." In the wilderness, Jacob wrestled with God and had his hip displaced (Genesis 32). And after his baptism by John, Jesus went into the wilderness to be tested by Satan (Mark 1:12ff).

The "wilderness experience" has become known as a time where one feels tested, perhaps to one's limit. Circumstances have gone terribly awry, or perhaps emotional or other challenges have led one to despair and doubt. Some emerge from the experience stronger; others emerge wounded. For still others, the wilderness leads them to abandon their faith.

When I was a pastor, I entered the church one morning to find the phone ringing. I hurried into the office and picked up the receiver, tossing my keys on the desk.

"Hello?"

Without any introduction or pleasantries, a loud, angry voice demanded, "Where did Cain get his wife?"

I didn't know if the guy was trying to be rude or if he was just deeply disturbed. I assumed the latter. "Excuse me?" I said.

"I said, where did Cain get his wife? If Adam and Eve were the first two people God created, and then Cain goes off and finds him a wife, then where did she come from?"

My mind went into professor mode, conjuring all the textbook answers, but then it dawned on me that this man wanted more than just an answer. He was going through some crisis of faith, and this intellectual snag had triggered something deep down inside. I decided to probe a little.

"Why do you want to know?"

"Listen." He sounded like he was running out of patience. "If you can't tell me in the next sixty seconds where Cain got his wife, then I'm throwing this Bible out the window."

"Well," I stammered, "the text doesn't tell us where these other people came from. It just describes them as being there. So we don't really know. But it sounds to me that there's more to this than you're letting on. Why is the answer to this particular question so important to you?"

I paused, waiting. His reply came in a rough growl: "I thought so." And then he hung up. By the tone of his voice, I imagined him walking over to the window and tossing a leather-bound, frayed Bible stained with notes and fingerprints into a nearby shrub.

I felt I was to blame because I didn't have the right answer.

In the book *Into the Wild*, Jon Krakauer describes the plight of an idealist (or eccentric person, depending on your perspective) named Christopher McCandless as he rebels against his father, gives everything away to the poor, goes on a journey of self-discovery, and befriends businessmen, hippies, and other outsiders before jaunting to Alaska. Then, against *everyone's* advice, he lives in the wild with absolutely no survival training or even respect for nature only to wind up (surprise!) dead from exposure. As I read the book, I wanted to feel empathy for McCandless. Part of me wants to drop everything and live in the wild. John Muir is one of my heroes. But I'm the guy who read a dozen books on day hiking and then bought hundreds of dollars of equipment before packing thirty pounds of supplies in a backpack that I hauled on a four-hour nature hike in a state park with my family. It was hard for me to excuse McCandless's recklessness.

What made him even more unlikable was the way he treated people who showed him a little compassion. One such character was an eighty-year-old retired military widower pseudonymously named Ronald Franz. He had a difficult life, losing everything dear to him, including his wife and son in a tragic accident. In response, he became an avid churchgoer, perhaps as penance, believing that faithful attendance would bring healing. It didn't. The underlying anger remained a tinderbox for him, just waiting for a spark. When McCandless arrived in the elderly man's life, the relationship became a balm, providing some comfort. Somehow McCandless managed to infuse new life in the retiree by encouraging him to seize the day. But right when it appeared that both men were healing a little from the wounds and dysfunction that brought them together, McCandless walked away. I pictured Franz, like the prodigal's father, looking out the window day after day for the return of his friend. Years passed, and then, out of the blue, Franz learned from a hitchhiker that McCandless was found frozen to death in a rusted and discarded bus in Alaska. As a result, buried tinderbox of anger burst into flame. It took the author a little while, but he finally got Franz to open up about the experience:

> "When [Christopher] left for Alaska," Franz remembers, "I prayed. I asked God to keep his finger on the shoulder of that one; I told Him that boy was special. But He let [Christopher] die. So on December 26, when I learned what happened, I renounced the Lord. I withdrew my church membership and became an atheist. I decided I couldn't believe in a God who would let something that terrible happen to a boy like [Christopher]." . . .
>
> "After I dropped off the hitchhikers," Franz continues, "I turned my van around, drove back to the store, and bought a bottle of whiskey. And then I went out into the desert and drank it. I wasn't used to drinking, so it made me sick. Hoped it'd kill me, but it didn't. Just made me real, real sick."[1]

In church we celebrate the atheists who find God, but we don't talk much about the apostates, those who toss their Bibles out the window because they've run into an intellectual snag or who give up on God because they've experienced the last straw in a string of hardships. These people are out there, and their numbers appear to be growing. A recent Gallup poll suggests that the number of Americans stating that religion is "not very important" to them has more than doubled since 2000, from 12 percent to 25 percent.[2] Historians such as Mark Noll have noticed the decline of religion in America for quite some time, arguing that Protestant influence peaked and started waning at around 1900.[3]

In response to, or perhaps more appropriately, in reaction to this trend, the church has attempted many strategies. Some fundamentalists have identified the problem as doctrinal, so they have waged war on universities and seminaries, attacking "liberals" in an attempt to get them fired and excommunicated from the church. The religious right has identified the problem as moral and political, so they have championed particular issues such as anti-abortion laws and anti-gay positions, believing that once we eradicate these behaviors, God will be happy with us again and our churches will grow. Entrepreneurial pastors have identified the problem as outdated worship and programs, so they have started megachurches with high-quality productions in worship and expensive children's and youth ministries. Despite the fact that the Southern Baptist Convention, the largest Protestant denomination in the world, has fired all of its so-called liberals; that the religious right has controlled the government for a significant period of time; and that mega churches have popped up across the country, growing from fifty to more than twelve hundred over the past forty years,[4] this recent poll suggest that none of these strategies is working—if by *working* we mean that active, churchgoing Christians are growing as a percentage of the population. In fact, since around 2000, the percentage of people claiming to be members of a church, synagogue, or mosque in America has dropped dramatically from 70 percent to 56 percent.[5]

Why is the number of Christians in America dwindling? As we enter what many are calling a post-Christian era, is it possible to turn the trend around?

I don't consider myself smart enough to be able to answer this question, but I can address it from my perspective as a pastor/professor living in the heel of the Bible boot. In my experience, people drop out of church and/or give up on God because life slams into the religion they've been taught, and they discover that their religion doesn't work. There's tension and conflict between their theology and their experience, and they don't know how to cope. Worse, many of them are ill equipped to labor through the tension, so they give up. They discover that the trite and clichéd answers they've been given in Sunday school aren't practical. The mass-market, one-size-fits-all approach to discipleship they have experienced has left them wondering, "*Is this all there is?*"[6]

There are many reasons for this epidemic. One comes from the nature of Christianity itself. Jesus taught us that authentic faith is hard. The narrow road leads to life. The broad road leads to death. I used to picture this concept as a person standing at a "Y" in the road—one almost like a footpath, leading off in one direction, and the other like a superhighway, angling away. At some point a person accepts Christ and begins his or her journey on the footpath. Once this decision has been made, that person is safe from the dangers of the broad path and walks straight to Jesus.

I no longer see it that way. Now I see the narrow way weaving in and out of the broad way, and the narrow way is perilous, much like the journey of Christian in John Bunyan's *Pilgrim's Progress*. Unfortunately, many want to simplify what this image has to teach us about salvation into an argument about "once saved, always saved," but in doing so one perhaps misses a significant insight stemming from the picture of a narrow road: it's easy to get off track. It takes work to stay on course. Neglect the work, and you run into Mr. Worldly Wisely, who will stop at nothing to direct you to Destruction City. People need to be taught how to remain on the narrow way.

This leads me to the second part of the problem, which is that many pastors have adopted a strategy of protecting their flocks from heresy by becoming paternalistic and telling them exactly where the narrow road goes. The problem with this, as I have mentioned, is that everyone's path is unique. Where God wants me to walk is different from where God wants someone else to walk. I have to develop the skills to find the path myself. To be more specific, when matters of theology and ethics are reduced to simplistic, three-point alliterations that make for great sound bites, the audience becomes a group of shallow theologians and ethicists unable to cope with the gray areas where most of life resides. If all you do is tell people what to think instead of *how* to think, then you create a dangerous situation. Parishioners, in fact, become far more vulnerable not just to getting lost but also to getting led astray.

When I was a youth intern at a large Alabama church, I remember listening to a pastor preach about a huge controversy in our denomination over a Sunday school lesson on the book of Job. The furor was over the fact that the writer of the lesson, taking his cue from the original Hebrew in the text, referred to Satan as "The Satan" or, as it can be translated, "The Accuser," making the point that the author of Job used this character as a prosecuting attorney rather than the embodiment of evil and the nemesis of God, as Satan became known in early Christian tradition. The pastor didn't explain all of this to our congregation. Instead, he ordered that the literature not be distributed in our church. He spent the hour in worship railing against the liberals in Baptist schools and how they were destroying everything. Then, when he reached a fevered pitch in his rhetoric, he yelled—and I quote because his words are seared in my synapses like a ranch symbol on calf skin—"I know what *Hasatan* means. *I* went to seminary. But you don't need to know what *Hasatan* means. Which is why we need to get *our* people writing for the Sunday School Board." The congregation yelled, "AMEN!" while bursting into raucous applause. I remember slowly sinking into the pew, aghast that these people were actually cheering for ignorance.

The Gospel of John contains a wonderful passage where Jesus gathers his disciples and says this,

> This is my commandment, that you love one another as I have loved
> you. No one has greater love than this, to lay down one's life for one's
> friends. You are my friends if you do what I command you. I do not call
> you servants [lit., "slaves"] any longer, because the servant does not know
> what the master is doing; but I have called you friends, because I have
> made known to you everything that I have heard from my Father. (John
> 15:12-15, NRSV)

In this passage, Jesus contrasts servants with friends by pointing out that
servants simply obey commands while friends do things for one another
out of love and understanding. He then turns to the disciples and says, "I
want you to be my friends, not my slaves." A part of the reason for this
is that Jesus wants them to understand and not blindly follow. Further,
in Matthew 22:36-40, where he elaborates on this new commandment of
love, he specifically points out that we are to love God with our mind. Now,
I'm not one to make a big deal of the categories, for I think the point is
to love with everything we've got. But I find it interesting that loving God
with our minds is mentioned. I'm amazed that modern Christians have
developed such insecurity about this, as if loving God with our minds is a
slippery slope to liberalism or atheism. Jesus wasn't afraid to command us
to do this, however, so we shouldn't be afraid to follow him on it.

One of the things I love about the Bible is that the writers ask hard
questions, sometimes of themselves and sometimes of God. They contemplate, throw fits, shake their fists toward heaven, weep, wrestle, fall prostrate,
and quake in fear. They shout "Hallelujah" one minute, and the next they
cry out, "My God, why have you forsaken me?" They are not afraid of
the conflict, tension, and sometimes unresolved nature of their questions.
In particular, I continue to be amazed at the wisdom of the early church
fathers to include all four Gospels, despite the fact that the writers painted
different pictures of Jesus that on a literal level are sometimes at odds with
one another. They did this because, for them, divulging the full witness of
Jesus' story was far more important than presenting a neat, harmonious
front. They weren't willing to sacrifice any aspect of the truth for conve-
nience. They believed that God was found in the tension and in the gray
areas. Unfortunately, many Christians have been trained to find harmony
in the Bible, and in so doing they miss out on its most valuable lessons.

When I have students in class who learn for the first time that in
Genesis 1 the narrator describes a flat earth held up by pillars, with a dome
in the sky behind which is not space but water, they scratch their heads

and say, "That's not right." And I say, "Well, yeah. Now what do we do with this?" They look at me and say, "You tell us what to do with this." I refuse, and they get mad and frustrated because their theological training has consisted of people telling them that evolutionists are going to hell and that you must interpret the first eleven chapters of Genesis in a literal way or you're going to hell, too. Interestingly, no one has ever pointed out the intellectual challenges of a literal approach—and there are many.

For example, in addition to the image of a whole flat earth with a dome of water in the sky described in Genesis 1, the author also declares that the animals were created first and then humanity. That sounds good, but if you keep reading, in Genesis 2 the author describes God creating Adam first and then creating the animals to take away Adam's loneliness (which doesn't work, by the way). If you are determined to interpret the texts literally, these two passages create a problem: they can't both be right. Biologists tend to make a big deal out of the fact that animals preceded humanity, affirming Genesis 1. But what does one do with Genesis 2, which states that humans came first and animals second? This goes against both science *and* the narrative of Genesis 1. And, as my phone caller at the beginning of the chapter pointed out, after God created the first family with Adam and Eve, in Genesis 4 Cain apparently wanders off and finds another whole community of humans. Where did they come from? When students discover this inconsistency for the first time, many of them feel duped.

In *Men in Black 3*, Agent K (Tommy Lee Jones) turns to Will Smith's character, Agent J, and says, "You know how I live such a happy life?" This takes J by surprise, because K is perpetually surly and grumpy, so he says, "How *you* live a happy life?" Unfazed, K reveals his secret to being happy: "I don't ask questions I don't want to know the answer to." It's funny, partly because it's essentially a stupid thing to say and partly because, well, a lot of people buy into it. It's a restatement of the axiom "ignorance is bliss."

When I first started teaching, I used to start the first day of class with a quiz as a way to get to know the students. I asked what I thought were humorous questions because the answers were obvious. Even so, the quiz was graded, and the students had to give serious answers. I mention this because I don't want you to think that what I'm about to say was an attempt by some students to be funny. This represents their actual answers.

Question number one was this: "Who founded Christianity?"

The answer is, of course, "Jesus."

Some of the brighter students would overthink the question and give me "Paul," which I would actually allow. But a sizeable number of students regularly got the answer wrong. They would say things like "Billy Graham" or "Moses" or "the Pope" or my two favorites, "Those guys who founded our country," and . . . wait for it . . . "Elvis." Yes, this is funny. But it's also tragic, because these were the same students who were convinced that you have to interpret Genesis literally or you are going to hell. And it was clear that they had never actually read Genesis.

In 1980, leaders at the Billy Graham Center at Wheaton College invited Charles Malik to give the address at the opening ceremony of the center. Malik is an Eastern Orthodox scholar. Mark Noll records the event in *The Scandal of the Evangelical Mind* because it became the driving impetus for writing his book. Anyway, you have to imagine a room filled with professors and dignitaries and donors. You also need to understand that Wheaton was originally founded as a reaction to the threat of Modernism in the early part of the twentieth century, so part of its heritage was a subtle anti-intellectualism.

It is for this reason that Malik showed up at the Billy Graham Center with both barrels loaded for bear. In Noll's words, "With great gentleness and magnanimity of soul, but also with great courage, Malik took us evangelicals straight to the woodshed."

Here's an excerpt of Malik's speech:

> The greatest danger besetting American Evangelical Christianity is the danger of anti-intellectualism. The mind as to its greatest and deepest reaches is not cared for enough. This cannot take place apart from profound immersion for a period of years in the history of thought and the spirit. People are in a hurry to get out of the university and start earning money or serving the church or preaching the Gospel. They have no idea of the infinite value of spending years of leisure in conversing with the greatest minds and souls of the past, and thereby ripening and sharpening and enlarging their powers of thinking. The result is that the arena of creative thinking is abdicated and vacated to the enemy.[7]

Malik outlined the situation succinctly with this statement: "If you win the whole world and lose the mind of the world, you will soon discover you have not won the world. Indeed it may turn out that you have actually lost the world."[8]

We would do well to remember that the early Christians responded to their critics by becoming smarter than them, not dumber. One reason for Christianity's triumph in the Roman Empire was the dazzling brilliance and scholarship of men like Justin Martyr, Origen, and Augustine. The first intellectual center of Christianity was Alexandria, the same location of the greatest library in the world, where men like Clement, Alexander, and Athanasius befuddled the critics of the faith.

Today, as Malik pointed out to his stunned audience at Wheaton, in most of Western culture, the phrase "evangelical scholar" is viewed as an oxymoron. Some of the reason is due to prejudices, but a large part is due to a growing sentiment in the church that one has to choose either a life of faith or a life that honors the mind.

Perhaps one of the reasons for this is an endemic fear of heresy. To allow people the freedom to think means we have to let them squirm and wrestle and even lose sleep in their pilgrimage to find the answer. We also have to give up control of the outcome, allowing them to use their imagination and wander in places that make them uncomfortable. I once had a student ask, "Are God and Satan the same being?" The question caught me off guard. I had a gut reaction that wanted to react aghast and say, "NO!" It took a lot of will power to hold back and say calmly, "Well, what do you think?" But in doing so, I gave the class confidence to ask other questions that they were afraid to bring up for fear of the reaction they had so often experienced in church. If we really believe in a Jesus who is the Truth, we have to have confidence that the Truth will find a way.

Somewhere along the way, our church culture has given the people in the pews the wrong impression that faith in Jesus is easy. That the Bible has an answer for every problem in the world. That if you have enough faith, you will be happy and successful and healthy. That as long as you show up to church, bring your Bible, pay your tithe, read your Sunday school lesson, conform to the social norms, and agree with the pastor's teachings, God will bless you. Unfortunately, when their experiences demonstrate otherwise, they feel betrayed. The feeling can be so strong that they resolve to abandon faith altogether, concluding that it's more honest and moral to be outside the church than it is to be in it.

Jesus didn't hold back when he described the tough road of discipleship. He used words and phrases like "take up your cross," "the road is hard that leads to life," and "it is easier for a camel to go through the eye of a needle than for someone who is rich to enter the kingdom of God." In other words, on the narrow way, faith is a constant struggle, and it will be the hardest thing you will ever do. Thomas à Kempis envisioned Jesus saying,

> Do you imagine that you can always have spiritual joys at will? My Saints did not, but had many troubles, countless trials, and great desolation of soul. But they patiently endured all these things, and trusted in God rather than themselves, knowing that "the sufferings of this present time are not worthy to be compared with the glory to be won hereafter." Do you wish to enjoy immediately that many others have only won after much sorrow and struggle?[9]

On the narrow way, understanding the question is far more important than finding an answer. On the narrow way, faith means you are assured of the cross, not the easy life. On the narrow way, Christ commands us to go beyond church to be salt and light in the world; to go beyond the Bible to incarnate the word; to go beyond the tithe to drop our last two pennies in the coffer; to go beyond the Sunday school lesson to love God with our minds; to go beyond conformity to be a friend of sinners; and to go beyond our pastor's theology to be thoughtful theologians in our own right. When we put these ideas into practice, we take the first steps necessary toward finding our faith. But be forewarned: those who dare to get on this path struggle deep down to the core of their being. Thomas Merton knew this all too well when he wrote, "If I find Him with great ease, perhaps He is not my God."[10]

Last, Paul phrased it another way in 1 Corinthians 13 when he admonished us to put away childish things and to see through the glass darkly. It's a profound image of someone giving up the black-and-white world of childhood for an enigmatic disc that encourages squinting, frustration, and even discouragement, but with the ultimate payoff of one day seeing Jesus, who is the Truth, face to face. It's a hard path, as my son found out when I led him to take his first step and abandon a childhood Santa. As a result, he experienced a crisis of faith that brought tears and disappointment. But in the process, my hope is that one day he'll replace his vision of the North Pole and a red-clad elf with a scene in Bethlehem and the mystery of the incarnation.

Indeed, Christmas will never be the same.

Inward Peregrinatio to the Wilderness

Question: Is there a God?
Fear: There is no God. (Or at least God's promises are not real.)

This section describes the longest and perhaps most difficult part of our journey of faith. I call it "the struggle." I don't mean to suggest that faith is all hardship, but the journey of faith is hard and long and filled with mountains and valleys. For some, I may be stating the obvious, but you would be surprised how many Christians have bought into the idea that faith and church are primarily designed to make them feel happy and good about themselves. There's actually a technical phrase for this—"Moral Therapeutic Deism." But, as this chapter introduces, faith is hard. If we are serious about maturing in our faith, then we need to be prepared for an arduous journey.

Sting (the singer, not the sword) once said, "Love is annihilation." He was actually echoing a strong sentiment in the contemplative tradition that John of the Cross, in particular, wrote about. It's the idea that for us to experience God, we must first die to self. The problem is that "self" is a powerful force in our lives, and the process of dying is typically traumatic and filled with suffering.

For this reason, most of us don't really want to die to self, which is why the wilderness is necessary. Typically, we find ourselves in this place because we were forced into it. We might even spend an agonizingly long time wandering around in it (the Israelites spent forty years here). The experience can seem punitive, but it's meant to be redemptive—even though it may not seem that way. Mother Teresa, for example, never found her way out.

The important thing is to keep going. Confront your hurdles in an honest way. Identify what you are wrestling with. And realize that at some point you have to let go. This will mean different things for various people, but to some degree it is the understanding that to find an infinite God, one must travel beyond the clichés and aphorisms, beyond narcissism and ego, and sometimes even beyond the left brain's abilities to form words.

To get there, you have to just keep moving forward.

Go Deeper

"The Wilderness" in "From Eden to Heaven Prompts" at
www.spilledcoffeeonancientscrolls.com

St. John of the Cross, *Dark Night of the Soul*

Augustine, *Confessions*

Notes

1. Jon Krakauer, *Into the Wild* (New York: Anchor Books, 2007) 60.

2. Poll taken in 2016 found at news.gallup.com/poll/1690/religion.aspx.

3. Mark Noll, *A History of Christianity in the United States and Canada* (Grand Rapids MI: Eerdmans, 1992) 364ff.

4. Scott Thumma and Dave Travis, *Beyond Megachurch Myths* (San Francisco: Jossey-Bass, 2007) 7.

5. Frank Newport, "Five Key Findings on Religion in the U.S.," Gallup, 23 December 2016, news.gallup.com/poll/200186/five-key-findings-religion.aspx.

6. For a thorough discussion on this topic, see David Kinnamen, *You Lost Me* (Grand Rapids MI: Baker Books, 2011).

7. Mark Noll, *The Scandal of the Evangelical Mind* (Grand Rapids MI: Eerdmans Publishing, 2010) 26.

8. Ibid.

9. Thomas à Kempis, *The Imitation of Christ*, trans. Leo Sherley-Price (New York: Penguin Books, 1952) 141.

10. Thomas Merton, *No Man Is an Island* (New York: Harcourt Brace, 1955) 232.

The Desert

Most people would like to be delivered from
temptation but would like it to keep in touch.
—Robert Orben

My first encounter with someone trying to beat a demon wasn't with a monk in the desert but with a professor in a Shakespeare class. We were studying *Macbeth*, Act 4, where the Bard introduces the audience to three witches. In his best whiny voice, Dr. Dobbins cackled,

> Make the gruel thick and slab,
> Add thereto a tiger's chaudron,
> For the ingredients of our caldron.
>
> Double, double toil and trouble,
> Fire burn and cauldron bubble.
>
> Cool it with a baboon's blood,
> Then the charm is firm and good.[1]

Returning to his normal voice, he asked with a wry smirk on his face, "Do you believe in the supernatural?" Stunned, none of us answered. He then went on to argue, "Because if the supernatural does not exist, then Shakespeare's use of witches here weakens the story. For in order for the plot to be plausible, witches must truly have powers to produce potions and to curse, even to prophesy."

I'm sure my eyes widened in bewilderment. Though my professor had often been eccentric, which is what made his class so much fun, this was bordering on the bizarre. I scanned the list of ingredients the witches were throwing into the cauldron: eye of newt, toe of frog, lizard's leg, tongue of dog. I grew up in south Louisiana, so to me this just sounded like they were making gumbo. But then I read further: liver of blaspheming Jew, nose of

Turk, finger of birth-strangled babe . . . okay, now they ruined it. They left out the roux.

My professor then proceeded to walk to an old reel-to-reel tape player he had set up on a table. "This was recorded in a hospital room," he said casually. He pushed a button and the plastic reels turned with a faint squeak. An eerie static filled the room.

"Who are you?" a muffled and distorted voice asked from the small speaker.

A woman hauntingly moaned in response.

"I said *who are you?*"

"I don't know what you want," the woman spoke dreamily.

"In the name of Jesus Christ, tell me your name," he commanded.

Now the voice of the woman dramatically changed, becoming softer, raspier, more baritone. Her answer, though, was unintelligible.

"Say that again!" the man ordered.

"Legion," she said defiantly.

"In the name of Jesus Christ, come out of her!" he commanded.

"Noooooooo," she wailed. "Go away. Please, go away and leave me alone. Why are you doing this to me?" Her sobs were audible.

"In the name of Jesus Christ, come out of her!" the man repeated over and over again.

I could feel goose bumps forming on my arms and the back of my neck. I couldn't tell if the man was harassing this poor woman, if she really had a demon, if she might have been mentally ill, or if she was playing along. The professor stopped the tape. "Looks like our time is up. Read Act 5 for tomorrow." I remember looking at my classmates, and we all had a *what-was-that-all-about?* gaze on our faces as we left the room. I have to give the professor credit; I still remember his lecture.

His question still haunts me: "Do you believe in the supernatural?" The obvious answer for most Christians is *yes*. But what do we mean by that?

Several years prior to my Shakespeare class, when I was in high school, a friend sat next to me in the commons area right before school.

"I just read the most awesome book," he said. "I couldn't put it down. You've got to read it."

I knew this guy normally wasn't a reader, so if it impressed him, it must be good. He was acting a little strange, though, like he was hiding contraband. He looked around to make sure the teachers were far away.

He then pulled out of his backpack a tattered paperback with the title *The Satan Seller*.

I took it home and began reading it that evening. My friend was right. From the first page, the author, comedian Mike Warnke, grabbed my attention with his enchanting tale of being a high priest in the church of Satan. He was a marvelous storyteller, dramatically describing his seduction, including the Satanic services he attended, spells he cast, demons he conjured, women he enslaved, orgies he attended . . . and then how a couple of military buddies exorcised the evil spirits from his life, set him free, and put him on a new path of charismatic glory. It was all the stuff a teenaged Christian boy could hope for in a story without it being considered a sin to read.

My fascination with Warnke was short-lived. I forgot all about him until the day I ran across an old article in *Cornerstone* magazine exposing Warnke as a fraud. It turns out that someone finally decided to verify the comedian's outlandish stories and discovered he made most of them up. Discredited, Warnke fell off the planet, though to this day he still claims that there is a kernel of truth to his testimony, admitting only to exaggeration in order to make his routine more entertaining. I visited his website and noticed that *The Satan Seller* is no longer listed among his products.

I wish stories of fraud like this were an anomaly in Christianity, but the formula is common, repeated over and over again with a different cast in each generation. Such stories should be a warning to Christians about being too gullible and, perhaps, of wanting to believe so badly in the realm of the supernatural that we are too willing to believe anyone with the gift of gab.

Still, the New Testament is filled with examples of dramatically supernatural events, a miraculous birth, healings, raisings from the dead, conversations with Satan, walking on water, the calming of the sea, and, on several occasions, exorcisms.

Modern interpretations of these events vary widely. For example, with exorcisms, those in the Charismatic/Pentecostal tradition believe that demons literally exist and that exorcisms still take place today. Others believe that though exorcisms were once common, they were a first-century phenomenon used by God to prove the validity of Jesus' ministry. As such, exorcisms are no longer necessary today. Many in the Reformed (Calvinist) tradition are pretty adamant about this view. Then there are those who believe that the world of demons was merely a cultural understanding of conditions we now understand better through medicine and psychology.

What first-century Jews described as demon possession, experts today diagnose as epilepsy, psychosis, or multiple personality disorder. Demons are not supernatural beings but a metaphor to describe something that torments us, like an ailment, an addiction, or even a trauma.

When I mentioned to a friend that I was working on a chapter about demons, the first question she asked was, "Do you believe demons really exist?" Interestingly, this question is never entertained in the New Testament. There, demons are a given, and, in fact, early believers understood much of the evil and suffering of their day in this context. Demons caused physical and mental ailments. Demons motivated people to sin. Satan himself entered Judas and persuaded him to betray Jesus. Demons inundated the culture of the Greeks and Romans through paganism. "That's not Jupiter," they would chide. "That's a demon pretending to be Jupiter. You've been duped, you Cretan!"

When the subject of demonology came up in the Ante-Nicene church, they didn't waste time pondering whether demons existed. They were far more concerned about how to get rid of them—so much so that exorcists were as common as youth ministers are today, only they at least had the sense not to wear tennis shoes with their Sunday best.

What exactly did the exorcists do? For that answer we turn to the "Elvis" of the Desert Fathers, an anchorite (solitary monk) known as Saint Anthony. His rock-star status came about as a result of a biography written by Athanasius, Bishop of Alexandria, who described Anthony's enthralling wrestling matches with demons in the desert. Before Anthony, anchorites had the reputation of being eccentric but holy old geezers. After Anthony, they became known more as demon-wranglers, inspiring a throng of men and women to seek a life of solitude and spiritual warfare. The movement exploded, causing one contemporary of the times to quip that the deserts of Egypt had become far more populated than the great cities of the empire.[2]

Anthony didn't develop his reputation merely by wrestling with the demons. He became famous because he regularly kicked their butts. Picture a young, wide-eyed fanatic with a long, straggly beard and lanky limbs kneeling in prayer. Satan shows up and the dual begins, lasting well into the night. At one point, Anthony taunts, and I quote, "I do not run from your blows, for even if you give me more, nothing shall separate me from the love of Christ." Seeing that Anthony is not one to be intimidated, Satan disappears and then reappears with friends. They take various forms—lions, bears, leopards, bulls, and serpents. The fight lasts for hours. Anthony feels worn out but coolly replies, "If there were some power among you it would have been enough for only one of you to come. But since the Lord has broken your strength, you attempt to terrify me by means with the mob; it is a mark of your weakness . . . ."[3]

Finally, a shaft of light pierces into the darkness, forcing the evil spirits to flee. Anthony recognizes at once that God has finally intervened, but he is troubled by the late arrival. "Where were you?" he asks. "Why didn't you appear in the beginning, so that you could stop my distresses?"

"I was here, Anthony," the voice replies. "But I waited to watch your struggle."[4]

Why God created a world filled with writhing is one of the great mysteries of the Christian faith. Many people have tried to explain it, and even in this biography Athanasius puts words into God's mouth that don't make sense. All I can tell you is that the struggle is somehow necessary for the exorcism and healing.

From experiences like this one, Anthony developed a demonology with insights that are still relevant even today. For example, to Anthony, demons represented not only a hostile force that was out to destroy humanity but also the sum of "all that was anomalous and incomplete *in* man."[5] In other words, take away the humanity of an individual and you wind up with the demonic. In addition, Anthony believed that demons had no real power to inflict harm. He pointed out that they couldn't even control a herd of swine when Jesus exorcised the Gerasene demoniac (see Mark 5 and Luke 8). Rather, as disciples of the Father of Lies, demons are experts at illusion.[6] And what they are best at doing is conjuring images that instill fear.

Fear, then, is ultimately what motivates the possessed person to behave the way he or she does: fear of being a failure, of losing everything, of being lonely, of being exploited, of being made a laughingstock, of losing control, of looking foolish. You name the fear, and there is a demon expert at conjuring an illusion for it that can lead to the most irrational behavior. In the New Testament, people possessed by demons throw themselves into fire, wander half-naked among tombs, and annoy Apostles by screaming at them as they attempt to evangelize the masses. Today, demoniacs may act a little more sophisticated, but they behave just as irrationally, with the result still the same—destruction. If you look hard enough, you can find modern examples of people wrestling with demons all around us.

Take for example an artist friend of mine, a child of the sixties who still has a sparkle in her eye from the unmentionable escapades of her youth. One long and lonely summer, she became convinced that her very ugly cat was possessed. This wasn't some hypothetical pondering. She really thought the cat was possessed because it was very, very skinny. Its hair was matted, its tail was unnaturally crooked, and it purred extra loud. What more proof do you need? Well, my very bright friend gave the cat a good reason to act possessed when she decided to test her hypothesis by dousing it with holy water. To give her credit, she approached this scientifically. First, she sprinkled regular tap water on the cat and carefully observed its reaction. Then, she took her special bottle of holy water from the Jordan River itself and sprayed the cat. She backed up to see if the feline acted any differently. I don't know if she was expecting smoke to rise from its fur or for it to go into convulsions or to become catatonic. But nothing happened. The cat didn't even projectile-vomit pea soup.

Unfortunately, there are more serious stories of the demonic. Back when I was attending seminary, there were rumors circulating when Ted Haggard stepped down as pastor and president of the National Evangelical Association because of immorality. Long before his fall, there were Jimmy Swaggart and Jim Bakker. Then there are the horrific tales of priests who sexually abused children in Boston and elsewhere.

These troubling cases are not isolated events. When we talk about these issues in my classes, I typically have an alarming number of students who share about a leader in the church who ran off with the secretary or who stole from the treasury. Recently, one woman even spoke about a pastor who hanged himself in the sanctuary just weeks after she had been baptized. She hasn't returned to the church since.

The Desert Fathers and Mothers offer us some guidance into the world of the soul. For though men like Anthony had a fairly limited and some-times bizarre worldview, they were in many ways wiser than us because of their ability to see a life filled with the supernatural. If we look carefully, maybe they can teach us something about defeating our own demons. Or, if you rather, maybe they can help us work through our personal issues by applying cognitive behavioral therapy to achieve self-actualization.

Perhaps Thomas Merton explained it best when he wrote,

> Old-fashioned idea: that the solitary life and indeed the Christian life is a struggle with invisible powers. All this is dismissed even by monks. Yet is the Bible so far wrong? I think I experience it more and more. As to what

these powers are, who can clearly say, but one experiences their persuasion, their use of our weakness to prompt us to choices that, if followed out logically, would wreck us totally. . . . A superficial existentialism can be a disaster.[7]

Granted, gleaning wisdom from the wise men and women of the past can be quite a challenge because, in my experience, sometimes those who dress like demons are really angels, and those who dress like angels are really demons—so one must develop certain critical skills. For example, in the age when Shakespeare wrote *Macbeth*, there was a popular book that was a special favorite of ministers titled *Malleus Maleficarum*, or *The Hammer of Witches*. Here's a sample:

All wickedness, is but little to the wickedness of a woman. . . . What else is woman but a foe to friendship, an unescapable punishment, a necessary evil, a natural temptation, a desirable, domestic danger, a delectable detriment, an evil nature, painted with fair colours. . . . Women are by nature instruments of Satan—they are by nature carnal, a structural defect rooted in the original creation.[8]

This text was essentially used to justify the notion that women were by nature evil and in league with Satan and were therefore guilty until proven innocent. It was the backdrop that set the stage for a dark and infamous period in church history known as the witch hunts.

One of the most well-known examples of this occurred in Massachusetts back when our country was still referred to as "the colonies." It was then that Elizabeth Parris and Abigail Williams conversed on a favorite subject of many preteen girls—boys. They dreamed about life with their future husbands: what they would look like, what they would do for a living, what kinds of house they would inhabit. And then one of the girls came up with the idea of getting some answers. For this, she used an egg and a glass as a means of divination. This seems silly to us today, but I imagine that, if you think back to your youth, you tried something like this. Maybe it was a Ouija board, or you and your friends attempted a séance, or you gazed into a crystal ball or asked questions of a Magic 8-Ball. I can remember that when I was in grade school, I stood in a darkened bathroom with a candle, spinning around three times while saying "Bloody Mary" because someone at school told me that if I did, a ghost would appear. I distinctly remember getting goose bumps but no ghost.

However, for Elizabeth and Abigail, something *did* happen. One of them saw a vision of a casket, and it scared her so much that she grew hysterical, which became contagious so that the other girl behaved strangely, too. They shouted blasphemies, went into trances, and convulsed on the floor, all of which alarmed the adults who lived around them. After consulting several physicians, the diagnosis was that these girls were being tormented by demons, so someone decided to bake a witch cake. This was a curious piece of white magic used to defeat black magic. It entailed baking a rye cake with the urine of the afflicted girls. The baked good was then fed to a dog, considered a messenger of Satan. If he ate it, then the spell was broken. Fortunately for the girls, and unfortunately for the dog, he ate it. The big question then became the identity of the witch or witches who conjured the demons. After much interrogation, the girls identified three women: Tituba, a slave, and two eccentric Puritan women named Sarah Good and Sarah Osburn, all of whom were quite innocent of anything worthy of capital punishment but were easy scapegoats because of their marginalized positions in society. They were executed. The Salem witch trials began with the innocent musings of a couple of girls and escalated into heinous acts of injustice, where fear and paranoia led to the execution of some twenty women before the governor finally stepped in and put a stop to the hysteria.

Though this story is probably the most famous anecdote of the witch hunts, it was tame compared to what was happening elsewhere in the Western world. The Puritan ministers as a whole were far more skeptical when it came to identifying and sentencing witches, but they get most of the blame. Though hundreds of cases were brought to court in the colonies, the vast majority of women were acquitted. Compare this to Europe, where in Bamberg, 900 witches were executed in a single year. In the province of Alsace, some 5,000 were condemned to death. This statistic says nothing of the tens of thousands who were tortured by devices that skewered, pinched, probed, broke, and sliced in ways that would make even a modern-day sadist queasy.

Which people in this story were really doing the work of demons? The answer: the ones who *demonized* their neighbors by refusing to acknowledge their fellow human beings as children created in the image of God; they stripped them of their humanity and viewed them as devils worthy of punishment. Some even justified their behavior by believing that torture and execution were valid forms of evangelism. In other words, by removing bits of flesh with white-hot tongs from these prisoners, they thought they were in some twisted way helping to redeem their souls. In a sober moment long after the witch trials, one of the judges, Samuel Sewall, publicly confessed his "blame and shame" in 1697, recognizing that perhaps the truly possessed were not the ones who were executed.[9]

It's easy for us to look back at these Puritans and shake our fingers at them for what they did, but are we any different when we strip the humanity from our neighbors so that we can justify treating them like devils? To avoid cavorting with demons, we must take great pains to recognize that *everyone* has been created in the image of God. I must confess that this is a difficult thing to do. There are politicians who make me so mad that I want to burn them in effigy—but that is demonizing. Even the worst politician out there is still one who has been created in the image of God. Our culture has no shortage of easy targets for demonization: Hollywood actors, pampered athletes, TV evangelists, the homeless, Muslims, undocumented immigrants, refugees, coworkers, supervisors, exes, mothers-in-law. These are but a few of the people groups that are deemed worthy of malice. But if we act on that impulse, then we do the work of demons.

A major task we all face in expanding the kingdom of God on earth is the job of ridding the world of the demonic. But how do we do that? Our friend Anthony gave us a hint. He taught us that the demons use fear to get us to do their bidding, and they create illusions to make us afraid and manipulate us. To counter this, we must use truth.

Luke 8:26-39 describes an exorcism that took place with a man who lived among the tombs in the country of the Gerasenes. It is a story filled with fear. The demons are the first to express this emotion as they approach Jesus right after he disembarks from the boat. "Do not torment us, and do not send us into the Abyss," they beg. Jesus then allows them to enter a herd of swine. We see fear at work again as the pigs panic and bolt for the sea where they drown one by one. When the people of the region hear about this, they approach Jesus and beg him to leave, for they are afraid of his power.

One of my friends, Steve Neves, created a sculpture depicting a scene from this narrative—the moment the demons left the demoniac. He chose to make it out of concrete, giving the figure a rough and unfinished look, like a cinder-block wall in need of a coat of paint. The man's face is caught between agony and relief, neither happy nor sad, but desperate. In the belly of the man is a hole, like someone has shot a cannonball through it. This, according to Steve, is where the demons lived. They are no longer there in his sculpture, an absence indicated by the gaping hole. Steve's piece offered insight that vowed to remember—exorcised demons leave holes.[10]

Though he is hunched over, the man is kneeling as in prayer. As you walk behind the sculpture, you see a demon face etched in the back, its eyes the only thing painted in the work. They are solid white, unfocused. The hole is now a mouth, and out of it swine escape in an arc as a putrid projectile, landing on the ground where they sink and drown in the grass. It is a haunting depiction that grabbed my attention; I wanted to know where this came from in Steve's life. So I asked him.

"I never really thought about it," he said.

"But look at this face," I said, pointing to his sculpture, "This is you."

Steve studied his sculpture and nodded thoughtfully. "You're right," he said. "I guess I'm trying to get away from my own demon."

I could tell he was getting a little uncomfortable as he shifted his weight. "I know much of my art in the past has depicted the pain and suffering I went through. I just didn't think about this particular piece being a part of that."

Steve tenderly rubbed his hands on the face of his sculpture and didn't say anything for a while. I didn't feel comfortable asking him anything more. I knew a little about what tormented him. Several years ago, he and his wife Dona had lost their infant son to cystic hygroma, a rare genetic condition. It is among a parent's worst fears, and it happened when they had first moved to Abilene, so there was the added stress of being in a new community with no close support group. To make matters worse, it happened to their infant child during a time when both of them had formed an intense bond with him. I well remember those early months with my own children. Your brain is swimming in euphoric chemicals. You have a hard time thinking of little else besides nurturing and protecting your baby. As a new father, I would wake in the night, worried that something was wrong, so I would walk into Nathaniel's nursery just to make sure he was still breathing. To be honest, I *still* do that from time to time even though he is a teenager. I can only imagine the horror of what it would be like to clutch a lifeless son or daughter, and I'm not sure how I would survive such a trauma.

However, as I looked at Steve eyeing his demoniac, I could see how my friend was trying to cope. He was using his art to embrace a truth in his own life—one that included a big hole in his gut that had been ripped open by demons. One that put a look on his face caught in a transition—sad and wondering when or if it will be okay to smile again.

As I have pondered Steve's art, it has dawned on me that my friend is a modern exorcist—and a good one at that. He's not what you might expect.

He doesn't walk around in a black robe. He isn't surrounded by mist and doesn't carry a bag of relics, like in the movies. Nor does he tell fantastical, funny stories about being a high priest in the church of Satan, like Warnke. Nor does he live in a cave and sport a long, scraggly beard, like Anthony. Rather than chanting psalms and hymns, his exorcism prayers are offered with cement, a trowel, and chicken wire. The effect is the same, though. It is a journey inward that is designed to help him face whatever he finds there with brutal honesty and, with the power of the Holy Spirit, to force that which torments him to leave.

* * *

This chapter began with my Shakespeare professor asking, "Do you believe in the supernatural?" Some twenty years later, I can say that at least now I understand the question a little better. It's not about whether witches really exist and whether they have real, demonic powers at their disposal. That's what we want to make the question because it's far easier. As a student, I really wanted to believe that Warnke did all those fantastical things, but I wasn't really believing in the supernatural, was I? I was believing in a lie, just like the Puritan ministers in Salem. To truly believe in the supernatural, we must look past the showy questions that get most of the attention and focus on the ones that matter so that we don't miss what's really going on in the supernatural world. Did Lady Macbeth really have blood on her hands that she could not wash off? That's not actually the issue, is it? Any freshman coed with access to CliffsNotes can tell you that it was Lady Macbeth's failure to overcome her murderous guilt that became her undoing. In other words, she feared that she would never be forgiven. Failure to work through the fear is what drove her mad, which is why it takes far more than just a little water to wash out the damn spots.

It is the truth that sets us free from this fear—and from the demons. When we push through the fear, we discover our true selves on the other side. The demon is exorcised. We are no longer its slaves. We can now move forward to become who we were meant to be, and the memory or trauma or pain that captivated us in the first place loses its hold as we transition from victims to witnesses.

This metamorphosis is easier said than done because we live in a culture that has gotten sophisticated in its ability to wield fear as a weapon to manipulate people. But stand firm. Keep moving forward. Power through the fear. In the process, learn that the witch is really just an eccentric old woman. That an ugly cat is just an ugly cat and you really need to get out more. And that after a deep sadness like the loss of a child, it is possible, over time, to find joy again.

* * *

Legend has it that the sixteenth-century reformer Martin Luther wrestled with his demon in the Wartburg castle while hiding from Charles V, who had put a price on his head. Luther attempted to overcome these bouts by translating the Bible into his native tongue of German. But the exercise didn't work. Satan still appeared in his room to torment him. I am told that if you go to the castle today, you can still see the ink stain on the wall where Luther threw a bottle at the Prince of Darkness during one of his apparitions. Given this context, Luther's famous hymn, "A Mighty Fortress Is Our God," takes on new meaning. The following is the third verse (italics mine):

> And though this world, with devils filled, Should threaten to undo us,
> We will not *fear*, for God hath willed His *truth* to triumph through us.
> The prince of darkness grim, *We* tremble not for him;
> His rage we can endure, For Lo! his doom is sure; One little word shall fell him.

Inward Peregrinatio to the Desert

Question: What demons do I wrestle with?
Fear: The demons will win.

When Jesus asks the demons to name themselves in Mark 5, it's interesting that they answer, "Legion." More than likely, Mark was the first to write down this story of Jesus, and it's also probable that his audience was the congregation in Rome very soon after the Neronian persecutions. In other words, this was the time when Christian homes were invaded by Roman soldiers and entire families were carted off and thrown in prison. Some of them met violent ends in the Coliseum. Credible stories exist of others enduring torture by being impaled, covered in pitch, and ignited. And still others were fed to wild dogs for the entertainment of Nero's guests.

It stands to reason that the biggest fear of the moment for Mark's congregation was that members of the Roman Legion would show up at their doorstep. When Mark's Gospel was first read to them and they heard the demons answer Jesus by saying, "Legion," a current of fear must have run through them. In crafting the story this way, perhaps Mark was trying to help his congregation name their own demons to get them to face their fear.

Naming one's demon has long been the proven strategy to begin an exorcism. It sounds overly simplistic, but you'd be surprised both by how difficult and how helpful it can be to figure this out. Some of us have made friends with our demons, and we don't realize how they are slowly eroding our lives away. Some of us have suppressed our demons deep in our psyche, where they are waiting to manifest themselves at the worst time when they can do the most damage. This is where journaling can help. Begin by asking, *What are some of my worst fears?* Then try to find the source of those fears. Often, that's where your demons lie.

The next step, when you are ready, is to identify how your fears are manipulating you, holding you back, or leading you to self-destructive behavior. For some, this is a journey best taken with a trained counselor.

Go Deeper

"The Desert" in "From Eden to Heaven Prompts" at
www.spilledcoffeeonancientscrolls.com

C. S. Lewis, *Screwtape Letters*

Athanasius, *Life of St. Antony*

David G. Benner, *Soulful Spirituality*

Notes

1. Shakespeare, *Macbeth*, Act IV, Scene 1.

2. Justo L. González, *The Early Church to the Dawn of the Reformation*, vol. 1 of *The Story of Christianity* (San Francisco: Harper and Row, 1984) 142.

3. Athanasius, *Life of St. Antony and the Letter to Marcellinus*, trans. Robert C. Gregg (Mahwah NJ: Paulist Press, 1980) 37–39.

4. Ibid.

5. From Peter Brown, *Making of Late Antiquity*, 90, quoted in introduction to *Life of St. Antony and the Letter to Marcellinus*, 7.

6. Athanasius, *Life of Saint Antony and the Letter to Marcellinus*, 53.

7. Thomas Merton, *Intimate Merton*, ed. Patrick Hart and Jonathan Montaldo (San Francisco: HarperSanFrancisco, 1999) 261.

8. Quoted in Stephen T. Katz, *The Holocaust in Historical Context*, vol. 1 (New York: Oxford University Press, 1994) 438–39.

9. Mark Noll, *History of Christianity in the United States and Canada* (Grand Rapids MI: Eerdmans, 1992) 51.

10. Much of the material in this section comes from my article "What Are You Afraid Of?" *Review & Expositor* 107 (Summer 2010): 413ff. It includes pictures of Steve's sculpture.

The Tower of Babel

> Men never do evil so completely and cheerfully as
> when they do it from a religious conviction.
> —Blaise Pascal

Genesis 11 begins with a curious story about humanity attempting to build
a tower to God. The writer probably had in mind a ziggurat, which is a
building with stair-step walls that angle upwards (similar to a pyramid)
until they reach a point. There were many of these structures in the ancient
Near East. But this particular ziggurat was different. It was intended to
reach all the way to heaven.

On the surface, this doesn't sound so bad. Why shouldn't humanity
strive to reach God? And why would God be upset at humanity trying to
get to him? A part of the answer lies in the hubris of humanity to take on
this engineering project. Though the text is ambiguous, perhaps humanity's
motivation is not visit God but to storm the gates of heaven to usurp him.

Clearly, God is not pleased with the project, and so God destroys the
tower and scatters humanity to the four corners of the earth. To make sure
they can't attempt such a thing again, God confuses their language so they
cannot work together anymore. And thus, we get the name of the tower,
"Babel."

At its essence, the tower of Babel is a place where spiritual pride
becomes the motivation for our strivings for God. And though you may
not find groups building ziggurats anymore, it's not hard to find very spiritual people who believe they have a better idea than God about how the
world and the church should be run. The New Testament is filled with
examples of such people. They are the religious elites who confronted Jesus
about his ministry. They didn't like Jesus' emphasis on love and grace and
breaking barriers that separated humanity. And they let Jesus know it.

In response, Jesus reserved his strongest words for these people
(Matthew 23). He charged them with making disciples who were "twice
as much a child of hell" as they were. And if that wasn't enough, Jesus sent
the Holy Spirit on Pentecost to reverse the curse of Babylon by having his

disciples speak in a language that everyone could understand, regardless of race, gender, ethnicity, education, wealth, religion, and all the other ways humanity has devised to exclude one another.

We would be wise to pay attention. These spiritual elitists are alive and well and numerous. And if followers of Christ aren't careful, we may very well find ourselves numbered. To keep this from happening, we must visit the tower of Babel from time to time, to sit and ponder whether we have stayed on course and kept the "main thing the main thing" with respect to the priorities that Jesus emphasized in his ministry.

* * *

I do not cuss. I don't say that to boast but merely to point out that this chapter is not an attempt to justify a bad habit of mine. When I was in grade school, I cussed a lot because I learned a bunch of grown-up words and thought it was fun to say them when adults weren't around. But then I befriended a boy named John who didn't cuss, and it impressed me. So in fourth grade I decided that I didn't want to cuss anymore, and I haven't ever since.

I will, however, admit to slipping one time since fourth grade. I was at a volleyball game for a church where I served as the youth minister. Our new pastor had just moved to town, so I invited him to join us. He seemed to enjoy himself and wasn't a bad player. In fact, at one point he managed to return an especially difficult serve. I wanted to compliment him, but in the heat of the moment my brain came up with two choices that it couldn't decide on: "good shot" and "good hit." My mouth put the two together, which prompted a bizarre look from the pastor.

I apparently learned to cuss at a very young age. My mother loves to tell the story that dates back to my toddler years. She and my father got into a fight that ended with my father storming out of the house and my mother visibly upset. Being a fairly sensitive toddler, I wanted to comfort her. I held Mom's hand and looked compassionately in her eyes and said, "Oh sh*t, Mommy?" It was at that point that she realized she needed to watch her language around me.

My son didn't pick up his first cuss word until he started school. Learning forbidden words appears to be a rite of passage, but it was one that I had hoped would elude him for a long time. I was wrong. While attending second grade, my son came home from school and sat beside me on the couch and said, "Daddy, I learned a word today, and some of the kids were saying it's a bad one."

"Really?" I said, trying to act unfazed. "What word did you learn?"

He leaned in close and whispered in my ear, "Sh*t."

I nodded. "Well, it's not a word I would use if I were you."

"Is it a bad word?" he asked, a little gleefully because this seemed to be secret, grownup information.

I found myself in a bit of a quandary because I've often wondered if there is even such a thing as a bad word. I decided to play it safe for the moment, so I said, "Yes, it's a bad word, and not one that a second-grader ought to use."

"I thought so." He nodded. I haven't heard him say it again, though I wonder if he secretly uses it around his friends, like I did when I was his age in order to feel more grown up.

What makes "sh*t" a bad word, anyway? Is it what the word refers to? Well, to be honest, sh*t is a good thing. Even though Leonardo da Vinci meant it in a derogatory way when he said, "Man is merely a poo machine," the truth is, if we didn't make poop, we'd die. Yes, poop is stinky. As it travels through the intestines it can be uncomfortable. Chimpanzees and politicians like to fling it. But to be intellectually honest, one cannot escape the hard truth that God made our bodies to make poop, and therefore it must be good. Every human being who has ever existed has made poop—men, women, saints, sinners, popes, apostles, even Jesus. Apparently there was a bit of a discussion in the seventeenth century as to whether Adam made poop in the garden of Eden. They actually have a phrase for it—"Edenic excretion." In his masterpiece, *Paradise Lost*, Milton wrote,

When Adam waked, so customed; for his sleep
Was airy light, from pure digestion bred
And temperate vapors bland, which th' only sound
Of leaves and fuming rills, Aurora's fan,
Lightly dispersed . . . .[1]

In this verse, Milton gives us his theory. While in Paradise, Adam's digestion was so efficient that he didn't need to poop, though it wasn't 100 percent. So while he slept, the little leftovers escaped as "temperate vapors" through his pores, and as they rose from his body, the goddess Aurora silently fanned them away. In other words, no grunts, plops, passing gas, odor, piles, or need for wiping. I'm assuming that meant no flaring hemorrhoids, either. Now *those* were the good ol' days.

* * *

A while back, a young pastor from Dallas came and preached in chapel. I'll call him Bob. In his closing illustration he recollected a time when he played college football and his fellow teammates were in awe over the fact that they had never heard him cuss. One guy bet another guy $50 that he could make the future preacher fall. He had a devious strategy that he thought was sure to work. He approached Bob, told him of the bet, and offered to split the winnings if Bob would just say the "s-word" in front of everyone. Using true preacher drama, Bob described the anguish he went through as he mulled over the temptation. *He was dirt poor. Twenty-five dollars was a lot of money. It was just a word.*

In the end, good triumphed over evil as Bob told his friend to get lost. It was a bittersweet victory because Bob could have used the money—but the story wasn't over. Because Bob was faithful in not saying a naughty word, God rewarded him with even more money. On that very day, when he went to the post office he discovered a letter from home filled with cash. God is good!

I have to admit that I was skeptical after hearing this story. Does God really go around rewarding young preachers with cash for not cussing? I don't think so. In fact, it seems to me that if you have been called to preach, the last thing you want to hear from God on the day of judgment is, "Congratulations. You didn't say *sh*t!*"

Contrast this with another speaker in chapel whom I invited a couple of years ago. I'll call him Tony Campolo. I met with him in the green room just prior to the service, and we had about ten minutes to chat. He sat across a speckled, Formica table, the kind you might see in a classic diner. His eyes made him look like he was thinking about a million things all at the same time.

"You know," he said as if we had been talking for hours, even though this was the first thing he'd said to me after, "Hello." His accent is a cross between Don Rickles and Jimmy Durante. "I've been to Abilene lots of times, which is unusual for a town this size."

"Really?" I responded politely.

"Yeah, yeah. In fact, you know that story I tell in my talk—the one about saying 'sh*t' in front of a youth group?"

"Heard it many times."

"Well, that happened here . . . in Abilene. I remember it. It was some sort of Baptist camp or something. I was talking and they were giving me this bored look, so I said, 'You know what your problem is? You're more offended that I just said the word *sh*t* than you are over the fact that 30,000 kids will die today because of starvation!'" He laughed as he conjured up the memory. "Boy, did I get a bunch of angry letters from those parents after that one. Not one of them about the starving kids, though."

Sure enough, in the middle of his talk to the college students that morning, he yelled out, "Sh*t!" I was sitting at the front of the auditorium, and I heard audible gasps. This surprised me a little. First of all, we have a dead dog buried on campus. He was one of the early mascots of the university and his name was "Dam-it." So, proudly displayed with the fire hydrant tombstone is a plaque that reads, "Dam-it. He's Dead." And second, well, this *is* West Texas, cattle and horse country. If we are used to anything around here, it's sh*t. But I must admit, in that moment I was concerned about the letters I might receive from the parents of offended students. But when Tony finished his spiel, the audience applauded in approval—something I've never heard them do in the middle of someone's sermon. And it was partly because Tony had the guts to risk cussing in chapel on behalf of the poor.

It was a proud moment for me as chaplain.

What is it about the word *sh*t* that's so bad that I don't include the vowel when I type it for fear of offending someone? Perhaps you, the reader, have been aghast during this whole chapter that a Christian publisher would even allow such a discussion. But before burning this book, humor me for a little while longer, because I have a serious point to make. It involves how our outrage for small offenses can sometimes blind us to the truly big offenses that outraged Jesus.

In fact, let's do an experiment. I'm going to type the word again, only this time I'm going to include the "i," and let's see if it gets past my editor.

Shit.

Did it make it? If so, was that less offensive for you to read? If not, take a pen or pencil and write it yourself. There. Now what do you think? It's just a word, isn't it? A word with no power by itself. But it has meaning. To learn about the word, I went to the library to do some "research." If you're looking up dirty words, I'm not sure you can call it that, technically speaking. "Research" sounds too much like something proper and work oriented. This is more like satisfying a kind of curiosity that might get you into trouble. Like sneaking into the girls' bathroom (if you're a boy) to see if they have any secret girl devices like urinals (they don't). Believe it or not, this is not the first time I've conducted such research. When I was in third grade, a classmate and I found ourselves relegated to a corner of the room all the time because we finished our assignments before everyone else did. Fortunately, the corner had a few books for us to look at, and one of them was a dictionary. One day my classmate and I looked up every dirty word we could think of, and to our disappointment, none of them were there except for one, which was defined as "detective" and "nickname for Richard"—not at all what we thought it meant.

When I went to the Hardin-Simmons library, I didn't have any better luck at first. A keyword search for *sh*t* didn't bring anything up, and neither did "cussing" or "swearing." Well, this is a *Baptist* university, down the street from a Church of Christ university and across town from a Methodist university. None of them had a book about cussing. This wasn't all that surprising, though I thought maybe the Methodists might come through for me.

I finally decided to ask the expert. I'll call her Elizabeth. She's a librarian. After a bit of small talk, I mustered up the courage to confess to her that I needed to look up dirty words. Without blinking, she walked briskly out of her office and straight to the *Oxford English Dictionary*, 2nd edition, as if she gets this question a lot. Sure enough, every dirty word I could think of was there, with long columns of definitions and usages.

Sh*t took up a whole page, and I was amazed to find the Texas pronunciation prominently displayed as the first alternate under the interjection form—"shee-y-it." It was also the one with the most syllables. I have to admit, though, the Old English version had the prettiest spelling of it: "scheitte."

Some form of this word, tracing back to the Anglo-Saxons, has been used for nearly a millennium, but it wasn't until the eighteenth century that authors began to be a little self-conscious about using it. They came up with the clever device of using a dash instead of a vowel, which, amazingly, works just as well as glasses on Superman in hiding the true identity.[2]

As you can imagine, the word can be used in a variety of ways: sometimes utilitarian—"I need to take a . . ."; sometimes derogatory—"you dumb . . ."; sometimes reflective—"I feel like . . ."; sometimes as a euphemism for something else—"don't touch that . . . ." But its main use is probably as an interjection, to express an extreme emotion of surprise, anger, or the like.

People who are averse to the word have to come up with something else to say, even when referring to the very literal definition of *sh*t*, so they have to resort to baby talk (doo doo) or Latin (feces).[3] "Crap" seems to be a more acceptable word to use. According to one tradition, this word comes from the name Thomas Crapper, who invented "Crapper's Valveless Water Waste Preventer," a slogan used for Victorian-era water closets (toilets). However, evidence exists that the word "crap" was associated with excrement at least fifty years before Crapper was born.[4] And, according to the majority of sane people who actually spend time debating the issue, Crapper wasn't even the inventor of this device. It appears that British patent number 4990 for the "device" actually belongs to Albert Giblin.[5] Some speculate that Crapper bought the patent from Giblin, thus calling into question the sanity of the man with the unfortunate last name who willingly stamped "T. Crapper" on a device that magnified his name and ensured that his children were treated to endless jokes from the other kids.

I think it's safe to say that more people would be okay with someone yelling "crap" than "sh*t." For one thing, "crap" is not listed among the seven forbidden words you can't say on television, made infamous by George Carlin. But to some degree, both are considered improper. Why?

In *Cursing in America*, Timothy Jay outlines some of the things that make words "dirty." Most of these are self-explanatory, so I won't go into too much detail about them. Cursing is defined as asking a divine power to injure someone. This is actually something you read about in the Bible quite often, as in Noah cursing Canaan to slavery because his father, Ham, saw Noah naked after he had passed out drunk. Other words are bad because they irreverently speak about something holy (blasphemy), as in the commandment that prohibits taking the name of the Lord in vain. The Hebrews were so scared of this one that when they ran across the proper name of God in the Bible (YHWH), they would say "Adonai," which means "Lord." Over time, they forgot how to say the proper name of God, and consequently so have we. In the New Testament, Jesus taught that those who blaspheme the Holy Spirit will not be forgiven.

Other words are avoided because the culture considers them taboo. This practice is more common outside of the United States, but we still say things like "he passed away" instead of "he died." Other words are slurs directed at people we don't like because their race, gender, nationality, or sexuality is different from ours. Insults are what we yell at the idiot who thinks he owns the road. Expletives are what we say when we stub our toe.

And then there are obscenities. In the past, what made a word obscene or profane was determined by the monarchy. Now the government has attempted to define this, but its three-point test is so steeped in legalese that no one really understands what the court considers obscene, despite mobs of angry pastors yelling insults and expletives at lawmakers in an attempt to explain it to them.

Last (and most important for our study), there is scatology, which is literally the "study of sh*t."

Believe it or not, there are only two of these dirty word categories directly prohibited in the Bible: blasphemy and insults. The rest seem to be fair game. I'm not suggesting that politeness and propriety should be ignored, but people who let a colorful word slip every now and then are no more spiritually immature than those who keep their language "clean." Because if we can draw anything from this long meditation on scatology, it is that sh*t by another name is still sh*t.

One dirty little secret about the Bible is that several authors and characters use a number of colorful words and phrases to make their point. But Bible sellers want to sell Bibles, and they know that it doesn't take make much to offend the Bible-buying crowd. They tone down the language, which is the real shame, because they remove some of the humanity from the text. Greek and Hebrew professors, however, love to point out these vulgar expressions, often because they are desperate to make their subjects interesting. Here are some of the biblical passages using bad words that your pastor never mentioned.

In 1 Samuel 25, David gets really mad at Nabal for not providing food for his men after they have protected Nabal's property. David invokes a curse, and the NIV puts it this way: "May God deal with David, be it ever so severely, if by morning I leave alive one male of all who belong to him!" (v. 22). What the Hebrew really says is, ". . . if I leave alive any by morning who pisses against the wall."

I have a few other quick examples. Genesis 30 is a bawdy passage involving mandrake roots. The Hebrew literally means "love apples." According to ancient superstition, mandrake roots were an aphrodisiac, a fertility herb that promoted pregnancy. Probably the reason for this is that the "female" mandrake root looks like a pair of naked legs. And the "male"? Well, it looks like the nickname for Richard. The writer of Genesis has a lot of fun with this in a passage filled with sexual double entendre that reaches a climax when Leah meets her husband Jacob out in a field and proclaims, "You must come in to me; for I have hired you with my son's mandrakes!"

While we're on the subject, in the New Testament the first big fight of the church was not over the nature of Jesus, his teachings, how people are saved, how to do missions, how to take care of poor people, or even what kind of worship style should be used in the church. Believe it or not, the early Christians got into a huge fight over . . . wait for it . . . what the penis should look like! Namely, they argued about whether men need to have their foreskins cut off (circumcision) in order to truly be Christians. At one point, Paul got so angry about the discussion that he literally wished that his opponents would lop everything off, not just the foreskin (Gal 5:12). By the way, as I mentioned earlier, one church father named Origen actually did castrate himself, not in response to Paul but in response to a literal interpretation of Jesus' statement in Matthew 19:12: "there are eunuchs who have made themselves eunuchs for the sake of the kingdom of heaven" (NRSV).

But we're here to talk about scatology, right? In Judges, Ehud stabs the rather large King Eglon of Moab in the belly so far that the fat folds over the knife handle and the "sh*t came out." In 1 Kings 18:27, Elijah uses a euphemism in a harshly satirical way against the prophets of Baal when their god fails to show up. Essentially, Elijah offers the excuse, "Maybe the reason Baal isn't answering you is that he's off taking a sh*t!" In 2 Kings 18:27, the Assyrian Rabshakeh warns the soldiers on the walls of Jerusalem that if they don't give up, things are going to get so bad that they will be forced to eat their own sh*t and drink their own piss. In Ezekiel 4, God commands the prophet to cook his food over sh*t, which grosses even Ezekiel out, so God allows him to cook it over cow manure instead. In Malachi 2, God expresses his desire to smear sh*t all over the faces of his priests because of the way they have profaned his altar. And then, not to be outdone in the New Testament, Paul says in Philippians 3 that everything he has lost on account of Christ he counts as nothing more than sh*t.

The original language and various translations refer to these words in different ways. King Eglon has "dirt" come out of his body. The Jerusalem soldiers are warned about eating human dung. Paul will count everything as "rubbish" compared to the surpassing knowledge of Christ. But the literal meaning of each of these words is nothing less than "sh*t." We don't use that word because it is not polite in our society. But why?

A popular theory harks back to the Norman invasion of England. When this happened, the French victors naturally viewed themselves as superior to the Anglo-Saxon victims. Over time, Old English or Anglo-Saxon (which, with its Germanic roots, became the basis for modern English) developed a reputation as being vulgar because it was used by lower-class, poor, uneducated servants. French words, used by rich, educated aristocrats, were proper. Whether or not this applies to scatology is not clear, but it does apply to food, which is why we say "I'm eating beef" (French *boeuf*) instead of "I'm eating cow."[6]

This brings up another question. What does it mean to be truly profane? To my knowledge, there is only one word that Jesus refers to as forbidden. It's the "f-word" (no, not that one!). It's "fool." In Matthew 5:22, Jesus warns that if we call someone a "fool," we will be in danger of the fires of hell. James picks up this theme in his epistle when he talks about the tongue starting unquenchable fires that destroy. The principle here goes beyond mere name-calling. It prohibits everything surrounding the act—making people feel stupid, shaming them, treating them as fools. Interestingly, Jesus gives us this teaching in his commentary on the commandment "thou shalt not murder," reminding us that there are more ways to murder someone than with swords and knives.

Words can kill, whether directed at others or ourselves. And it's not so much the actual word but how the word is used that determines whether it is a blessing or a curse. Even a noble vocabulary spoken in righteous anger can be profane if it's designed to strip an individual of his or her humanity and dignity. Perhaps true profanity, then, is found not so much in saying the word "sh*t" but in treating people like it.

* * *

Believe it or not, this silliness has a serious point, because just about everyone goes through a stage in their spiritual formation where they are seduced by legalism and dualism (seeing the world as black and white). And many, many people fall prey to this way, believing it is a path to spiritual maturity.

For example, when I was a budding youth back in the 1970s, real Christians didn't cuss or drink alcohol or use tobacco or see R-rated movies or listen to secular music or read anything that one couldn't buy at a Christian bookstore (this was back when they actually sold books). You were also required to tithe, attend Sunday school and church, and, if you were really righteous (which I was), attend Sunday evening service and midweek prayer meeting. If you wanted super-Christian status, you went out on "visitation" where you knocked on doors and invited people to church and handed them a religious tract if you thought they were "lost." The way you determined whether or not they were lost was by how many of the aforementioned rules they had broken. If they broke them all, they were definitely lost. There were some rules that, if you broke them, you were lost no matter what. For example, if you listened to the band KISS, you were definitely going to hell no matter how often you went to church because, as every good Christian youth knew, KISS stood for "Knights In Satanic Service."

The problem with this approach is that it leads us down a path that is antithetical to the message of Jesus. Legalism promotes the idea that rules are more important than people and that faith is nothing more than adhering to social norms. Dualism likes to divide the world into categories like saved and damned, good and evil, orthodoxy and heresy. When this happens, we tread on dangerous ground—so much so that Jesus essentially cussed out those who practiced it in his day. He used words like "woe to you" and "child of hell" and "blind guides" and "brood of vipers," just to name a few. He concluded, "How can you escape being sentenced to hell? Therefore I send you prophets, sages, and scribes, some of whom you will kill and crucify, and some you will flog in your synagogues and pursue from town to town, so that upon you may come all the righteous blood shed on earth . . ." (Matt 23:33b-35a, NRSV). Part of what he got so mad about is how the religious leaders of his day made their religion something other than loving God and loving their neighbor.

It's easy to do. In some corners of Christianity, if you are not recycling every scrap of paper and metal that touches your hands, you are looked down upon. In others, if you don't vote Republican and send vitriolic emails to godless legislators who are trying to prevent the Ten Commandments from being posted in the courthouse, you are an apostate. In still others, rejecting certain doctrines like the sovereignty of God or substitutionary atonement can land you on the "obviously non-elect" list. I'm not trying to belittle theology or recycling, but one must remember that cussing, politics, doctrine, and even social issues such as abortion or treatment of homosexuals existed in the days of Jesus. Yet the litmus test that he chose to determine whether one comprehended the true message of the gospel was this: *Did you feed the hungry, comfort the sick, visit the imprisoned, and clothe the naked?* (Matt 25:31ff).

This is consistent with many other statements Jesus made whereby he demonstrated that all the law and the prophets hinge on two imperatives: love God and love one another (Matt 22:36-40). Put another way, if our ethics or our worship or our doctrines or our church polity or our politics or anything else we do in the name of Christ doesn't lead to love, then there is something fundamentally wrong.

* * *

In the Bible, there is probably no greater legalist and dualist than Jonah. Most of us are familiar with the prophet getting swallowed by a whale (actually, it was a big fish), but the real hook of the narrative comes at the end of the book when Jonah sets up camp just outside of Nineveh to watch God rain down fire and brimstone on the Ninevites. In Jonah's mind, the Ninevites deserve this because they are, well, Assyrians, the sworn enemy of the Jews. They are pagans. They are heretics. And they stink. Jonah's contempt for them can be seen in the fact that when he preaches on the street corners of Nineveh, he basically says, "You're toast." That's it. No grace or hope.

He reveals at the end of the book why he did this—fear. Fear that the Ninevites would repent and turn to Yahweh. Despite Jonah's best (or worst, depending on your perspective) efforts, the Ninevites put on sackcloth and ashes and repent. Their remorse extends to every facet of society. Even the dogs, cats, pet gerbils, and cattle are dressed in sackcloth and ashes. Never in history has a more effective sermon been preached.

But Jonah is in denial. He sets up camp and hopes beyond hope that the wrath of God will still pour down upon his enemy. In response, God decides to play a practical joke on Jonah. Now, not everyone sees it this way. In fact, I doubt any serious biblical scholars will give my interpretation much credence. But I think what God does is funny. After all, he has already played one big, hilarious practical joke on Jonah by having the big fish vomit the prophet on the beach. Just picture it! It's funny. At least, back in seventh grade you thought it was funny. That's why you snuck the rubber barf into the lunchroom and hurled it onto the table along with a mouthful of milk and masticated food, thus making all your friends pee in their pants from laughter as you were carted off to the principal's office.

You are sophisticated now, and, thus, Jonah spewed on the beach covered in stomach contents isn't funny to you. But I'm sophomoric enough to think it is—along with what happens at the end of the book where God causes a plant to grow over Jonah, providing shade while he's waiting for the Ninevites to roast, and then sends a worm to eat the plant. When Jonah wakes up the next day, he is the only one roasting. To me, this is like pulling the chair out from someone while their bum is slowly descending in anticipation of a soft landing. At some point, the victim realizes that the chair is not there, but by then it's too late, and their bum continues to descend. Their arms flap up, as if that's going to help. Their eyes widen. And their face grimaces as they brace for a hard landing that is not only going to hurt a little but will also make them look foolish. Thus the humor.

Jonah, however, is a man with no sense of humor, so he throws a huge temper tantrum. He accuses God of loving the enemy, and if God is going to be that kind of God, then Jonah wants no part. He concludes, "Just go ahead and *shoot* me!"

Really good humor is also really serious, and the sober and painful point of God's practical jokes is that Jonah has become so pious and self-righteous that he has wandered far from his true calling as a prophet, which is not to wish the wrath of God on people but to awaken them to the needs of the widows and the orphans. God chastises,

> You are concerned about the bush, for which you did not labor and which you did not grow; it came into being in a night and perished in a night. And should I not be concerned about Nineveh, that great city, in which there are more than a hundred and twenty thousand persons who do not know their right hand from their left, and also many animals? (Jonah 4:10-11, NRSV)

This is how the book ends—with a question. It's a question directed at the reader, imploring us to consider what "bushes" we care more about in our lives than "persons who do not know their right hand from their left," i.e., children.

When you hear the name "Huckleberry Finn" you probably conjure an image of a tall, lanky boy with cutoffs and rolled-up shirtsleeves with a stalk of wheat sticking out of his mouth. You may also have fond or not-so-fond memories of the character depending on how much you enjoyed *The Adventures of Huckleberry Finn* by Mark Twain. If you had asked me a year ago, I would have fallen into the latter category because I had to read the book for an English class in high school, and, for some reason, books that a teacher required me to read were not near as much fun as books I read on my own, even if they were the exact same books. So my memory of the work was one of plodding through a dialect hard to decipher because, well, no one I know speaks that way. But my wife suggested that we give the audiobook a try on a long trip to the Grand Canyon. I was skeptical until she mentioned that Elijah Wood was the voice actor. "Elijah Wood! *The* Elijah Wood! Mr. Frodo Baggins! The Ring Bearer!" I imagined myself sitting in a house with a round door, drinking good tea and eating butter scraped over too much bread and listening to the cutest of hobbits trying to sound like he was from the Deep South. How could I pass this up?

To my astonishment, Elijah Wood didn't sound like Frodo at all. He sounded like he *was* from the Deep South. It was a pleasant surprise, and we were all swept away to the Mississippi where Huck staged his own murder in order to escape a town where everyone was trying to "civilize" him, and his "Pap" was beating him to a pulp.

The genius of Twain's story is how he used Huck as a moral voice to comment on a violent and cruel culture that claimed to be steeped in Christianity. This irony was most evident in a friendship forged with a runaway slave named Jim. In the story, Huck knows that he has to do the "right thing," which is to turn Jim in, but he can't because then everyone would find out that Huck isn't really dead, and he'd have to go back to his Pap, who would be so angry there's no telling what he might do.

So Huck and Jim travel down the Mississippi River seeking freedom. At first it seems like the good life. No one tells them what to do, and the Mississippi provides a never-ending supply of fish to eat. But Huck's conscience bothers him. He is having a blast with Jim, but something tells him he shouldn't be. The voices in his head keep nagging him that this isn't right.

Huck's moral dilemma only gets worse as he keeps putting off the decision. Then one day, circumstances demand that Huck make a choice. In an elated voice, Jim shouts for joy when he thinks he sees "Cairo," a town in a free state where Jim believes he can finally live as a free man. Jim also dreams of making enough money to buy back his wife and daughter. When Jim verbalizes how excited he is that he might actually get his family back, it makes Huck feel even worse. Deep down inside, Huck knows he has to do the "right" thing, so he tells Jim he's going to take the canoe and paddle ashore to make sure that this is indeed Cairo. But it's a deception. Huck really plans on turning Jim in.

As he paddles away, Jim calls out.

Pooty soon I'll be a-shout'n' for joy, en I'll say, it's all on accounts o' Huck; I's a free man, en I couldn't ever ben free ef it hadn' ben for Huck; Huck done it. Jim won't ever forgit you, Huck; you's de bes' fren' Jim's ever had; en you's de ONLY fren' ole Jim's got now. (Chapter 16)

Huck is crestfallen. He's torn between what his heart is telling him to do and what his conscience is telling him to do. Twain masterfully builds suspense as Huck is immediately confronted by two men who are looking for runaway slaves. They have seen a shadowy figure on Huck's raft and demand that Huck allow them to investigate.

It's at this point that Huck has to make a moral choice. He has resolved to turn Jim in. Now that he has the opportunity, he just can't, so he concocts a wonderful lie that the man on the raft is Huck's father who has smallpox. Huck cries and begs the men to tow the raft to town so that he can get medical help. Now the men who were hell-bent on checking out the raft are doing everything they can to paddle away as quickly as possible. Before leaving, they toss Huck a good sum of money to assuage their guilt for abandoning him.

When Huck returns to the raft, Jim is elated. "But lawsy, how you did fool 'em, Huck! Dat WUZ de smartes' dodge! I tell you, chile, I'spec it save' ole Jim—ole Jim ain't going to forgit you for dat, honey."

Huck feels demoralized because once again, he has failed to do the right thing.

Huck's moral quandary gets worse and worse. He can no longer live with himself. He feels he has to come clean. Once again, Twain's scathing wit comes to bear in Huck's inner thoughts.

So I was full of trouble, full as I could be; and didn't know what to do. At last I had an idea; and I says, I'll go and write the letter—and then see if I can pray. Why, it was astonishing, the way I felt as light as a feather right straight off, and my troubles all gone. So I got a piece of paper and a pencil, all glad and excited, and set down and wrote:

Miss Watson, your runaway n----r Jim is down here two mile below Pikesville, and Mr. Phelps has got him and he will give him up for the reward if you send.

HUCK FINN.

I felt good and all washed clean of sin for the first time I had ever felt so in my life, and I knowed I could pray now. But I didn't do it straight off, but laid the paper down and set there thinking—thinking how good it was all this happened so, and how near I come to being lost and going to hell. (Chapter 31)

Far from resolving everything, however, Huck just can't bring himself to follow through. His love for Jim is too strong. Still, he knows that by being faithful to Jim he will incur the wrath of God.

But somehow I couldn't seem to strike no places to harden me against him [Jim], but only the other kind. I'd see him standing my watch on top of his'n, 'stead of calling me, so I could go on sleeping; and see him how glad he was when I come back out of the fog; and when I come to him again in the swamp, up there where the feud was; and such-like times; and would always call me honey, and pet me and do everything he could think of for me, and how good he always was; and at last I struck the time I saved him by telling the men we had small-pox aboard, and he was so grateful, and said I was the best friend old Jim ever had in the world, and the ONLY one he's got now; and then I happened to look around and see that paper.

It was a close place. I took it up, and held it in my hand. I was a-trembling, because I'd got to decide, forever, betwixt two things, and I knowed it. I studied a minute, sort of holding my breath, and then says to myself:

"All right, then, I'll GO to hell"—and tore it up.

Recently, one of my students gave an imploring speech in chapel begging the student body to care about the problem of slavery in the United States. She gave some startling statistics, including one source that estimated that some 50,000 slaves are trafficked into or transited through the United States every year. Moreover, there are hundreds of thousands of slaves living here, and most of them are children ages twelve to fourteen, the majority forced into prostitution.

The auditorium was dead silent as she made her case, and I was proud of her. Here was a young Christian woman who got it. In response to the human suffering that she saw, she devoted her life to becoming a lawyer so that she could work for an organization that used the courts to put an end to this evil.

After chapel, I had a brief word with her, letting her know how impressed I was. While I was still filled with pride, a handful of freshmen approached me.

"Dr. Pigott," their spokesman began, "we want to talk to you about something."

"Sure." I paused and leaned against a chair. I could tell they were obviously agitated about something. I thought, perhaps, the mere mention of "sex slave" in chapel had bothered them. I never know what it's going to be when students want to talk to me after a service.

"Dr. Pigott," the spokesman continued, "we don't think it's right for a Christian campus to have a sign with the word 'Dam-it' written on it." (Remember, our campus has a grave to a dead mascot named "Dam-it." It's a joke that goes back several generations, and it's part of our tradition.)

But these freshmen obviously didn't see the humor in it, and I found myself becoming livid. I have to admit that I didn't handle the confrontation very well.

"You mean to tell me," I said, trying to hold back my righteous anger, "that after hearing a talk about the hundreds of thousands of children suffering in this world because of slavery, you are offended over a silly little marker on campus?!"

The young man immediately got defensive, and he launched into a speech about how this matter needed to be taken seriously. He even quoted Scripture as proof text. I was incredulous. I finally huffed away and told them that they needed to reevaluate their priorities.

Later, as I ran through the confrontation in my mind, I realized how much of a hypocrite I had become. I was no better than Jonah. For when Jesus commanded us to love our neighbors as ourselves, he didn't give us any loopholes. And when a lawyer actually tried to find a loophole by asking Jesus, "Who is my neighbor?" Jesus responded with a story that made the sworn enemy of the Jews (Samaritans) out to be the heroes. To make matters worse, Jesus made the Jews in the story out to be the villains because they refused to show compassion. It was a slap in the face for the lawyer with a clear message: *There are no loopholes.*

That's what makes this so hard. We want loopholes, and if we can't find them, we want distractions like Jonah's shade tree. Because if we can get into an argument about how we deserve a plant to shade our head, then we don't have to think about the fate of the "least of these" in Nineveh. We argue about doctrine or worship styles or what color the carpet in the sanctuary should be or what movies or music or words good Christians should avoid or what books should be banned. If we do that, then we won't notice the broken people in the world whom we have been called to love, like the stranger passed out on the side of the road.

Or the slave trafficked through our city.

Or the child starving in Ethiopia.

Or the sworn enemy of our country.

Or even the expletive-averse freshman who confronts us after chapel.

Inward Peregrinatio to the Tower of Babel

Question: How has legalism or dualism led me astray?
Fear: Nothing matters.

At the tower of Babel, we must contemplate the super spirituality and self-righteousness that has led us astray. It may seem like building a tower to heaven is a good idea, but if our intention is to usurp God, or to distract us from what is really important to Jesus, then we have gotten off track. To illustrate how easy this is, I highlighted cussing, but there are a myriad of minor habits or vices I could have chosen. It's important that as we grow in our faith that we identify our "towers," or those trivial things that lead us astray.

One good litmus test is provided by both Jesus and Paul. Jesus essentially taught us that there is nothing more important than loving God and loving our neighbor. Paul says in 1 Corinthians 13 that faith, hope, and love are among the most important elements of our worldview. And of those, nothing is more important than love.

So test your theology and ethics in this way. Do my opinions, actions, thoughts, and spoken words lead me to a deeper love and grace? If not, then that ought to be a red flag.

My guess is that you can think of a bunch of examples where leaders in the church became so obsessed with the color of the carpet, where to put the piano, room assignments, and the like that they acted un-Christlike. While just about everyone who has been in church for any length of time has a similar anecdote to tell, not many stop to ask, "How has legalism or dualism led me astray?"

Our faith should lead us to challenge our presuppositions, to learn how to listen to others who think differently, to love radically, and to be obedient to the spirit of the law rather than the letter of the law.

Go Deeper

"Tower of Babel" in "From Eden to Heaven Prompts" at
www.spilledcoffeeonancientscrolls.com

Walter Rauschenbusch, *Christianity and the Social Crisis*

Ronald Sider, *Rich Christians in an Age of Hunger*

Mark Twain, *Huckleberry Finn*

1. John Milton, *Paradise Lost*, ed. Gordon Teskey (New York: W.W Norton and Company, 2005) 106.

2. Margaret Fleming, "Analysis of a Four Letter Word," in Reinhold Aman, ed., *Opus Maledictorum: A Book of Bad Words* (New York: Marlowe & Company, 1996) 24.

3. C. S. Lewis wrote, "As soon as you deal with it explicitly, you're forced to choose between the language of the nursery, the gutter and the anatomy class." Quoted in Geoffrey Hughes, *Swearing* (Oxford: Blackwell, 1991) 1. The context was sex, but the sentiment still applies.

4. Hughes, *Swearing*, 27–28.

5. "Thomas Crapper: Myth and Reality," *Plumbing & Mechanical*, 13 July 2000, pmmag. com/articles/91485-thomas-crapper-myth-and-reality (accessed 19 December 2017).

6. "Swear Words, Etymology, and the History of English," *Oxford English Dictionary*, blog. oxforddictionaries.com/2015/06/17/swear-words-etymology-and-the-history-of-english/ (accessed 29 November 2017).

Victory

The Empty Tomb

Ah! . . . He'd make a lovely corpse!
—Mrs. Gamp, in *Martin Chuzzlewit*
by Charles Dickens

I spent a couple of my grade school years in New Orleans on the West Bank, in a sprawling little community known as Harvey. The street I lived on practically dead-ended into the Harvey Canal, so that above the trees you could see the tops of some of the bigger boats floating by from time to time. And if it rained a lot, which it often did in South Louisiana, you could literally paddle a canoe from the doorsteps of my house.

One of our favorite family excursions at this time was crabbing, the essential tools of which were an ice chest filled with snacks, Cokes, and Dixie beer, along with raw chicken necks. Mom and Dad would drive us down to one of the piers jutting out into Lake Pontchartrain. Many times they would invite another family to come along. For those of you who have never done this before, crabbing is a lot like fishing but without the slime, which is to say that it's nothing like fishing. The only equipment you actually need is a crab net, a large circular net about the size of a beach ball made of something like kite string and attached to a large round wire. In the middle of the net is a smaller round wire, and at the center of that you attach a chicken neck. I thought this was a little strange at the time, because if crabs fed off of chickens, it seemed to me that the bottom of a lake was a stupid place to live.

The net lies flat, making it easy for the crab to crawl onto it. When you lift the net it creates a funnel-like bowl that the crab finds difficult to scale. Crabbing consists of simply dropping the net in the water and waiting for the crabs to find the necks. There is no art to watching a bobber dip under the water and tugging the line just right to hook anything. You just pull the net up from time to time to see how many crabs you've caught.

If something happens to be in the net, the excitement begins because this is where crabbing becomes a sport. Once you drop the net on the pier, it becomes flat again, allowing the crab to immediately scurry away. The adults, sitting in their lawn chairs with sunburned faces and feeling happy, yell, "Get the crabs! Get the crabs!" The children, giggling wildly, make a mad dash for the crabs, which can move surprisingly fast. The crustaceans instinctively know the shortest distance to the edge of the pier, and every now and then a crab will win, rolling over the edge and making an obscene crab gesture with its claw before plopping back into the water. The goal is to beat the crab. To do this, you must step on the crab (it's important to have shoes on, as my brother found out the hard way) with just the right pressure to stop it from moving but not so hard that you crack its shell, because this will kill the crab. If you do that, the adults get really mad because they want the pleasure of boiling it alive later in the day.

Once you have prevented the crab from escaping, you must tentatively reach behind it while it's clawing at your shoes for dear life. The trick is to pinch the back legs together. You have to grab both legs. If you grab just one leg, the crab can pull itself up and pinch your hand (something else my brother found out the hard way). As you pinch, the two legs will click to a stop while still far apart, and with a little pressure you can pick it up. The anatomy of a crab is such that its pinchers can't reach that far back. In fact, the claws will typically flex back, making the crab look like a body builder about to bench press, and lock in that position until you drop it in the ice chest.

When you've caught enough crabs, or the adults have run out of beer, you climb in the car and head home for the crab feast. The star of this meal is, of course, the freshly caught crabs that are slowly freezing in the ice chest while blowing snot bubbles out of their mouths. Dad typically put a large pot of water on the stove, tossed in a couple of bags of Zatarain's crab boil (a pouch filled with spices) along with a lot of salt, and then dropped in the live crabs. As much fun as I had catching the crabs, I always felt sorry for them at this point. I can't imagine that being boiled alive is a good way to go, but there they were, a bowlful of shells and eyes, looking at me, slowing turning red, and clawing at one another. On one occasion, I remember one of my dad's friends standing behind me as I stared at the crabs.

"Those crabs could crawl out easily enough if they wanted to," he said. "Did you know that?"

I shook my head.

"Know what keeps them from getting out?"

"No idea," I said.

"As soon as one of them begins to pull himself up, the others grab a hold of him and drag . . . him . . . back . . . in." He said the last phrase slowly and menacingly.

I'm sure my eyes widened at the thought. To this day I don't know if he was just pulling my leg, repeating old folklore, or telling the truth. It seemed real enough to me as I stared at the crabs grabbing at each other as they slowly rolled in the churning water, a picture of the living dead.

The few years I spent in New Orleans introduced me to a lot of interesting, sometimes bizarre things. One of them was voodoo. I didn't pay much attention to it at the time, but every now and then I'd see an ad or a storefront or a picture that had something to do with voodoo, and it always made me feel creepy. In addition, while I was in New Orleans the James Bond movie *Live and Let Die* came out, and voodoo played a prominent role in the plot—specifically zombies.

I remember one summer a friend and I decided that we were going to go zombie hunting, and if we happened to find Bigfoot along the way, we'd bag him, too. Neither one of us owned a gun—not even a BB rifle—so we made our own out of sticks, rubber bands, and rocks. Our weapons were a great example of fourth-grade technology that could launch a projectile in the general vicinity of "in front of you" for a solid three feet before hitting the ground. Those zombies had no hope.

Of course, we knew nothing of zombie lore, and as I recall, we scared ourselves so silly by jumping at every snap, crackle, and pop in the woods that we wound up dropping our weapons and sprinting home as fast as we could to find something safer to do. *Now* I know that you can't kill a zombie with a rock. It's far more complicated than that. But to learn exactly how to defeat a zombie, we have to go back in time.

The Bible actually has a story about a zombie—well, sort of. In the Gospel of John, Jesus visits Mary and Martha on the occasion of their brother Lazarus's death. Jesus says to Martha at their initial meeting, "Your brother will rise again."

Martha answered, "I know he will rise again in the resurrection at the last day."

Jesus said, "I am the resurrection and the life." He then proceeded to the tomb where Lazarus was buried, said a prayer, and commanded Lazarus to come out.

Here, the author says something fascinating: "The dead man came out" (see John 11, NRSV).

It's not "And Lazarus came out" or "the man came out" or "Jesus' friend came out" or "the guy came out." It's "the *dead man* came out." It makes no sense on a literal level. Dead men don't come out. Dead men . . . well, they just lie there. They're dead. The phrase may be a reference to Jesus' teaching that in order to live, one must first die. John loves to play with spiritual truths embedded in literal events in his narratives.

When I picture this story being told to the early Christians, I imagine them clapping and laughing when the storyteller said, "the dead man came out," because it was an inside joke. It was both ludicrous and true. Lazarus embodied the idea of the *dead living*—which is the call to the abundant life in Christ here and now. It was in stark contrast to the *living dead*, the nameless, faceless souls slogging their way through life.

The early Christians cherished the story of Lazarus because of the way it demonstrated the promise of the resurrection, a concept that mystified the Romans. They made fun of this doctrine, imagining something akin to the film *Night of the Living Dead*, where zombies roam the earth with rotting limbs and half-fleshed skulls. In response, the early apologists defended the doctrine of the resurrection. Origen wrote,

> By the command of God the body which was earthly and animal will be replaced by a spiritual body, such as may be able to dwell in heaven; even on those who have been of lower worth even of contemptible, almost negligible merit, the glory and worth of the body will be bestowed in proportion to the deserts of the life and soul of each.[1]

In other words, following Paul's lead, the early church fathers argued that the resurrection meant that which was old would be made new. The old, corruptible bodies would be replaced with new, incorruptible bodies that would be similar yet different. This is why the two disciples on the road to Emmaus didn't quite recognize Jesus at first. His resurrection body was slightly different.

This fascination with what happened to the body after death led to a lot of curious practices. One of them was based on the concept that the corpses of the saints were objects stuck between two worlds, so, beginning in at least the second century, believers scrambled underground into the maze of catacombs beneath Rome to hold worship services.[2] Such a service was called a *refrigerium*, which, believe it or not, referred not to the fact that the bodies were stored in this cold, dark place but that worshipers "refreshed" themselves (the root meaning of the word). A major impetus for this was to honor martyrs on their death day, which the early Christians actually referred to as a "birthday" since they viewed it as the moment of being reborn. One can imagine a huddled group in an earthy room illuminated by flickering candles. Shelves carved into the walls contained skeletons and perhaps partially decomposed bodies. There, the Christians retold the story of how Sister Mary was dragged from her home and brought before the magistrate. Despite her fears, she confounded the wise with her brave statements of faith. For her obstinacy, the guards escorted her to the coliseum where she was tossed to the lions. Remember how she fell to her knees and prayed for her captors as the animals pounced on her? In retelling her story and gazing at her bones etched with teeth marks, the believers saw Mary resurrected before them. They might even talk to her a little and ask her to put in a good word for them with Jesus since she got to go straight to heaven. Next, they broke bread and passed a cup of wine as they shared Communion with one another, eventually saying good-bye to Sister Mary until next year.

We know these services became ever more popular throughout the years of persecution in the ante-Nicene period (100–325 CE). Along with the practice grew the notion of having "saint days" and venerating the remains of the martyrs. Augustine defended this observance, declaring that the skeletons were "temples of faith." Honoring them was no different from honoring a living holy man because of his wisdom. Cyril of Jerusalem went even further, declaring that the corpse had an "intrinsic power" because of the "virtuous soul that once inhabited it."[3] As a result, a multitude of miracles were attributed not only to the remains of the saints but also to handkerchiefs or aprons that touched them and even to the dust that collected on their tombs.[4] This notion gave rise to the pilgrimage, where a believer in need of refreshment traveled a great distance to visit relics in the hopes that some of that power might work a much-needed miracle.

Unfortunately, this practice also gave rise to fraud. In the fifth century, two heads of John the Baptist appeared, yet both were accepted as credible. By the eleventh century, the number had grown to three, and the church in Constantinople housed two of them. Guibert of Nogent attempted to bring some sanity to the issue by declaring, "Now what could be more absurd than to suppose that this great saint had two heads. Let us therefore take this matter seriously and admit that one of them is wrong."[5]

Unfortunately, his voice of reason fell on deaf ears. In the Middle Ages, relics became big business and sources of prestige, so much so that saintly body parts were considered more valuable than gold. Cathedrals *had* to have them in order to survive financially. Royalty desired them in their realm in order to rise in social status. Like the scramble to drill oil wells in Texas, the slogan became, "If you don't have a dead saint, get one"—and by any means necessary. For some, this meant they were willing to steal, extort, or bully to get what they wanted.

For example, when Hugh of Lincoln went to the abbey of Fécamp, he asked the abbot if he might visit the arm of Mary Magdalene. At the time, it was kept safely wrapped in bandages. When it was presented to him, he pulled out a knife and ripped off the covering. The monks, of course, tried to stop him, but they could not prevent him from hacking at it and, when that failed, gnawing on it with his teeth, "first with his incisors and finally with his molars." When the abbot, in shock, confronted him, Hugh coolly replied something to the effect of, "Well, I just consumed the body and blood of Christ in Mass. How is this any different?"[6]

* * *

As stories of miracles circulated and the dead saints were viewed more and more as still active in the world, the line between heaven and earth blurred. Consequently, the line between hell and earth blurred, too, for if dead good guys had power, perhaps dead bad guys did as well.

Beginning in the New Testament, we read that the powers of hell were manifested through demons. In particular, demons could bewitch people with unexpected illnesses and rebelliousness of all sorts. In the ongoing battle against these forces, saints played a major role in limiting their effects.[7] Some saints were better at this than others, and every now and then even the good saints had to be disciplined for sleeping on the job, thus the origination of the practice known as the "humiliation of the saints."

Imagine you are the abbot of a monastery in southern France and you've had a bad year. The yield of grapes from the vineyard has declined because of bad weather. The plague has wiped out half of the local village. The number of new novitiates is down. To top it all off, donations to the monastery have plummeted just when the roof needs fixing. It's time to get Saint Jean-Luke off his butt so that he can start performing some much-needed miracles, so you draw up a schedule for the brothers to visit the sarcophagus for a little dose of tough love. As each monk enters the room, he gives the Jean-Luke's bones a tongue-lashing: "You call yourself a saint! You're nothing but a lazy, good-for-nothing son-of-a-Pelagian! Your pious parfum has become putrid. Your mother was a hamster, and your father smelt of elderberries.[8] *Faut péter dans l'eau pour faire des bulles!*"[9]

Hopefully, the saint gets the message and things start looking up a little. If not, you can always sneak down the road in the dead of night and steal the bones of Saint Jude from a rival monastery. When those monks complain, tell them that Jude appeared to you in a vision, claiming that he wasn't being properly taken care of. He asked you to come save him. If they protest, go a step further by proclaiming that Saint Jude demands that they repent by eating nothing but macaroni and cheese for a century, after which he may consider coming back. That ought to keep them quiet for a while.

During the first half of the Middle Ages, stories involving saints and demons were mostly fanciful. Take the mid-thirteenth-century story about a pious woman who entered a church in Nivelles one night to pray. At about midnight, some townspeople delivered a corpse and dropped it at the back of the church auditorium, a common practice before the invention of funeral homes. The pious woman simply shrugged it off and knelt, eager to get back down to business. While she was praying, however, a demon possessed the corpse and it sat up in the coffin. I don't know about you, but if I were by myself praying in a church in the middle of the night and a dead body popped out of a coffin and looked at me, I wouldn't stick around to find out what happened next. This particular woman, though, stayed to confront her assailant. Her first line of defense was to make the sign of the cross and shout, "Sit down, you wretch, for you have no power against me!"

In response, the demon caused the dead body to hop up and retort, "Truly, now I will have power against you, and I will revenge myself for the frequent injuries I have suffered at your hands!" You can almost hear the trill on piano keys as this melodrama plays itself out. In my mind, I picture the dead body trudging forward, growling, with arms outstretched. The woman places the back of her hand to her mouth and looks frantically about. The scary music swells. Drums echo the dead body's footsteps. He gets closer. Closer! She scrambles backwards, and her hand, by chance, falls on the base of a staff, on top of which is a cross. Her eyes narrow with confidence and she latches onto the staff, raises it in the air, and smacks the side of the dead head with great force. The body topples to the ground and the demon flees. Cue happy music and a close-up of the woman smiling and batting her eyes.[10]

The fourteenth century brought about a major change of tone in these kinds of stories, mainly because Europeans were forced to grapple with a very real and horrific bout with the Grim Reaper known as the Black Death or Black Plague. Tiny fleas transmitted bubonic and pneumonic plague throughout Europe, wiping out a third of the population overall, and sometimes entire villages and towns. Because medical knowledge typically did more harm than good, the population was virtually defenseless. Wave after wave of disease swept through the countryside, forcing the church and culture to reckon with death in incomprehensible ways. Bands of flagellants roamed the countryside, torturing themselves in an attempt to appease God, who seemed biblically enraged. When that didn't work, they turned their attention to killing and torturing the Jews, who must have had something to do with it since "they killed Christ," an opinion that gave impetus to a growing anti-Semitism. The most common prescription from the medical experts at the time was to run far, far away. Unfortunately, there really wasn't any safe place to run. Besides, by the time the plague struck a town, it was too late. Caregivers attempted remedies ranging from bloodletting to salves, but to no avail.

To say that the plague changed the world is an understatement. Every aspect of civilization—religion, culture, economics, architecture, literature, art—was affected by the psychological impact of the plague. For example, before the plague, a fragile skeleton was often used to depict death in Italian art. After the plague, this image was replaced with a picture of an old woman dressed in black, with hair like snakes, claws for feet, and a scythe clutched in her talons with which to reap the dead. Indeed, every culture revised death from something innocuous to something far more menacing. In Tuscany, for example, Giovanni del Biondo portrayed a Madonna as a decomposing corpse.[11]

The Black Plague also heightened the notion that dead bodies, when removed from this world in an untimely and traumatic way, became restless, unwilling to make the transition to the next world. Consequently, they loitered in this one. Before the plague, stories abounded of naughty priests who returned to confess their sins so that they could rest and of knights who returned to preach against violence. There was even a touching story of a baker who returned to help knead bread for his widowed wife in the middle of the night. She was so frightened by him, though, that she had the townsmen chase him away with rocks, inter his body, and dismember it so it that he'd leave her alone. This couple obviously had some issues.

After the Black Plague, the returning dead were a little, well, scarier. The *danse macabre* became a popular iconographic scene found in cemeteries, where zombies with flesh rotting off the bones, entrails hanging out, skin pocked with holes dug by worms, and mouths pulled back in evil grins led humans away, presumably to their doom. A possible origin of this scene can be traced to a story whereby three bratty young playboys accidently wandered into a cemetery and were greeted by three rancid dead guys. The zombies slowly lifted their arms and pointed with fingers of half bone, half flesh. In an unnatural voice they growled, "What you are, we once were; what we are, you will become."[12]

Naturally, the living would like the dead to stay dead and leave the living to enjoy what brief amount of time might be left. But how do you control these unnatural forces? Eventually, the belief arose that to keep cadavers in the ground, one must force them to remain in the ground until all the flesh rotted off their bones. Elaborate rituals developed to call upon the power of God to keep the dead . . . well, dead. But in times of unusual stress, like a plague, keeping the dead buried became problematic. Mass graves were dug in order to dispose bodies quickly before they could pile up too high. Sometimes, mass graves were reopened to accommodate more victims, and this desperate practice led gravediggers to notice something odd. It appeared that some of the bodies had eaten through the shroud encasing the head, and fresh blood could be seen oozing from their mouths. In fact, people who were skinny while alive were now fat cadavers. How did they get that way? Obviously, the blood around the mouth was a clue: these people were actually vampires! To make sure that the vampire was unable to feast anymore, they would shove a brick in its mouth, thus ensuring that it could no longer feed, causing it to starve . . . um, to death.[13]

Today, we typically view these practices as superstitions of the past, but some things don't change. No matter how modern our society becomes, coping with death still creates a significant emotional challenge. What do we do with the fresh memories of a person who just yesterday was talking and laughing? Elisabeth Kübler-Ross, in her groundbreaking book *On Death and Dying*, was one of the first to contemplate our society's uneasiness with death. In a modern hospital, after we say good-bye, the deceased is whisked away from loved ones to funeral homes where elaborate work is done to preserve the body for a few more days so that he or she still looks alive. It's a tough battle because nature wants to decompose the flesh, but when everyone shows up for the funeral, the loved one is in nice clothes, has a gentle smile, and looks to be at peace. In this way, we create the illusion that the person is not really dead but merely asleep, dreaming happy thoughts.

The inescapable reality, of course, is that no amount of formaldehyde and makeup can remove the specter of death. The dead make us uncomfortable. They are shrouded in mystery. Even though we put them deep in the ground, or cremate them, the dead still linger—in our memories, in our dreams, in the voices in our heads. They can still reach out to us and curse us like zombies. Like the living dead, they can claw at us and pull us toward them, and if we are not careful, they can turn us into specters just like them. Void of esteem and purpose and hope, they hold us back, convincing us that we can never escape our past, our fate, our DNA. The critical voices, the emotional wounds, the bad habits they passed on to us can become an overwhelming burden. To our horror, we realize that we are becoming just like them—that their prophecy that we will never amount to anything might very well come true.

However, like the saints who have shared in the resurrection of Christ, they can also reach out to bless and inspire us. The lessons they taught us, the gifts they bestowed upon us, the joyful experiences we shared with them all shaped and formed us for the better. Where our lives intersected theirs can become an impetus to live life to its fullest, to recognize how fleeting and short our time is. In doing so, we honor them.

Let's face it. Most people who were dear to us were a little saint and a little sinner. They both blessed and cursed. The struggle, then, is to allow them to reach out and bless us while also keeping them in their graves when they attempt to curse us. This can be more challenging for some relationships than for others.

Several years ago I received a message on my phone. The voice was so stressed with emotion that it was almost unintelligible. "Come quick! He's stopped breathing!" My mom hung up without providing any more information. I knew she was talking about my dad, but I didn't know where they were going to take him. I called home and no one answered. I called the hospitals, and it became apparent that his name had not yet been entered in the databases. I scrambled for the nearest one—Hendrick. As I entered the emergency room, I was greeted by my mom and sister and taken to a harshly lit room, filled with chrome metal and glass. My dad had an opaque plastic hose coming out of his mouth, hooked to a machine that hissed and chugged. Mom's face was swollen from crying.

The three of us sat in the sterile room for quite some time, waiting for a doctor to tell us what we already knew. My sister volunteered to stay the night with Dad, and I told her I could relieve her first thing in the morning. Because Dad's health had slowly deteriorated over the last couple of years (and he had not responded to his condition gracefully), Mom had been through a lot of trauma lately. She just wanted to go home.

I remember feeling numb as I went home. I didn't feel sad. Dad and I had a strained relationship that dated back to my latter teen years. It was then that I made the decision to get baptized in a Baptist church. He, being Irish Catholic, was staunchly against it, but he couldn't do anything about it since I was no longer living at home. I still remember approaching him at work because I had heard from Mom how mad he was. His eyes narrowed when he saw me. He feigned that he was busy as I approached, and then he dismissed an employee nearby.

"What's wrong, Dad?" I asked, trying to break the ice.

What happened next forever scarred a relationship that was already strained. Dad was a man consumed by addictions, one of which was work. He wasn't home much, and when he was at home he was too tired to be bothered. But his words cleanly severed the imaginary bond of affection between father and son that I had always hoped was there.

He said, "I never want to talk to you again."

The aftermath is blurred for me, but I remember that he relented in his own way. A few days later, he took me to a park and we walked and talked. We patched things up as best as we both knew how, but the truth is, Dad never really talked to me again. I lived far away from home, so my contact with him was in the form of sporadic visits and phone calls. When I was at home, Dad went to work. When I called, Mom always answered the phone.

I could share many stories of attempts and failures to reconcile, but at least you now have an idea of why I wasn't sad. For me, the dad who cheered me on at Little League baseball games, who never missed a football game, who endured school plays, and who imparted to me a love for music with his 8-track tape collection, had died a long time ago. The man lying in the critical care unit was a stranger. That's not the way I wanted it. I'm pretty sure it's not the way he wanted it, but I don't know how I could have done anything differently to reestablish the bond we had when I was a child and we snuggled in the den, his thick arm holding me closely as we watched really bad 1970s sitcoms.

The following morning, I got up early to relieve my sister at the hospital. The machine was still breathing for Dad. Monitors hummed, whirred, and beeped, translating what was going on inside his body into numbers and graphs—secret codes known only to nurses and doctors. At that moment I felt very alone as I looked at my dad. His skin felt cool and damp. His eyes popped open every now and then as if he suddenly remembered something, but then he'd groggily close them, seemingly deciding that whatever it was, it didn't matter. The nurse told me it was an involuntary reflex. I was unsettled by it at first, but then I realized that it gave me the chance to look at his eyes. I don't remember ever being able to get so close to him that I could just stare into his eyes. They were hazel—almost gray. And his pupils were wide open, expressionless, as if he was already gone, which at that moment was probably true.

I leaned in close and kissed his forehead. "I love you, Dad," I said. The machine answered with a mechanical hiss. In an attempt to offer comfort, I stroked Dad's hair and held his hand. I realized how metaphorical the moment was, a fitting picture of our relationship over the last thirty years: the son reaching out for approval, the silent father.

"Good-bye, Dad," I said.

More clicks and whirrs from the machines.

Eventually the nurse came in and removed the tube from his mouth as our family had decided. Dad struggled for an agonizing couple of minutes. Despite my best efforts, I lost it, and embarrassingly so. "Oh, Dad," I said, and clasped my hand to my mouth as if it would somehow help contain all the emotions that were trying to gush out of me at once. His breathing became shallower, and then I watched him take his last breath.

The nurse came in and patted me on the shoulder. She stoically attended the machines, turning them off one by one. Then she drew the curtain and left the room so that it was just me, holding a hand that became cold surprisingly fast.

Silence.

It's been many years since this episode, and Dad has surprised me by showing up from time to time. Many times I dream about him. Sometimes I'll be shopping at a grocery store and I'll see the back of him as he turns the corner down another aisle. Sometimes I'll recognize his voice in my thoughts or see him staring back at me in the mirror. I realize that Dad's not *really* there. Yet there is a reality to the experiences as well. Dad is reaching out to me from the grave. He is gone, but he is still with me. What do I do with that?

Like Jesus commanding Lazarus to come forth, resurrection is about making the dead live again. From the beginning of the Jesus Movement in the first century, the church has understood this to be its primary mission. We can see this in what is arguably the first catechism, titled *Didache*, or the *Teachings of the Twelve*. The precise dating is uncertain, but it could be a first-century work designed to help novice Christians learn the basics of faith. I love how it begins—"There are two ways, one of life and one of death, and there is a great difference between the two ways" (J. B. Lightfoot translation).

The text describes the Christian life as recognizing that we have two paths before us. It's a bit simplistic, but effective nonetheless. One is a path that leads to life, and the other is one that leads to death. On a pragmatic level, the text is describing how imperative it is that we make sure our choices lead to life.

For example, I could allow the memories of my dad to put me on a path that leads to death. I could stew on all the mean things he said to me, on the many times he rejected me and ignored me. I could allow these thoughts to make me angry and bitter and in a foul mood all the time, but they would lead to a life of the living dead. Instead, I need to turn what could be a curse into a blessing. No one can tell me how to do this. I have to figure it out for myself.

There are memories of my dad that claw out to me from the grave and direct me to the path of the living dead. They speak to me with a disapproval that is never satisfied with what I do. Or worse, they glare at me in silence. But there is also a part of my dad that I want to reach out and bless me. This is the part that taught me how to ride a bike, that took me to the Sugar Bowl of 1973 to watch Notre Dame beat Alabama 24-23, that showed me how to drive a golf ball and cheered me at every Little League game I played in, even when I struck out. The dad who put me on his shoulders and paraded me around the yard while I laughed wildly. The dad who gave me his gift of humor for you, reading these words right now, to enjoy.

By redeeming my experiences with my dad, I do not ignore or suppress the pain and anger, but I transform them into something miraculous. I acknowledge the wound but also the cure, which is love and grace and forgiveness. Through this, that which was dead is now alive. That which was lost is now found. All that my dad was *not* for me, I can be for my children. In turn, a curse is turned into a blessing that brings life to me and to my family. That which held me in the grave and sought to plunge me into despair is conquered, and I emerge from the cave, bandages flapping in the wind, a dead man living.

Unbind me and let me go.

Inner Peregrinatio to the Empty Tomb

Question: Am I fully alive?
Fear: I am dead.

The empty tomb provides a place for us to contemplate what it means to be fully alive (to be the dead living) and what is holding us back to make us the living dead.

For many, there is an issue that therapists call the elephant in the room. It's the hidden, obvious problem, dysfunction, wound, or addiction that is boiling us alive. It's hidden because often we have no idea it's there. It's obvious because once we see it, we smack our foreheads and wonder why we hadn't noticed it before.

To move forward, we first have to identify the zombies. Often we inherit the issue that is boiling us alive from our parents. Their critical voice or addiction or insecurities are passed on to us, and they become the zombies dragging us back to the grave.

Second, we need to develop a sense of urgency about life. Though we know otherwise, many of us who act as if we will live forever discover our mortality too late. The tomb reminds us that each day brings us one day closer to death. Rather than getting depressed about it, we need to see each day as a gift—one that beckons us to let go of what holds us back so that we can be free to strain forward for what lies ahead.

Part of what it means to move ahead is making peace with our past. In particular, we need to make peace with those who have cursed us as we move from victim to witness through the process of forgiveness. We let go. We immerse ourselves in grace. We declare to the memory that it no longer has a hold on us. We can see it still, but only as a witness.

We don't stop there. We must now turn the curse into a blessing by growing from the experience, learning from it, and, in some cases, seeing the good that can come from it. But even if we can't see any good, we can still grow stronger.

Go Deeper

"The Empty Tomb" in "From Eden to Heaven Prompts" at
www.spilledcoffeeonancientscrolls.com

Randy Pausch, *The Last Lecture*

C. S. Lewis, *The Weight of Glory*

Notes

1. Origen, *De Principiis* 2.10.3, in Henry Bettenson, ed., *The Early Christian Fathers* (Oxford: Oxford University Press, 1956) 255.

2. Admittedly, scholars debate whether this actually happened. James Jeffers in *The Greco-Roman World of the New Testament Era: Exploring the Background of Early Christianity* (Downers Grove IL: Intervarsity Press, 1999) 46, argues that it was just too stinky to hold a worship service in a catacomb.

3. In Jonathan Sumption, *The Age of Pilgrimage* (Mahwah NJ: HiddenSpring Books, 2003) 23.

4. Ibid., 25.

5. Ibid., 29.

6. Ibid., 41.

7. "Demons," *Late Antiquity: A Guide to the Postclassical World* (Cambridge MA: Harvard University Press, 1999).

8. I'm indebted to the Frenchman in the film *Monty Python and the Holy Grail* for this wondrous insult.

9. "Go fart in water and make bubbles." I am told that this is a serious French insult. Go figure.

10. See Nancy Caciola, "Wraiths, Revenants, and Ritual in Medieval Culture," *Past & Present* 100 (August 1996): 11.

11. "Black Death," *Dictionary of the Middle Ages*, vol. 2., ed. Joseph R. Strayer (New York: Charles Scribner's Sons, 1983).

12. Caciola, "Wraiths, Revenants and Ritual," 25.

13. Ariel David, "Italy Dig Unearths Female 'Vampire' in Venice," *ABC News*, 3 March 2009, abcnews.go.com/Technology/story?id=7084910&page=1 (accessed 18 May 2018).

The Banquet

> Whereas Christ turned water into wine, the church
> has managed something more difficult: it has turned
> wine into water.
>
> —Søren Kierkegaard

Isabel de Flores, born in the sixteenth century, had two things going for her: she was beautiful and she was rich. However, her mother became very concerned when Rose, as the family called her, did not seem interested in men. For some reason she preferred to hang out at the church and befriend nuns. When other girls were talking about dresses and romance, Rose was talking about sin and suffering. The family, and her mother in particular, spent ten years trying to get Rose to give up her austere interests, but to no avail. Rose even went so far as to take a vow of virginity, which, if kept, pretty well ruined her chances of getting married because, and this goes without saying, though men in that time liked to marry virgins, they did not like to *be* married to virgins.

In 1606 Rose joined a convent and became a Dominican of the Third Order. At this point Rose's pursuit of God took a bizarre turn though there were already hints that she was deeply disturbed about something. For example, rather than flaunt her beauty, Rose did everything in her power to make herself look ugly, from the clothes she wore to the caustic lime she smeared on her face to splotch her skin. When she became a nun she chose a strict life of seclusion, relegating herself to a hut in her family's garden. There she donned a silver-studded ringlet that dug painfully into her head; she slept regularly on a bed of broken glass, stones, potsherd, and thorns. Rose believed that by subjecting herself to such torture she could draw closer to God and earn grace for her fellow sinful countrymen and women.

Perhaps more bizarre than Rose's masochistic tendencies was the reaction from the church that eulogized her. She became a role model of piety for other young women. The people of Peru, especially, embraced her as a spiritual superhero. Perhaps unsurprisingly, Rose's lifestyle took a toll on her health, and she died at the young age of thirty-one. Several miracles occurred soon afterward that were attributed to Rose, so in 1668 Pope Clement IX beatified her, declaring Santa Rosa de Lima to be the patron saint of South America.[1]

To her credit, Rose of Lima pursued God with admirable tenacity. She devoted herself to serving the poor and the sick. Her chosen lifestyle is consistent with the penitential theology of the Roman Catholic Church, so in speaking of Rosa I do not want to seem disrespectful or antagonistic. Even today, her life continues to deeply influence the lives of thousands who look to her for spiritual guidance. But I am disturbed by a part of the message for which she lived and died—a common notion in both Catholic and Protestant circles that misery equals piety. In other words, the kingdom of God is all about suffering. Now, don't misunderstand me. I'm not saying that suffering is altogether evil. Pain can act as a warning. It helps to establish boundaries, and it has been understood as a necessary part of spiritual formation. Suffering can be a means to an end, but it is not the end. In other words, life isn't supposed to be about suffering.

As a young Catholic attending parochial school, I remember the teacher placing a large picture of Jesus above the blackboard. His face looked contorted with pain. On his head sat a crown with long, pointy thorns, some of which were clearly embedded in his skull. Blood drained down the sides of his face in dark crimson lines. Every now and then, the nuns would point to the picture and warn us that each time we did something bad, we pushed another thorn into Jesus' head. The thought horrified me as a six-year-old, and I remember staring for long periods of time into the face of Jesus, wondering why he was perpetually upset with me.

As I read the New Testament, I get a different vision of Jesus than what I was led to believe in parochial school. Shockingly, Jesus developed a reputation of being a glutton and a drunkard (Luke 7:34). Understand, Jesus never committed the sins of gluttony or drunkenness, but he obviously loved eating and drinking and hanging around those who did the same. The very thought of this unnerves people today as it did when he walked the earth (see Matt 11:19). They can't imagine the Savior mingling, laughing, or even telling a joke, much less drinking. Nor can they fathom Jesus actually encouraging such behavior.

Let's take a closer look. In John 2:1-11, Jesus attends a wedding feast. We're not told who's getting married, but, based on Mary's behavior, it was probably a relative or someone close to the family. A social *faux pas* occurs as the wine runs out. More than just a minor nuisance, this meant that the bride and groom would forever be labeled as the couple who rudely denied their guests common hospitality—a serious offense in first-century Jewish culture.[2] Mary approaches Jesus and requests that he do something about it. His response is very interesting.

First of all, he says, "Dear woman, why do you involve me? . . . My hour has not yet come" (John 2:4). Clearly, for Jesus to perform a miracle at this time involved some sort of risk. Nevertheless, he then turns six stone jars filled with water into wine. Understand, this added between 120 to 180 *gallons* of alcoholic beverage to the party! The master of the banquet expresses amazement that the good stuff had been held back. For the general rule was to give the guests the fine wine at first, and then, after they started to feel drunk, to bring out the stuff that was sold in a cardboard box. By then few would know the difference.

The critical problem for teetotalers entails getting past the fact that Jesus encouraged the drinking of alcohol at a party. It's as if he bought a round of drinks at a bar or brought a keg to a Super Bowl bash. The question we must ask ourselves is, "Why?" Not "Why did Jesus do this?" but "Why are we so uncomfortable with Jesus' doing this?" Why is it easy for us to picture a God suffering but so hard for us to picture him celebrating, eating, and drinking?

If given the opportunity, I bet some modern-day church leaders would like to rewrite this passage to make it a bit more religiously correct. Just for fun, let's imagine what that might read like. We'll pick up the narrative where Jesus responds to his mother's statement, "They have no more wine."

"What? You mean they're actually serving alcohol here? Woe be unto them!"

Jesus entered the room and commanded the servants to take up every glass containing alcohol. They poured the poisonous liquid into a stone water jar and it measured nearly twenty gallons.

Jesus prayed and then said to the servants, "Now draw it back out and take it to the master of the banquet."

They did so, and the master of the banquet tasted it.

After wrinkling his nose and spitting on the ground he said, "What's this? Have we run out of wine?"

"No sir," the servants said. "Well, yes sir. You see, the wine has been turned into water."

"But why? Who would do such a thing?"

Then Jesus answered him and said, "You should be ashamed of yourself for serving alcohol at this wedding. Don't you know it will rot your insides out and destroy the nation? From now on, serve only water, or ginger ale with lime sorbet."

The bridegroom asked, "What's sorbet?"

Jesus answered and said, "There are some things too difficult for you to understand now. But in the meantime, don't drink alcohol, and while you're at it, stop all this dancing, get rid of all the jewelry pierced anywhere but your ear, have your tattoos surgically removed, shave all that facial hair, and, by all means, PUT OUT THOSE STOGIES! From now on when you get together for a party, just have a covered dish supper, play a few board games, and then go home before 9 PM."

So the feast stopped and everyone went home, each to his own house, pondering these words.

Smiling gleefully, the modern-day religious person puts his pen down, hoping that he has communicated better what John obviously meant to write.

Before I continue, please do not misunderstand the intent of my sarcasm. I fully recognize the pain and misery caused by the abuses of alcohol. Both of my grandfathers died of alcohol-related problems, and I've had to work through my own issues as a child of parents who struggled with alcoholism. I also remember, as an unchurched person, my disdain for Christianity because Christians seemed against everything . . . especially fun.

Jesus, however, is far from boring. When I read the Gospels for the first time as a teenager, I was amazed at how different Jesus appeared compared to what I had heard about him at church. The Jesus in the Bible turned water into wine. It was the religious people who were staunchly against this, desiring, so to speak, to turn wine into water.[3]

The kingdom of God is about a ministry of fermentation in which water *is* turned into wine. The author of John understood this. Why else would he record this miracle as the first of Jesus' ministry and then follow the narrative with a succession of examples? The answer? Because water becoming wine stands as a metaphor for what the kingdom of God is all about. The first example occurs when Nicodemus, a religious professional, is lectured on the subject of what it means to be born again. Afterwards, he is turned from hardened skeptic to believer. The next occurs when Jesus speaks to the Samaritan woman at the well and transforms an idolater into a true worshiper. Next, Jesus transforms an enemy into a friend as a royal official, probably an officer serving Herod, pleads with Christ to heal his son. The soldier expresses such faith that Jesus also transforms his dead son into a living boy. The next narrative describes how an invalid relegated to a life of begging is able to stand up and walk home for the first time in his life.

In each of these cases, a person is transformed from water into wine. Before, their life was a struggle, with some misery and sadness. Then Jesus came along and transformed it into something robust, colorful, spirited, and intoxicating.

Many Christians are afraid of wine. Case in point: we serve grape juice at the Lord's Supper. As one who grew up Catholic and then became Baptist, I have never quite understood this. I remember my first experience at a Baptist church when they served the Lord's Supper, and the pastor explained why they served grape juice. He started off by saying that he didn't want to cause alcoholics to stumble by giving them a taste of something that might prompt them to go "off the wagon." His second argument was to explain how grape juice was a far better symbol for the blood of Christ. Wine was rotting juice, which was why it was fermented, a better symbol for death. Grape juice was fresh, a more fitting symbol for the life that Jesus offered.

At the time I remember pondering, "Hmm, the Baptists think that they are smarter than Jesus?" I was sure that Jesus was well aware of the existence of fruit juice, and of alcoholics, yet he still chose wine. So the question is, why are we so afraid of the wine?

Part of the answer can be found in people like Carry A. Nation.

Most people have forgotten who she was, though I'm sure there are some who still remember her antics. Carry faced untold traumas as a girl from a mother who believed she was Queen Victoria of England. In addition, her father, Martin Moore, owned slaves in the South at the outbreak of the Civil War. As a result, they were forced to move to escape the violence, and when they returned, the land was ruined, the slaves gone, and the family destitute. Nevertheless, her father managed to eke out a living boarding travelers.[4]

When Carry became a young woman, the son of one of these boarders stole a kiss from her when no one was looking. Carry ran away, yelling, "I am ruined!"—having no idea just how prophetic her words were. Carry fell madly in love with the man, and soon, she and Dr. Charles Gloyd were married despite the strong protests from Carry's father. Gloyd was an alcoholic, a Mason, and constantly broke. All three of these things became a source of intense bitterness for Carry, who left Gloyd while she was pregnant with their first child. More than any other trauma in her life, this one shaped Carry's future, for she was still very much in love with Gloyd. She blamed the Masons and the alcohol for destroying her marriage and vowed to do everything she could to prevent this from happening to other women. Later, out of financial necessity, she married a minister named David Nation. She hated the man, and the two fought constantly, which allowed Carry to hone her skills.

One day Carry had a conversion experience she described as electricity "pouring on her head." She ran around laughing, crying, and praying ecstatically. She intensified her attacks on her husband, which eventually led to their divorce. She joined the Woman's Christian Temperance Union and was appointed an evangelist to the prison. There, she sang to the prisoners, just about all of whom were jailed for public drunkenness,

> Touch not, taste not, handle not;
> Drink will make the dark, dark blot,
> Like an adder it will sting,
> And at last to ruin bring,
> They who tarry at the drink.[5]

As Carry got to know the prisoners, she became especially enraged at the hypocrisy of so many men found drunk in Kansas, presumably a prohibition state (before nationwide Prohibition began in 1919). She decided to target the saloons that were not so secretly operating under the noses of the authorities. When the saloonkeepers laughed at her protestations and the local law ignored her, Carry took matters into her own hands. She began by throwing bricks and rocks through windows. Then, invigorated by the sound of broken glass and the discovery that she enjoyed smashing things, she escalated her attacks. One day she hid under her cape a metal rod, a cane, and some rocks and walked into a local bar that displayed a large portrait of a nude woman. Dramatically, she flung her cape back, tossed rocks at the picture, and smashed the mirror and bar with the rod and cane. When she was done, she dashed across the street to another "hell-hole" but was run off by the police.

Exhilarated, Carry had now found her calling—but rocks and canes were too crude. Carry discovered that a hatchet proved more effective for both destructive purposes and for establishing her image as God's warrior. Soon, she was leading bands of conservative, religious prohibitionists—mostly women—into the bars and warehouses, wielding her hatchet in one hand and a Bible in the other, singing "Onward Christian Soldiers," pointing fingers, and shouting the war cry, "Smash! Smash! For Jesus' sake, smash!" By now, the journalists had found their iconic image, and soon, pictures of Carry on a rampage were published all over the country, with the headline, "Hatchetation!"[6]

Carry's movement swelled, propelling her to national notoriety. She traveled the country, spoke at gatherings, smashed more liquor bottles, handed out miniature hatchets decorated with white ribbons, and spurred a cause that ultimately resulted in the Eighteenth Amendment being added to the Constitution in 1919 (Prohibition), which was then repealed by the Twenty-First Amendment in 1933. What bothers me most about the story of Carry Nation is not that she was violent and likely mentally ill. Given her experiences growing up and the delusions of her mother, a modern psychologist likely could have diagnosed her specific illness. What bothers me is that fact that believers in Christ followed her and put her on a pedestal, honoring her as a saint.

If our cause includes a mentally ill person wielding a weapon to vandalize property while shouting "Smash for Jesus," then perhaps we need to rethink our approach.

Unfortunately, this is not a lesson many in the church have learned; in fact, the spirit of Carry A. Nation is alive and well. My guess is that you've recently seen a story in the news about supposed Christians supporting the abuse and marginalization of migrants, refugees, and other vulnerable populations or involved in some hateful protest. Perhaps you've read of a controversy involving conservative evangelicals supporting a politician or cause that is making you shake your head.

As a church, we simply haven't learned. Turning wine into water has been the mission of subgroups of Christians since the Judaizers of the first century. Since then, it has happened whenever angry, mean-spirited, vitriolic voices speak for the church, whenever faith is merely misery and suffering for the sake of misery and suffering, whenever legalistic stances become more important than compassion, and whenever vengeance trumps grace.

The only time Jesus became angry or chased people with a whip was when religious people were exploiting sinners. In contrast, whenever Jesus came upon an actual sinner, he expressed audacious grace. It's time the church reclaim this strategy and follow Jesus, who confronted sin by loving sinners; who sought to embrace broken people, not ostracize them; who did not patronize sinners by serving fruit juice but treated them with respect; who did not shame them, make them grovel, or force them to inflict pain on themselves but instead sought to restore their dignity and heal them.

When believers have the courage to follow Jesus in this way, water is turned into wine. But be careful: it is an intoxicating experience.

Cheers!

Inner Peregrinatio to the Banquet

Question: Is this all there is?
Fear: Yes

In *Against Heresies*, Book 4 (20, 7), Irenaeus wrote, "For the glory of God is a living man; and the life of man consists in beholding God." There are different ways of interpreting this, but one way can be expressed like this: "The glory of God is a human fully alive." For Irenaeus, this meant participating with God in the drama of life to become what God intended you to become.

For those of us who grew up in the church, there is the sense that to be a good Christian we must attend church faithfully, read our Bibles, pray, witness, tithe, and serve on church committees. Though these are good things, the truth is that life in God is not confined to these things. In fact, these things can potentially get in the way of becoming a "human fully alive" especially if the church one attends is oppressive and manipulative.

"It [was] for freedom that Christ . . . set us free," Paul writes in Galatians (5:1) in response to the legalism of his day. In fact, in this letter he is angrily confronting those who want to make the gospel merely a Jewish movement. For Paul, the gospel was for the whole world. His God was far, far bigger.

That's the invitation of the banquet, to see God as far bigger than we ever imagined and to see our life with God as something far bigger as well. Approaching the banquet table is an exercise in freedom. Scientists shouldn't be afraid of searching for truth. Artists shouldn't be afraid of exposing the human condition. Musicians shouldn't be afraid of mining the depths of human emotion. Businessmen shouldn't be afraid of making money. God created us for such endeavors. And as we pursue them alongside this ever-increasing vision of the glory of God, we become fully alive.

There are great risks. One can make an idol out of truth or humanity or passion or money, but true joy comes as we become fully alive in God. He delights in it. He wants us to experience a kingdom that is not confined to a temple or a church building but only by our ability to dream. And God wants us to dream big.

Go Deeper

"The Banquet" in "From Eden to Heaven Prompts" at
www.spilledcoffeeonancientscrolls.com

Brother Lawrence, *The Practice of the Presence of God*

C. S. Lewis, *Till We Have Faces*

Notes

1. "St. Rose of Lima," *Britannica Online*, britannica.com/biography/Saint-Rose-of-Lima. See also *New Catholic Encyclopedia*, vol. 12, "Rose of Lima," Catholic University Press of America, 2002; and Michael Walsh, ed., *Butler's Lives of the Saints* (San Francisco: Harper and Row, 1985) 260–61.

2. *Expositor's Bible Commentary*, ed. Frank E. Gaebelein, 9:42.

3. Interestingly, in the Ante-Nicene period (AD 100–325), heresy became a major problem for the church, and one of the hallmarks of heretical groups was that they used water instead of wine in the Lord's Supper. See Joseph B. Tyson, *Marcion and Luke-Acts* (Columbia: University of South Carolina Press, 2006) 35.

4. Ishbel Ross, *Charmers and Cranks* (New York: Harper and Row, 1965) 173–78.

5. Ibid., 178–81.

6. Ibid., 181–85.

Return

Heaven

They say that God is everywhere, and yet we always
think of Him as somewhat of a recluse.
—Emily Dickinson

So far, the only time I've witnessed a disturbance in a chapel service was the day I invited a speaker to address the issue of creation care. Essentially, this is the idea that God has placed us on this earth to take care of it. God created the planet. It belongs to him. We are his stewards. Therefore, Christians ought to be concerned about environmental issues. Admittedly, this topic is not a popular subject in Texas. Those of us who are interested in environmentalism are derided as "tree huggers." Texans try to corral us for the most part in Austin, an oasis for all things "weird." Nonetheless, I thought that as a university we should talk about it, so I invited a conservative and outspoken Republican to introduce the subject, thinking that maybe his credentials would give him some credibility with the audience.

I was wrong.

He had almost reached the end of the sermon when a young man stood up in the back of the auditorium and began frantically waving his arms. I must admit that the speaker handled it well. He politely acknowledged the student, to the dismay of the rest of the audience. Then, clearly agitated, the student yelled, "If God is going to judge the world by burning it up in a ball of fire anyway, why should I care?"

He had a point: if God is purposely making things worse on the planet because Jesus is coming back sometime after lunch, and if he is going to rapture the church, leaving the wicked behind, and if he is going to punish the wicked by making the earth a hellish place to live, then it does seem that we are wasting our time recycling, reducing pollution, conserving water, cleaning up litter, and reducing our carbon footprint. Maybe global warming is God's plan to create a hell on earth. If so, then Christians who try to stop it might just find themselves fighting on the wrong side.

There are a lot of "ifs" in this presupposition, and since we are talking about possibly making major decisions about the future of our planet based on them, perhaps we ought to know where they come from.

Many Christians are under the impression that the church has always believed that the world is going to meet an end as I just described, but the truth is that some of these ideas are fairly recent. In fact, there have been a plethora of ideas about the millennium, the identity of the antichrist, the beast, the mark of the beast, the two witnesses, and the woman in celestial clothes over the centuries. So let's go back and take a hard look at the book that started it all: Revelation (add ubiquitous explosions, smoke, fire, screams, and ominous music here).

Revelation is part of a genre known as apocalyptic literature, written with colorful metaphors, fantastic creatures, and a dualistic plot pitting good against evil. The style became popular as oppressed people groups needed to encourage one another in the face of severe persecution. Think of it this way: you could be thrown in jail for treason if you wrote something, or even had something in your possession, that described horrible things happening to the emperor. But if you possessed a story about a creature called the antichrist who got harassed by fantastic creatures, well, that was different. Still, you and your friends would know who you were *really* talking about.

In order to begin to understand Revelation, you have to understand the context in which it was written—a time of official persecution against the church, when Christians were arrested merely for the crime of being a Christian. Some of the rationale for this came about as a result of some pretty nasty rumors. For one, Christians were believed to be atheists because they rejected the Roman pantheon and they did not have a temple to worship at or an idol depicting their god. In the Greco/Roman mind, no idol meant no god. Second, Romans thought Christians hated them. Believers, for the most part, resisted patriotic parades, refrained from the theater and the games, and refused to serve in government or fight in the military. Most Christians kept to themselves, and the Romans, being a bit paranoid, took it personally. Third, it became clearer and clearer that Christians were not Jews. At first there was a great deal of confusion about this, even among the Christians. But as Christian gangs and Jewish gangs rumbled in the streets of Rome, it was obvious that these two groups didn't like each other. Their feud was problematic for the Christians because whereas before, the Romans lumped Jews and Christians into one large group, now the Romans viewed them as separate. As a result, laws granting special privileges to the

Jews no longer applied to the Christians, like an exemption from emperor worship.

These misunderstandings were reason enough to wind up on "Most Wanted" posters all over the empire. But it got worse. The Romans heard that the Christians gathered together regularly for something they called an "agape meal," which was much like a Wednesday night covered dish supper and prayer meeting. The Christians intended the title of their service to express close fellowship; however, the Romans heard "love feast" and their imaginations ran wild. If that weren't bad enough, Christians called themselves "brother" and "sister" and drank the body and blood of Christ. This behavior could only mean one thing: Christians were participating in incestuous orgies and then consuming the deformed babies of these immoral trysts. Wouldn't you want to throw these people to the lions?

Granted, the rumors were far from reality. Much like today, though, malice is far more fun to believe than the truth. And little did the Romans realize that they were laying the foundation for the invention of social media.

On June 18, AD 64, a fire broke out in Rome that lasted over a week and burned significant portions of the city. The emperor at this time, Nero, heard about the fires while relaxing at his palace in Antium (Anzio), about forty miles away. He supposedly hurried back and organized an effort to extinguish the flames, even opening his personal garden and public buildings as a shelter for the homeless. Unfortunately, Roman bloggers had already decided that Nero suffered from madness, so before the embers had cooled they also decided that somehow Nero had started the fire. The only thing left to do was to speculate, er, *determine* how he did it.

Nero fancied himself a poet. He also loved buildings. So perhaps he ordered the fire to demolish some ugly building he didn't like in order to erect a new palace and accessorize it with a few fancy parks. While the fire swept through the city, he recited poetry. No, no, no. That's not it. Nero fancied himself as a great crooner, so perhaps he dressed in a fancy toga, played the harp, stood on top of a Palatine tower, and passionately sang about the destruction of Troy while the fire raged around him. Ahh, that can't be it, either. I've got it: Nero loved to play the violin, so he must have gathered a bunch of his buddies, played a recital, and, as a dramatic backdrop to his virtuosity, burned Rome to the ground. That's it! Grab your pitchforks and torches and let's throw the bum out!

To make matters worse, economic hard times soon followed, and Nero's job rating plummeted. He needed to do something, so he decided to beat the bloggers at their own game. Nero astutely recognized that the few sections in Rome that did not burn to the ground contained a high concentration of Christians. He hired his own bloggers to start a counter rumor that the real culprits behind the fires were the abominable, orgy-crazed, incestuous baby eaters.

Of course! That made much more sense than the beloved emperor starting the fire, so it became open season on the Christians. "Mad" Nero led the hunt. He started by throwing them to the lions, but that was too clichéd. Nero soon took a more sophisticated approach by having them crucified, like their god, hoping that the Roman elitists would enjoy his use of irony. But he had to be mindful of the real Romans living in the flyover provinces as well, so he had Christians dressed in the skins of wild animals and tossed to the dogs as entertainment for his house parties. To illuminate his guests' way through the garden, he had Christians impaled on stakes, covered in pitch, and ignited. Nothing brought tears of joy to a real Roman quicker than seeing a godless heathen torched. After all, the rising smoke was a pleasing aroma to the pantheon.

Fortunately for the Christians, Nero didn't stay in power for long, but his success in using the Christians as a scapegoat became a standard strategy in the political playbook of successive emperors. Now, whenever anything went wrong, like the barbarians won a battle or a volcano wiped out a city, it became convenient and effective to blame the Christians. The gods were obviously upset that good, moral Roman citizens allowed the abomination of the Christians to go unchecked. It was time to round up the perverts and punish them.

In the aftermath of these persecutions, a man named John, living on the island of Patmos, saw a hopeful vision that proved, despite the fact that it was taking Jesus a long time to return, God had not forgotten the church—that, in fact, everything taking place was a part of God's plan. To demonstrate this, John the Revelator used colorful scenes to reveal what was really happening. In other words, it may have appeared that the bad guys were winning because they had powerful armies and prisons and coliseums filled with animals ready to devour the enemy, but the truth was that the power Christians wielded was far greater. On the surface, it may have looked as though their prayers were like ethereal smoke rising to the heavens, having no real impact. But as John describes in Revelation 8, the incense burners (commonly used in first-century Christian worship) would be tossed by the angels on the heads of their enemy, causing rumbling, thunder, lightning, and earthquakes. And it may have seemed like the Lamb of God was meek and mild (Rev 5), but he would return as a great Warrior King riding on a white horse, striking fear in the enemy in a great battle that would end in the enemy's destruction (Rev 19).

One can see how this message would have vast appeal to a church suffering horrific violence at the hands of the government. And one can see how easy it would have been for the early church to relate the characters of the drama in Revelation to their own struggle with evil. To them, Nero was the beast. The mark "666" may have been a symbol for most evil (7 means perfect and 6 is one less than 7, indicating imperfect, and repeating it 3 times was the superlative). Or it may have been a code. The Hebrews used letters for numbers. The Hebrew equivalent of "Nero Caesar" adds up to 666.[1] In Revelation 17:8, John describes the "beast, which you saw, once was, now is not, and yet will come up out of the Abyss and go to [his] destruction . . . ." Interestingly, there was a popular belief among the early Christians that Nero would come back from the dead to persecute them even more severely.

Ultimately, the book of Revelation gave the early Christians much-needed hope to remain faithful. It also reminded them that, despite the way circumstances looked, God was still in control. And in the end, God will win. The nebulous style of the book allowed them to talk about it, read it, copy it, and pass it along in a covert way that helped them remain safe.

Despite its popularity, some early Christian leaders criticized the book of Revelation and felt that it should not be viewed as Scripture. It was written in poor Greek. Its authorship was questioned. The message of violence and retribution seemed to contradict Jesus' message of grace and forgiveness. As early as the second century, some eastern bishops discouraged Christians from considering the book authoritative. And Eusebius, who was a *huge* fan of the Emperor Constantine, didn't like Revelation because he felt that it described nasty things happening to Roman emperors. Nonetheless, the book enjoyed enough appeal that it was eventually accepted and became a favorite over the centuries for groups that felt oppressed or persecuted by large, powerful institutions believed to be corrupt and evil. Of course, those fascinated with conspiracy theories have also enjoyed attempting to decode the numerology, metaphors, and perceived secret messages encouraged by the imaginative narrative.

* * *

Probably no idea has captured so many would-be masters of cryptology and self-professed symbologists as the meaning of the millennium. In Revelation 20:4, John the Revelator tells us,

> And I saw the souls of those who had been beheaded because of their testimony about Jesus and because of the word of God. They had not worshiped the beast or its image and had not received its mark on their foreheads or their hands. They came to life and reigned with Christ a thousand years. [Add more thunderclaps, smoke, fire, screams, and ominous music here.]

What does that mean?

Well, there are a lot, and I mean *a lot*, of prophets, theologians, revolutionaries, crackpots, and best-selling authors who would like to tell you *exactly* what it means. All you have to do is buy their book or join their movement, sell everything you own, and hand it over to Fearless Leader. After all, you're not going to need all that stuff once the Apocalypse starts, anyway, and your sacrifice will ensure that none of the impending acts of God will harm you.

Before you empty your bank account and max out your credit cards, however, it's important to consider what the vast majority of Christians who first read the book of Revelation understood it to mean, and it's quite simple: one day Jesus is coming back, and when he does he'll stop all these horrid things from happening to us, and we'll live with him during a time of peace and prosperity when all that stuff about the lion not eating the lamb will come true.

They disagreed over the details, of course. Will Christ's reign be visible or invisible? Will people be resurrected physically or spiritually? In general, though, this "millenarianism" was widely accepted; all the black hats in the narrative were generally understood to have something to do with the Roman Empire, and all the white hats had something to do with the Christian church.[2] But then a funny thing happened on the way to the Apocalypse. Constantine decided he wanted to be emperor, and in a famous battle he marched against Maxentius near the Milvian Bridge that crossed the Tiber River outside of Rome. Prior to the fight, God spoke to Constantine and said, *"en toutōi nika,"* which is Greek (because by now, God was no longer Jewish) for "in this sign, conquer." The sign was the "*chi rho*," which looks like a tall "P" and a small "x" superimposed on one another. If you're creative, you can make it look like a cross. It comprises the first two letters of the word "Christ" (ch and r), and Constantine understood it to mean that Jesus wanted him to be emperor so that he could save the Christians. According to tradition, he had his soldiers paint this insignia on their shields to give them special powers. Sure enough, as the two armies clashed, Maxentius found himself pressed back toward the Milvian Bridge despite the fact that he had the larger army. To add insult to injury, his soldiers became disheartened when they saw their commander-in-chief floating away, face down in the Tiber River.

Constantine won.

In gratitude, he built Jesus a bunch of churches, gave the bishops lots of money, convened the first ecumenical council of the Christian church to encourage the bishops to stop fighting among themselves, and in general made it chic to be a Christian in the Roman Empire, all the while still retaining his title as high priest of the pagans.

The very real problem this posed to those who loved the book of Revelation was that those who were perceived to be the bad guys of the Apocalypse were now the good guys. What could they do? There must be bad guys.

As always, the esteemed Augustine had an answer. Borrowing heavily from Tyconius (a lay leader in a condemned heretical movement known as the Donatists, but don't tell anyone), Augustine came to the conclusion that the millennium had already started. He believed there was no need for Satan to be bound in some future event because Satan had already been bound when Jesus came the first time. His demise was the reason the church was doing so well. Augustine was wisely cautious about the details of the Apocalypse. He believed that events would remain in tension as two cities battled it out with one another: the city of God and the city of the world. Essentially the city of God is the church, the community of the faithful, and the city of the world is everyone else. The millennium was not to be understood literally but represented a time of struggle. At some point (no one really knows when), Satan will be unloosed during a time of final persecution when things will get really, really bad. Augustine did not believe, as many did, that Nero would come back as the antichrist to inflict pain on the church. Instead, all the godless in the world will essentially attack the church. Then Jesus will come back again (second advent). A final judgment will take place. The bad guys will suffer eternal punishment, and the city of God will enjoy eternal bliss. This view is often called "amillennial," but in practice it's actually closer to "postmillennialism," something I'll describe a little later.[3]

Postmillennialism would remain the dominant eschatology (that is, the dominant perception of what the end of time would be like) for most of Christian history. However, in the latter part of the twelfth century, Joachim of Fiore thought up a paradigm-shifting interpretation of the book of Revelation that would play a key role in our day. Rather than viewing Revelation as primarily historical as had been the custom since John wrote the book, Joachim surmised that the book was mostly about things yet to take place.

Do you know what this means?

Well, I'm not really sure. Neither was Joachim, but he was determined to be the first to find out. In doing so he opened a Pandora's box that inspired and obsessed prophets who burned tons of candle wax while pouring over apocalyptic passages and trying to decipher how they related to current events. In other words, before the Holy Trinity of Hal Lindsey, C. I. Scofield, and J. N. Darby, there was Joachim of Fiore.

Joachim lived in the middle of the Middle Ages (twelfth century) during a time of great civil unrest. An old threat to Christianity had resurfaced in a frightening way in the shape of the Crusades. Though Christian armies had largely been successful in taking back the holy lands, especially Jerusalem, the Muslim Saladin was methodically taking them all back again, creating a great deal of frustration and finger-pointing in Europe. Essentially, people were convinced that God was mad at them. In addition, a great fight was taking place between popes and holy Roman emperors over who God had really placed in charge of ruling the world—church or state. At issue for Joachim was the impiety and corruption he saw in all of this that had to mean something epic was about to take place. A final ingredient in this apocalyptic stew was the fact that Joachim viewed himself as a mystic akin to John the Revelator, a man blessed with mysterious visions filled with insights for the spiritually wise and elite.

Somewhere around 1183 or 1184, Joachim had one of his most famous visions: in it, God revealed the full meaning hidden in the book of Revelation and explained that it harmonized the Old and New Testaments in a beautiful way that showed how all the scary events going on at the time were part of God's plan.[4] Eventually, this insight worked its way into a rather novel interpretation in which Joachim divided history into three ages based on the Trinity. The first began at the time of Adam and was characterized by the law and humanity's relationship with the Father. The second age of the Son began, curiously, in the Old Testament with King Uzziah and was known as the "gospel" stage. The final age of the Spirit began with Saint Benedict (sixth century).

Though the mystic did not blatantly contradict the revered Augustine's eschatology, he modified it just enough to suggest that perhaps Satan wasn't completely bound by Christ in the first advent, and, therefore, the Millennium hasn't started yet. Which means that certain events must first transpire before the thousand-year reign of Christ can begin. This notion captured the imagination of many, many to come.

Joachim saw the events in his day as leading to the conclusion of the second age, when the beast and the false prophet would be tossed into the Lake of Fire, thus beginning the third age and the millennial reign of Christ. If one looked carefully enough at what was going on in the world, the signs were quite obvious. Revelation 13 describes a beast with seven heads rising from the sea, and, well, it just made common sense that the fifth head was Holy Roman Emperor Henry IV, who at that moment was sending Pope Gregory VII the message that, contrary to what he thought of himself, the bishop of Rome was *not* the most powerful person in the world; the emperor was. And to prove it, Henry IV marched against Rome and forced Gregory VII to flee.

The sixth head was certainly the Muslim Saladin, Sultan of Egypt, who at that time was telling Henry IV that, contrary to what he might believe, the Holy Roman Emperor was *not* the most powerful man in the world; the Sultan was. And to prove it, Saladin sent the Crusaders in Jerusalem running for their lives.

The wise Joachim had deciphered from the hidden messages in Revelation that both men were mere puppets in the hands of the Almighty God, who was patiently waiting for the last head of the beast to emerge, an anti-pope who was going to unite the world against the real pope.[5] Joachim's ideas and subsequent movement were popular for a while, but two papal denouncements and a condemnation from the Fourth Lateran Council brought them to an end. Nonetheless, this didn't stop Joachim's views from surviving. Monks clandestinely copied his works, read them by candlelight in darkened corners, and whispered to one another about how right he was. Because look—[fill in the blank] was even now attacking the faithful. It was only a matter of time.

* * *

About three centuries later during the Reformation, Augustine's view was still quite popular, but Joachim's vision got some major endorsements. Unfortunately, it came from the sort of people who only strengthened its reputation of being a vision from the ravings of a heretical lunatic. For in the chaos of the sixteenth century, several self-professed prophets saw themselves in the pages of Revelation as characters in a drama yet to be fulfilled.

Among the most infamous was the result of delusions of grandeur expressed by German visionary Melchior Hoffman, who believed he was the reincarnation of Elijah and began to preach to the inhabitants in Strasbourg that the Day of the Lord was at hand. When he predicted that he would soon be imprisoned and that six months later the New Jerusalem would become a reality, the city officials decided to take him up on it by throwing him in jail. Their plan backfired as a flock of malcontents migrated to Strasbourg because, after all, the first part of Hoffman's prophecy had just come true. Thus, he must be a prophet. They listened wide-eyed as he described the coming day in which the children of God must take up arms against the children of darkness.

Unfortunately for Hoffman, the six months came and went, and no New Jerusalem appeared. His fanatic followers refused to be discouraged. A baker named John Matthys convinced the riotous crowd that it was silly to think that the kingdom of God would come to a little place like Strasbourg. It was obviously coming to the nearby podunk German town of Münster. So they abandoned the reincarnation of Elijah and left him to rot in jail while they attacked Münster, expelled the Catholics along with their bishop, and prepared for war. Matthys then announced to his followers that he had just received a vision with the clear message, "death to the godless!" By which he meant that all the people in Münster who refused to join their cause must be killed. A colleague gently took him to the side and explained that this would be a bad idea, after which, Matthys announced to the crowd that he had just received a new vision with the clear message, "expel the godless." By which he meant, never mind what I said before; let's just kick them out of town and take over their homes.

By now, the bishop had returned, and he brought along a few thousand well-armed friends. Matthys, true to form, announced a third vision to his followers in which God assured him that he was invulnerable to the weapons of the godless. Courageously, he led a group of armed fanatics outside the city walls in a bold attack against the Catholics. As it turned out, Matthys was wrong about the whole invulnerability thing as he was summarily killed. His buddy, Jan of Leiden, took the opportunity to declare himself "Ruler of the New Zion," and for the first time in this movement he managed to do something right for a change as he successfully defended the city against the bishop's army. But the Catholics were in no hurry, so they wisely camped outside and waited.

Jan took the opportunity to declare that he too had seen a vision. You see, the New Jerusalem had a problem. Lots of men were dying, leaving lots of widows. The population of the town was dwindling. And, well, the town needed more children to join the children of light, but there weren't enough men to go around. Plus, the Ruler of Zion had a major crush on the widow of Matthys, but Jan was already married, so the Holy Spirit told Jan that God wanted to bring back polygamy. The men cheered, and Jan immediately wed the widow of Matthys. It didn't take long for him to conclude that he needed to spread the love. The next woman who caught the eye of the Ruler of the New Zion, however, resisted his advances. This rejection was treason, so she was taken to the town square and beheaded. To make his point more clearly, Jan proceeded to jump up and down on her headless body, giving it a few swift kicks for good measure. Now, all of a sudden, it became a lot easier for Jan to get a date.

Time, though, was running out. Well, more important, the food was running out. Soon, just about everyone was having visions about this or that as others were passing out due to starvation. Eventually, a couple of Münsterites decided that they didn't want to be numbered among the children of light anymore if it meant starving to death and having their daughters join Jan's growing harem, so they made a deal with the Catholics. The bishop's army was led through a breach in the town's defenses, and the children of light were slaughtered. Jan, along with two other leaders, were tortured and executed, their bodies left to rot in cages hung in public. If you go to Münster today you can still see the cages, though the skeletons have long been removed. They were left hanging to proclaim a warning to any others who might envision themselves as characters in the Apocalypse.

With fans like this, Joachim's eschatology was labeled dangerous, like the mercury used by the hatters of the day. Dabble in it long enough, and it will drive you mad, so the best thing to do is leave it alone. This apprehension can be seen in the attitude of the major reformers like Luther and Calvin and Zwingli, who not only condemned this particular eschatology but also tended to shun the book of Revelation as a whole. Luther questioned its authorship, and though he continued to accept its canonicity, he described it as a book that the Holy Spirit had nothing to do with, adding that Christ was "neither sought nor known in it."[6] He later softened this view a bit, especially when he had fun associating the papacy with the anti-christ. In addition, Calvin's assessment of the book can be seen in the fact that he never got around to writing a commentary on it. Some claim that he ran out of time, but let's face it: at the very least it was a low priority for him. Finally, Zwingli simply viewed Revelation as an "unbiblical work."[7]

* * *

Times changed, though, and in the nineteenth century interest in eschatology resurrected. New threats challenged the church in the form of the Enlightenment. Science became the new authority of truth, and, slowly, more and more of the mysteries formerly attributed to God were explained. In addition, new technologies were created. Muskets replaced swords, and toilet paper replaced ripped pages from almanacs. In this new era, J. N. Darby did something no one had been able to do yet in the history of Christianity: he brought some respect to eschatology. In the process, he created an entire industry that would eventually include books, computer games, prophecy conferences, TV shows, movies, and Kirk Cameron.

The paradigm change began with Darby, who grew disillusioned with the Irish Anglican Church after studying the book of Acts and noticing that the present-day church failed in many ways when compared to the dyna-mism and purity of first-century believers. His tendency toward literalism in understanding the Bible and his fascination with apocalyptic passages led him to the same conclusion that a man named William Miller had popularized earlier in the United States: that most of the stuff in Revelation hadn't happened yet.

As a result, Darby endeavored to figure out if perhaps all the bad stuff going on in his world was somehow predicted in the Scriptures. He rejected the then-popular postmillennialism, which assumed that everything would just keep getting better and better in the world until a final showdown with Satan prompted Jesus to come back, despite the fact that this view was held by some pretty stalwart theologians like Jonathan Edwards.[8] Ever the contrarian, Darby adopted a rather pessimistic view of this world in which everything must get worse.

He started hanging around with other disgruntled evangelicals in Ireland who loved to get together and gripe. Soon this group captured the attention of a wealthy widow named Theodosia A., Viscountess Power-scourt, or Lady Powerscourt for short, who thought it would be fun to get all these pessimists together at a large conference so that they could hear a succession of speakers complain about how bad things are. Little did she know that she was laying the foundation for cable news networks.

Eventually, the group got tired of complaining all the time and started to talk about what they could do about the stuff they were complaining about. They concluded that they were far too depraved to be able to do anything (most of them were Calvinists) but that perhaps God might intervene. This insight is where things get really interesting because the speakers started to present their ideas about how God was going to assault all the people they didn't like, especially the Catholics.

This made them feel much better.

Soon, J. N. Darby rose to notoriety among these speakers for two reasons: (1) his novel eschatology captured their imagination, and (2) Lady Powerscourt wanted Darby to be her boyfriend, so she made sure he had ample opportunity to speak at the best spots during these prophecy gatherings, aptly named the Powerscourt Conferences.[9] Alas, their love never blossomed, mainly because Darby fancied himself a fighter, not a lover.

Eventually, Darby's insights developed into a grand scheme of understanding all of history known as premillennial dispensationalism. It's so complicated that my spell checker doesn't even recognize these two terms as actual words. Essentially, Darby divided history into seven dispensations and explained that today we are in the sixth age of grace, also known as the "church age," characterized as a rather dull period where nothing much happens until we get close to the end, when all hell breaks loose—literally. In a last gasp of desperation, Satan and his forces will unleash a torrent of maelstroms against the church.

Since the church represents the faithful, Jesus won't be able to stand watching them suffer for long, so Darby concocted the idea that Jesus will return soon in the sky. He will "rapture" the church, allowing the chosen to flutter to heaven to join him. Together, they will gleefully watch the rest of the world get tortured over a period known as the "tribulation." After the Millennium, Satan will be released for one big, high-noon showdown with God called Armageddon. It won't be much of a fight, however, for after a little sword rattling, God will merely zap Satan with fire. Now we get to our happy ending where the New Jerusalem is established and everyone runs around and hugs Jesus, sings contemporary Christian worship songs written by David Crowder, listens to preaching tapes, and watches Pixar movies. There will be no pain, suffering, crying, or evolutionary scientists in this world.

Darby's views would have probably remained popular only among his beloved Plymouth Brethren and friends had it not been for an American named C. I. Scofield, a Confederate soldier, lawyer, U.S. attorney general fired under suspicion of embezzlement, prisoner busted for forgery, divorced man, and Dallas pastor.[10] In 1909, Oxford published his commentary along with the King James Version of the Bible, which became known as the Scofield Reference Bible, and it was a huge success with few rivals in publishing. What Scofield managed to do, whether he planned it or not, was use the KJV to bring respectability to a once-taboo topic typically associated with fringe groups. For in his commentary on Revelation, Scofield promoted Darby's eschatology with a few minor changes that made it more applicable to the times. For many, his notes were as inspired as the biblical text itself. In addition, he added copious headings in the text, offering yet another layer of authoritative interpretation. Many pastors found themselves having to defend any of their interpretations that were at variance with Scofield's notes, especially on eschatology. The famous Fundamentalist T. T. Shields of Toronto once complained that it generally took a believer about three to six months to go from total ignorance to "oracular religious certainty" with the Scofield Bible.[11]

I of all people know that my snarky summary of dispensationalism doesn't do it justice. However, I hope that as I have described its development I have revealed that, though it draws from some historical roots, overall it's a fairly new idea and that, for most of the history of the church, this brand of eschatology was viewed askance. I'm not attempting to discredit it—far from it. I admit that it's possible that Darby might be right, but there are a myriad of other interpretations that might be right as well. Let's face it: Revelation is probably the most nebulous book of the Bible. It's important because it's part of the canon, and there are certainly truths to glean from its pages. But because it is so obscure, it is also important to balance the potential tenets from Revelation with the more concrete passages in the rest of the Bible. Moreover, it's a good idea to approach the book with a great deal of humility. I don't know of any two interpreters of Revelation who agree on absolutely everything about it. In addition, do we really want to base major decisions about the environment and foreign policy on our interpretation of *this* book?

Finally, I find it interesting that the Gospel writers make it clear that everyone was clueless about the first advent of Jesus, even his closest disciples. When Jesus died on the cross, everyone abandoned him because he didn't fit their preconceived notions of who the Messiah ought to be. When the resurrection occurred, it took absolutely everyone by surprise, even the inner circle of Peter, James, and John. I've often wondered if, by baptizing a specific eschatology, we are making the same mistake. As our necks ache from glancing skyward all the time, looking for the rapture, are we blinding ourselves to the way Jesus has chosen to reveal himself in the second advent?

Revelation is a classic story about the struggle between good and evil that was written during a time when the church was deeply discouraged because Jesus was taking longer to return than they expected, and the church was facing oppression and persecution from its culture. Thus, I believe the book was designed to offer hope more than anything else. I believe our emphasis should be not on trying to decode the book but on allowing it to encourage us with its message that, no matter how bad our circumstances might get, God is always with us.

This hope is portrayed in a beautiful scene that John the Revelator conjures at the end of the book when he describes the church gathered around the table for the messianic banquet, a dominant theme found throughout the teachings of Jesus and foreshadowed in the agape meal of early Christian worship. Despite real threats from the empire, Christians gathered because the fellowship (*koinonia*) experience far outweighed the risk. They drew strength from the power of a feast that for them became the living metaphor of the kingdom of God, the most beautiful of sacred places.

Thus the feast became the Christian eschatological strategy for transforming the world, for as more and more come to the table, the closer we get to realizing all the promises of the gospel. At the table, the marrow of life is enjoyed. At the table, the hungry are fed, the naked are clothed, the sinner is reconciled, weeping is turned to laughter, sorrow to joy, brokenness to healing. And as Jesus raises his cup, he commands, "Make the world like this table for when I return."

It has been a long time since he uttered those words. But still we hope. And we wait eagerly for his return. We have no idea what it's actually going to be like, except for the fact that it will be joyous. We know that he will create a New Jerusalem unlike anything we could possibly imagine. John the Revelator tried, and he described the place in splendorous ways at the end of Revelation with streets of gold and jewel-encrusted artifacts. There is a city gate that will be open. Always open. And in the middle of it all will be a tree. It's the very tree that God felt we shouldn't have access to after we ate the forbidden fruit in Eden, but now it's out in the open and freely available to anyone and everyone.

It's the tree of life.

As I imagine this scene unfolding one day, I see people walking through the gates with mouths gaping and eyes wide open at everything they see—until they get to this tree, at which point they stop and stare for a moment as the truth of it sinks in. Then, eventually, with nods and laughter, it dawns on them. They've been here before. In fact, this tree was where the journey began. In Eden.

With that, they will proclaim, "There's no place like home!"

Inward Peregrinatio to Heaven

Question: What is my future?
Fear: There is no future.

Eschatology is literally the study of "the end." Unfortunately, for some it has connoted what I call the Disney fairy princess approach, i.e., wait around for the handsome prince to rescue you. Yet, if there is *one* thing that the passages on eschatology teach us about "the end," it is that when the second advent occurs, Christ expects results.

To "that end," what do you want your legacy to be? If our eschatology is merely attempting to decode the book of Revelation, then we've totally missed the point. A part of eschatology is dreaming about *your* end. It's also about imagining how your story fits into the larger narrative of God at work in the universe, which Revelation reveals will be a happy ending. What part do *you* play? This is a question that it is never too early or too late to ask. Abraham was past retirement when he was shown the stars and told he would be the father of a great nation, and Jeremiah was but a youth when he dreamed about the almond tree.

What's it going to be? What are you making of your life? Or, more important, what do you want to make of your life? If you had ten million dollars and could do anything you want, what would it be?

Now figure out a way of doing that without the ten million dollars.

Go Deeper

"Heaven" in "From Eden to Heaven Prompts" at
www.spilledcoffeeonancientscrolls.com

N. T. Wright, *Surprised by Hope:*
Rethinking Heaven, the Resurrection, and the Mission of the Church

C. S. Lewis, *The Great Divorce*

John Milton, *Paradise Regained*

Notes

1. Arthur W. Wainwright, *Mysterious Apocalypse* (Nashville: Abingdon Press, 1993) 129.

2. See Dan R. Stiver, *Life Together in the Way of Jesus Christ* (Waco TX: Baylor University Press, 2009). His chapter titled "Last Things," beginning on p. 427, provides an excellent historical summary of the major views on millenarianism.

3. See Wainwright, *Mysterious Apocalypse*, 34–39, for an excellent summary of Augustine's views.

4. Stephen E. Wessley, *Joachim of Fiore and Monastic Reform* (New York: Peter Lang, 1990) 5.

5. Ibid., 39–40.

6. Wainwright, *Mysterious Apocalypse*, 11–12, 55, 109.

7. Ibid., 109.

8. Ibid., 77–81.

9. Jonathan D. Burnham, *A Story of Conflict: The Controversial Relationship between Benjamin Wills Newton and John Nelson Darby* (Carlisle, England: Paternoster Press, 2004) 122–23.

10. LeAnn Snow Flesher, "The Historical Development of Premillennial Dispensationalism" *Review & Expositor* 106 (Winter 2009): 37.

11. Ibid., 39.

Epilogue

We don't read and write poetry because it's cute. We read and write poetry because we are members of the human race. And the human race is filled with passion. And medicine, law, business, engineering, these are noble pursuits and necessary to sustain life. But poetry, beauty, romance, love, these are what we stay alive for. To quote from Whitman, "O me! O life! . . . of the questions of these recurring; of the endless trains of the faithless . . . of cities filled with the foolish; what good amid these, O me, O life?" Answer. That you are here—that life exists, and identity; that the powerful play goes on and you may contribute a verse. That the powerful play *goes on* . . . and you may contribute a verse. What will your verse be?

—John Keating in *Dead Poets Society*

At the end of the *Lord of the Rings* trilogy (in the book *The Return of the King*), before Frodo leaves on the ship that will take him far from his home forever, he hands his best friend, Sam, a book. In the movie, the book is a large, beautifully illustrated red book titled *There and Back Again*. The original author was Bilbo, Frodo's uncle, who went on a grand adventure that included the slaying of a dragon. Before Bilbo left, he handed the book to Frodo and told him to pick up where the story left off, so the next section of the book included Frodo's even grander adventure of destroying the Dark Lord of Mordor.

Now it is Sam's turn. As Frodo flips to the end of the book, he thumbs through several blank pages. Sam's eyes widen as Frodo challenges him to pick up the pen and complete the book. The insecure Sam is reluctant. What can he possibly add?

But that's the question we all ask, isn't it?

* * *
—

When Jesus left his disciples, he handed over the fate of his movement to them. Given the past record of the disciples, this was a pretty gutsy move, because they hadn't really proven themselves to be all that trustworthy. All of them, including their leader Peter, abandoned Jesus at his more vulnerable moments.

But you and I know what happened next. We know that Jesus had to die on the cross and resurrect from the dead in order to demonstrate that he truly was the Son of God. And the disciples, for the first time it appears, finally *get* what Jesus was talking about. At first, the disciples gathered at homes and recounted their experiences with Jesus: "Remember that time when Jesus healed that paralytic." "Remember when he walked on the water." "Remember when he was arrested." And if you ever needed any clarifications, you just asked one of the apostles who was actually there!

Around AD 70, a writer sat down and thought to himself, "I'd better get some of these stories down on paper before all the eyewitnesses die." So, without knowing that he was about to transform Christianity in the most profound way since its beginning, a man traditionally identified as Mark sat down and wrote, "The beginning of the good news of Jesus Christ, the Son of God" (Mark 1:1, NRSV).

These words may not mean much to you. On the surface, they don't seem all that revolutionary. But Mark created a completely new genre of literature called "the Gospel." Granted, Mark doesn't use the word "gospel" in his writing because it's an Anglo-Saxon word originating from "God-spell," which means literally "story of a god." But the Greek *euangellion*, which means "good news," is found in this verse, and eventually the idea of "good news" and "the story of a god" were merged together in this new genre; a "Gospel" is the story of Jesus, the Son of God, and it is good news to those who hear of it because it is a story of how God became a man to reveal himself to us. The Gospel is as much a narrative about Jesus as it is a collection of his teachings.

Here is where something beautiful happened because this story about Jesus and this collection of his teachings have Mark's fingerprints all over it. Mark's Gospel exhibits Mark's personality. In the process, we get the story of Jesus through Mark's eyes. There are some fascinating aspects presented in his writing. For example, Mark's narrative is a series of exciting conflicts that start off rather small, around Galilee, but then escalate as Jesus' movement gets bigger and bigger. Jesus takes on all the religious leaders in the temple, and then he takes on the Roman Empire itself with Pilate. In the end, everyone is clueless about what's going on until the resurrection where we get this dramatic "aha!" moment. In the hands of Mark, the gospel is a grand epic.

Then other writers decided to copy this new genre: specifically (according to tradition) Matthew and Luke. But these two writers were a little uncomfortable with some aspects of Mark's narrative, so they sat down and came up with their own Gospels. Matthew didn't like Paul's dismissive attitude about the law, reflected both in Paul's letters and in Mark's Gospel. Thus, among other reasons, Matthew wrote his Gospel to address this. Jesus is portrayed as the new and improved Moses, even heading to Egypt after the Bethlehem infanticide (notice the similarities to Exodus). But Moses only received the Law and revealed it to the Israelites and led the people to the promised land. Jesus was the kingly Messiah, worthy of worship, who was to be the master interpreter of the Law and who will usher in the new kingdom. How did Matthew start his Gospel? With a genealogy, which most of us skip because it's boring. But look at this first verse: "An account of the genealogy of Jesus the Messiah, the son of David, the son of Abraham" (NRSV).

What you may not know is that "messiah" literally means "anointed one," and it was a designation for all the kings of Israel. David was anointed with oil by the prophet Samuel, and as you look at the names listed in this first chapter of Matthew, the dynasty of David is front and center. The message is clear: the Messiah King came from the lineage of David to establish a new throne and a new kingdom. Matthew emphasized this point at the end of the Gospel where the followers surround Jesus on a mountain in Galilee (like the Israelites around Moses at Mt. Sinai), and he had Jesus declare, "All authority in heaven and on earth has been given to me" (28:18, NRSV).

Then Luke entered the fray and inserted his personality into the story. He traced the lineage of Jesus not to Abraham and David but to Adam. Why? Because, to Luke, Jesus was the Messiah for everyone. He wasn't just a fulfillment of Jewish prophecy. He reached out to Gentiles too. To women. To lepers. To Samaritans. So Luke began his "story of a god" with Mary and Elizabeth.

Not to be outdone, John wrote his Gospel much, much later than the others. By now, the context of Christianity had changed quite a bit. The church was established and growing. A second generation of leaders had arisen. New crises were erupting. In response, John began his Gospel, "In the beginning was the Word, and the Word was with God, and the Word was God." In this Gospel, the story of Jesus doesn't begin with John the Baptist, out in the wilderness, and then escalate to the temple, as in Mark's story. Nor does it begin with a genealogy to demonstrate that Jesus is better than Moses as the Messiah King, as in Matthew's story. Nor does it begin with Elizabeth and Mary, as in Luke's Gospel, to demonstrate that Jesus is for everyone. John starts the story of Jesus at the beginning of time, revealing how before the Messiah came to earth, he participated in the creation of the universe. The point: Jesus is cosmic. He is "I Am," as he declared to the Sanhedrin at the end of John's Gospel, reminding readers of the burning bush that spoke to Moses in Exodus.

Each writer added to the story in a dramatic way, providing different perspectives of the life and message of Jesus. As we examine these different approaches, an incredibly creative and beautiful narrative emerges—one that reveals as much about the personalities of Mark, Luke, Matthew, and John as it does about Jesus. All of them together present for us a fuller witness of the "story of a god."

This left the early church fathers with a bit of a quandary, however. Should they choose just one of the Gospels to be *the* gospel, making things neat and tidy? Or should they include all four? Their genius answer was the latter, even though some (like Marcion[1]) argued that having a variety of viewpoints weakened the message. But the early fathers and mothers correctly understood that since God is so big, it was going to take a lot of different perspectives of him to present the full drama and beauty and truth of the story. So they didn't shy away from the tension.

This tension continues to grow because writing the narrative about the "story of a god" isn't over. It's still going on. That's what Mark, I think, attempted to convey in his Gospel. The most ancient manuscripts of Mark have his Gospel ending abruptly in verse 8: "So they went out and fled from the tomb, for terror and amazement had seized them; and they said nothing to anyone, for they were afraid" (16:8, NRSV).

This uneasy ending prompted later redactors to finish the story for Mark and add their own verses. But what if Mark intentionally ended the book unfinished for a reason? The cliffhanger begs the reader to do something. The women leave the tomb afraid and silent. The end. And the reader (or listener) very much wants to know what happens next! Maybe that's the point, because now the question is put to you: "Are you just going to sit there and let it end that way?" What if Mark's intention was to hand the book off to you, the reader, and say, "Okay, now you add your part of the story," giving you the opportunity to add your insights and experiences and miracles and personality? And as you do, the "story of a god" gets even more beautiful and profound and complete.

What part of the story are *you* going to live?

You see, these sacred places you have visited are designed to equip you to wrestle with questions about yourself, God, and your calling. At some point, you must take what you have learned, even though it will feel insufficient, and go live your adventure. To me, this is what is at the heart of salvation. It's not just a ticket to heaven, as some have made it. It is an invitation to the "abundant life," as Jesus described in John 10:10. I happen to like the way Thomas Merton put it: "Perhaps the Book of Life, in the end, is the book one has lived. If one has lived nothing, one is not in the Book of Life."[2] It is a sentiment that is also echoed by an early church father named Irenaeus who wrote, "The Glory of God is a human fully alive."[3] For this to happen, conjuring an image I mentioned at the beginning, you have to get in your own coracle (boat), launch into the Irish Sea, bring the oars in, and allow the wind and the waves to guide you to your destiny. The inner peregrinatio must become an outer peregrinatio at some point.

So, as Frodo challenged Sam, I challenge you. I leave you with a book filled with blank pages and a blunted quill that needs sharpening. You are the protagonist, and the story is unfolding even as you read these words. Go beyond the gate, into the unknown. Face your fears. Experience highs and lows. Make friends. Fall in love. Be transubstantiated. Challenge evil. And win the day.

The fate of the world rests in your hands.

1. Marcion was a second-century church leader who started his own brand of Christianity after being ostracized by the proto-orthodox church for his heterodox ideas. Among them was a rejection of the Gospels of Mark, Matthew, and John in order to protect a harmonious narrative about Jesus.

2. Thomas Merton, *Intimate Merton*, ed. Patrick Hart and Jonathan Montaldo (San Francisco: HarperSanFrancisco, 1999) ix.

3. *Against Heresies*, book 4, 20:7.